SOCIO-MEDICAL HEALTH INDICATORS

EDITED BY:

Jack Elinson
Athilia E. Siegmann

Routledge
Taylor & Francis Group
LONDON AND NEW YORK

First published 1976 by Baywood Publishing Company, Inc.

2 Park Square, Milton Park, Abingdon, Oxfordshire OX14 4RN
52 Vanderbilt Avenue, New York, NY 10017

Routledge is an imprint of the Taylor & Francis Group, an informa business

First issued in hardback 2019

Library of Congress Catalog Card Number: 78-74484

Library of Congress Cataloging in Publication Data

Main entry under title:

Sociomedical health indicators.

Includes bibliographical references.
1. Social medicine--Methodology. 2. Health status indicators. I. Elinson, Jack. II. Siegmann, Athilia E.
RA418.S675 362.1'01'8 79-12982

ISBN 13: 978-0-89503-013-9 (pbk)
ISBN 13: 978-0-415-78623-2 (hbk)

MIX
Paper from responsible sources
FSC™ C013985
FSC www.fsc.org

Printed in the United Kingdom
by Henry Ling Limited

FOREWORD

In view of the magnitude of use of and expenditures for personal health services, now approaching $600 annually per capita in the United States, never was so much spent for and demanded by so many with so little objective criteria of the impact on well-being. The persistence and continuing expansion of the personal health services must rest on a faith analogous to the persistence and support of churches and synagogues. Both presumably offer assurance, solace, and relief from pain in coping with life's vicissitudes. The difference is that faith in the intrinsic value of churches and synagogues is not being questioned (except by a small minority of atheists and agnostics). The faith in the efficacy of health services in having any impact on health levels is now, however, being questioned as costs of these services continue to rise. It is feared that health services are being wasted and overused and should be rationed for "real" and severe illnesses when financed by public funds.

The following chapters promise to be the beginning of the shift from pure faith in the efficacy of health services to some objective criteria of need in relation to services. They may also become a counterweight to the increasing likelihood that the need for health services will be defined by physicians, administrators, and budget bureaus with decreasing trust in such definition by the public. A medical-administrative utopia would be one in which there are explicit and validated criteria of perception of need and efficacy of services, on which a price tag could be put, contributing to rational public policy discussion of trade-offs.

It is, of course, unlikely that the utopia of completely validated criteria will be attained, but the following chapters show promise of extracting ourselves from the morass of unvalidated criteria in which we now find ourselves. There may then be the possibility of some equitable balancing off of public perceptions and desires and physician and administrative criteria.

Odin W. Anderson, Chairman
Committee on Organizational Consequences of Varying
National Programs for Providing Health Services

PREFACE

In 1971 the Medical Sociology Section of the American Sociological Association initiated a program, with the support of a grant from the Carnegie Corporation, to examine various problems relevant to the emergence of national health insurance. In selecting problems on which to focus, we not only selected important areas where we felt the social and behavioral sciences had something unique to contribute, but we also agreed to emphasize problems which we felt were receiving too little attention relative to their importance for emerging national concerns. We developed and provided financial assistance to eight subcommittees that dealt with such areas as how to enhance the humanization of medical care, to improve research on professional organization and control, to examine the role of emotional problems in the use of primary medical services, to better understand how to modify patient health behavior and achieve greater conformity with medical advice, and to gain wider appreciation of the broader determinants of health status. The fact that these areas are receiving much more attention now than they did then attests to the fact that we chose wisely, and even possibly that our efforts had some influence.

When we began in 1971, we felt strongly that evaluation of health care policy and practice required more attention to examining outcomes. We appreciated that measures of outcome were limited and poorly developed relative to the need for appropriate indicators and the importance of the issues of evaluation we faced. Thus, we viewed the issue of sociomedical indicators as a key concern, and established a committee to work in this area under the very able chairmanship of Jack Elinson. As chairman of this committee, Elinson initiated a seminar on the topic at the Columbia School of Public Health, which served as an initial basis for the work contained in this monograph.

Until very recently, most commentary on broad health care policy outcomes depended on citation of infant and adult mortality statistics. While some data were also available from household morbidity interviews on bed disability days and limitation of activities, the dominant indicators were insensitive to levels of functioning and disability, reduction of pain and discomfort, and feelings of well-being and satisfaction. Without better indicators of functioning and health status, we could do little on a broad basis to examine the value of varying medical care programs or means of organizing health care delivery systems. The papers in this monograph attest to the rich possibilities we have yet to exploit and the fact that we are now thinking more seriously than ever before about the ways to monitor appropriately the vast investments we make in providing medical care and to examine the value of alternative possibilities. We hope that this thoughtful monograph will be one more stimulus to the increasing development of more sophisticated sociomedical indicators and more serious evaluation of the performance of the health services.

David Mechanic, Chairman
Carnegie Grant Steering Committee

TABLE OF CONTENTS

PART 1
Social and Behavioral Criteria

Introduction To The Theme: Sociomedical Health Indicators

Jack Elinson

This monograph is devoted to expositions by some active investigators of their current work on sociomedical health indicators. It will be seen that their work, concededly in various stages of early development, has begun to move from conceptualization to operationalization. Dissatisfaction with the limitations of conventional biomedical measures of mortality and morbidity is no longer enough (1, 2). Snide commentary on the vagueness of the humanitarian definition of health presented by the World Health Organization should also be passé. The contents of this volume demonstrate that serious efforts to breathe some life into the WHO definition are finally being made.

The use of the term "sociomedical health indicators" requires some explanation. We use it primarily to distinguish those dimensions of health which are primarily social from those which are primarily physiological. To be sure, all of the indicators considered here have been, and continue to be, matters of medical concern; and all have a physiological basis. At the same time, our goal is not merely to address, but rather to emphasize societal concerns with the effects of deviations from physiological states deemed desirable from a medical point of view, and furthermore, to develop measures which reflect these societal concerns.

Among the desiderata for sociomedical measures is that they be applicable not only to individuals, but also to large aggregates of individuals, such as workers in particular industries, persons covered by insurance schemes, and populations of communities, states, and nations. In short, it is hoped that these measures will eventually be useful as social indicators. Not all of the measures considered here have arrived as yet at that advanced happy state, although some are more immediately applicable than others, e.g. the measure of "reproductive efficiency" proposed by health economist Charlotte Muller and coworkers.

It will be noted that the authors are, in the main, either doctors of medicine or doctors of philosophy, but predominantly the latter. The doctors of medicine–Katz, Wolfe, and Martini–have all been involved in collaboration with social scientists in research on health services; in particular, the relation of health services to health status. Perforce they have had to conceive and develop sociomedical or sociobiological measures appropriate to their research endeavors. John Jago, Doctor of Dental Surgery, collaborating with the sociologist Lois Cohen, has also been exposed to both public health and sociodental research training. The social scientists among the contributors are drawn from economics, sociology, and social psychology. There is represented also a new breed of "sociomedical scientist" who combines graduate training in a social science with training in public health—Bergner, Brunswick, Greenblum, Patrick, and Siegmann—resulting in points of view which integrate the two fields, attempting to bring together social and medical concerns.

This volume is, in part, one of the products of the work of a committee on sociomedical health indicators which I chaired at the invitation of David Mechanic and Odin Anderson. The Section on Medical Sociology of the American Sociological Association, stimulated by a grant from the Carnegie Corporation in 1971, created a set of working committees whose ostensible purpose was to express the relevance of the work of medical sociologists to the polity. Mechanic and Anderson felt that one of these committees should consider the question of health indicators (see the Preface). In a real sense the authors of the papers in this volume may be seen as members of an extended committee on sociomedical health indicators.

Members of the original committee whose work is not presented here but who nevertheless contributed to its deliberations in a seminar inaugurated in October 1972 at the Columbia University School of Public Health included Sam Shapiro, Margery Braren, and Seth Goldsmith. Others who made presentations at the initial seminar and whose work is published elsewhere include Robert Parke and Nicholas Zill of the Social Science Research Council's Task Force on Coordination of Research on Social Indicators established by Eleanor Sheldon; Dean Krueger, who instituted a clearinghouse on health indexes in the Division of Analysis of the U.S. National Center on Health Statistics; Martin Chen, a psychometrist with the U.S. National Center on Health Services Research; Annemarie Crocetti, then with the Columbia Center for Community Health Systems; Charlotte Ellis Beauchamp, then with the Harlem Hospital Center's Department of Patient Care and Program Evaluation; and Margot Jefferys, director of the Social Research Unit, Bedford College, London.

We shall not use this space for a comprehensive scholarly review of efforts to develop measures to assess the health status of populations. It will be sufficient to mention in passing such landmark ideas as those presented by Stouman and Falk (3) who, forty years ago, offered a profile of health indicators including health service indicators, and, twenty years ago, by Halbert Dunn (4), a former director of the U.S. National Office of Vital Statistics, with his notion of "high-level wellness," and various sounders of the clarion call to produce concepts of positive health, a recent particularly cogently reasoned plea being that of Monroe Lerner (5).

Some readers will note a major omission: the complex subject of mental illness and mental health has not been addressed per se. Beginning with Marie Jahoda's *Current Concepts of Positive Mental Health* (6), to the imaginative efforts of Norman Bradburn's *The Structure of Psychological Well-Being* (7) and Norman Matlin's "The Demography of Happiness" (the *Puerto Rico Master Sample Survey* report) (8), there have been serious efforts to conceptualize and operationalize wholesome and less wholesome mental health attitudes as distinguished from the prevalence of circumstantial interaction between mental hospitals and practitioners and their patients (9, 10) and from psychiatrically oriented community surveys (11-14).

Another significant area not directly considered by any of our contributors is that of the "quality of life." Serious work has been undertaken in this area (15). It is an open question as to whether all such variables dealt with by these investigators should be considered under the rubric of "health," important as they are. Indeed, health may be viewed as only one component of the quality of life, and perhaps not its most important one. I recall a noted social philosopher referring to health as being among the more trivial values of mankind; and another who demeaned the pursuit of health care, if not of health, by his concern with our being driven into becoming a "hospital state."

Yet another area related to health status which is not covered in these pages is the area of preventive health practices or preventive health behavior (16). Smoking, drinking, eating, and physical exercise are behaviors which in some quarters are considered sufficiently related to health status to be dealt with in their own right as health indicators, as for example, in the Canadian volume on social indicators (17), and the health chapter in Terleckyj's volume (18).

Indicators of mental and emotional health, quality of life, and preventive health behavior are not addressed here; they are worthy of extended treatment, but were considered as being beyond the scope of the present effort.

Covered here, as the table of contents reveals, are modifications and expansions of traditional health indicators as well as new ones based on social and behavioral criteria.

When infant mortality rates were relatively high, a charting of the trends in infant mortality seemed indicative of a population's health. What affected a tiny proportion was assumed to reflect the health status of the total population. Whether or not this assumption was ever valid–given the miniscule size of the numerator–the likelihood of its being so today is considerably less. Charlotte Muller et al. seek to build a more sensitive and reflective indicator in their measurement of "reproductive efficiency" (RE) in which the numerator is enlarged by including not only infant deaths but also fetal deaths and surviving children with congenital abnormalities or of low birth weight. There are difficulties in obtaining the necessary data with sufficient completeness for the several components (in particular, fetal deaths), and in avoidance of double counting, e.g. low-birth-weight babies who appear again as infant deaths. Nevertheless, reasonable estimates can be made. Thus, an RE of about 75 percent is estimated for available United States data, suggesting much greater sensitivity and opportunity for modification than infant mortality alone.

For the other end of the age spectrum, Sidney Katz and C. A. Akpom consider measures of sociobiological functioning as more reflective of the health status of older people than the names of the multiple chronic diseases with which they might be afflicted. Indeed, with respect to evaluating the health status of older people, the names and numbers in the WHO International Classification of Diseases and Causes of Death are a Procrustean bed. Building on the work of the Commission on Chronic Illness in the 1950s, Katz and Akpom, using Guttman scaling techniques, noted a hierarchy of independence in performance of activities of daily living (ADL) which enabled them to create an easily understood and readily applicable index of high reliability. Moreover, they find theoretic significance in parallelisms for their Index of ADL with patterns of child development and with behavior of primitive societies. The Index of ADL has already been widely used to evaluate the effectiveness of treatment, not only by Katz and his colleagues, but by many other investigators as well.

Martini et al. of Professor Backett's Department of Community Health at the University of Nottingham analyzed routinely published statistics in the United Kingdom on deaths under one year, total mortality, deaths in hospital, multiple diagnoses, and certified incapacity; their results showed that sociodemographic influences contributed more to the variance than did medical care. Indeed, with respect to mortality, sociodemographic variables explained four times as much of the variance as did medical care. This and similar findings highlight the general conclusion that traditional health status measures are too insensitive to medical care to be useful in evaluating health services. The lack of appropriate indicators of the effectiveness of health services, particularly in the area of primary medical care, has pushed investigators such as Bergner et al. to developing new measures more relevant to the purpose.

There is a dilemma in developing health status indicators that can simultaneously serve two masters: one, the evaluation of specific health action programs; and two, the assessment of the health status of the general population. As Bergner et al. point out, *in developing countries* mortality and morbidity can still be used as outcome measures for both purposes. *In developed countries,* on the other hand, the relative impact of health care programs on health status of the general population is so much reduced that measures of process or structure of medical care tend frequently to be used as proxy measures, ". . . even though the relationship between the process or structure and outcome may not be known." The "Sickness Impact Profile" (SIP) formulated by Bergner et al. is an effort to overcome the insensitivity of mortality and morbidity as measures by providing a sensitive indicator of the outcome of medical care, one which, furthermore, claims to be culturally unbiased and is expressed as changes in behavior. The SIP has been tried out in medical clinics and is being studied as to its relation to clinical judgments. Its utility in serving the second master, the assessment of the health level of a population, remains to be extensively explored.

The SIP is based on self-report, i.e. subjective accounting of experienced behaviors. It is concerned with the reporting of actual behaviors as impacts of sickness. Conceivably such behaviors may be reported by others, as for example, mothers for children. Brunswick, on the other hand, directs attention to personal or subjectively experienced wellness or illness as *Ding an Sich.* To establish this concept she refers to the phenomenon as "ontological health" to remind us that subjectively experienced health is not the same as the kind of health more commonly the concern of physicians, or "medical health." Her empirical study of Harlem adolescents may be regarded as part of an effort to create ontological health status measures which are both age and race specific.

Donald Patrick argues that collective decisions satisfying the Rawlsian principles of equality and social minimum must incorporate what he calls "a social metric for health." This social metric is to be derived from the determination of social preference or value priorities which, in turn, are to enter in collective decision-making processes. He describes and assesses various methods for constructing social metrics. Measurement efforts, he feels, should be directed toward the goal of evaluating the worth of social arrangements in terms of satisfaction provided to the society's members.

Just as Donald Patrick notes that we need measures of social preferences for health status, Howard Kelman says we are lacking evidence about consumer preferences for health *care.* The paucity of appropriate measures to evaluate the effectiveness of health services, coupled with the impression that criteria for assessment of quality of medical care reflect primarily the values and interests of the dominant professional providers, have stirred up a controversial area of assessment by consumers or recipients of medical care. The "small frantic voice of the patient," in the words of the Ford Foundation's William McPeak (19) at the opening of the Stanford University Medical Center, is more and more heard throughout the land, however distortedly amplified through so-called consumer representation on health care planning bodies. Kelman observes that the extent to which spokesmen accurately reflect consumer views is not known; what is needed, he argues, is good empirical data as to what consumers actually regard as the quality characteristics of health care. These should not simply be assumed by the professional.

In the paper by Carr and Wolfe we come finally to the position that what really matters is whether social arrangements are such that people receive the services that are deemed necessary to deal appropriately with defined health problems. The gap between needed services and services actually being received is "unmet need." The nature and extent of unmet needs are measures of fulfillment of societal obligation. If these unmet needs are determined both professionally, as Carr and Wolfe do in their evaluation study in Nashville, and by persons with health problems who are said to be in need of services, as we may infer from the suggestions of Patrick and of Kelman, we shall be on our way to a more complete assessment of health status and needs for care. The United States National Center for Health Statistics, through its Division of Health Examination Statistics, seems to be moving in this direction.

The two concluding papers in this issue offer perspectives (a) from conceptual and methodological points of view, by Thomas W. Bice, and (b) from the point of view of administration and planning, by Athilia E. Siegmann. It is to be hoped that these efforts will contribute not only to evaluation of social action programs and decisions about health services and health policy, but also—through conceptual clarity and operational measurement—to what may be an emerging science of health and society which I have called "sociosalustics" (20-22).

It will be noted that most of the papers on sociomedical health indicators deal with measurements applicable to developed countries. A parallel effort is indicated for methods of assessing health status in the developing countries.

REFERENCES

1. Moriyama, I. M. Problems in the measurement of health status. In *Indicators of Social Change*, edited by E. B. Sheldon and W. E. Moore, pp. 573-600. Russell Sage Foundation, New York, 1968.

2. Elinson, J. Toward sociomedical health indicators. *Social Indicators Research* 1(1): 59-71, 1974.
3. Stouman, K., and Falk, I. S. A study of objective indices of health in relation to environment and sanitation. League of Nations, *Quarterly Bulletin of the Health Organization* 5:901-996, 1936.
4. Dunn, H. L. Points of attack for raising the levels of wellness. *J. Natl. Med. Assoc.* 49(4): 225-235, 1957.
5. Lerner, M. Conceptualization of health and social well-being. In *Health Status Indexes,* edited by R. L. Berg, pp. 1-12. Hospital and Educational Trust, Chicago, 1973.
6. Jahoda, M. *Current Concepts of Positive Mental Health.* Basic Books, New York, 1958.
7. Bradburn, N. *The Structure of Psychological Well-Being.* Aldine Publishing Company, Chicago, 1969.
8. Matlin, N. The demography of happiness. *Puerto Rico Master Sample Survey of Health & Welfare,* Series 2, No. 3. Department of Public Health, University of Puerto Rico, 1965.
9. Hollingshead, A., and Redlich, F. *Social Class and Mental Illness.* Wiley, New York, 1958.
10. Goldhamer, H., and Marshall, A. W. *Psychosis and Civilization.* Free Press, Glencoe, Ill., 1953.
11. Leighton, D. C., Harding, J. S., Macklin, D. B., Macmillan, A. M., and Leighton, A. H. *The Character of Danger.* Basic Books, Inc., New York and London, 1963.
12. Srole, L., Langner, T. S., Michael, S. T., Opler, M. K., and Rennie, T. A. C. *Mental Health in the Metropolis: The Midtown Manhattan Study.* McGraw-Hill, New York, 1962.
13. Dohrenwend, B. S. Social class and stressful events. In *Psychiatric Epidemiology: Proceedings of the International Symposium Held at Aberdeen University 22-25 July 1969.* Oxford University Press, London, 1970.
14. Langner, T. S., and Michael, S. T. *Life Stress and Mental Health.* Free Press, Glencoe, N.Y., 1963.
15. Andrews, F. M., and Withey, S. B. Developing measures of perceived life quality: Results from several national surveys. *Social Indicators Research* 1(1): 1-26, 1974.
16. Becker, M. H., editor. The health belief model and personal health behavior. *Health Education Monographs* 2(4): 324-508, 1974.
17. Statistics Canada. *Perspectives Canada.* Information Canada, Ottawa, 1974.
18. Terleckyj, N. E. *Improvements in the Quality of Life.* National Planning Association, Washington, D.C., 1975.
19. McPeak, W. W. The small frantic voice of the patient: Speech given at dedication of Stanford Medical Center, September 17, 18, 1959. *Stanford M.D.* 9(1): 5-9, 1970.
20. Elinson, J., and Herr, C. E. A Sociomedical Response to Edward S. Rogers: Public Health Asks of Sociology. . . . Paper read at the American Sociological Association Annual Meeting, San Francisco, September 1969.
21. Elinson, J. Methods of sociomedical research. In *Handbook of Medical Sociology,* edited by H. E. Freeman, S. Levine, and L. G. Reeder, pp. 483-500. Prentice-Hall, Inc., Englewood Cliffs, N.J., 1972.
22. Jago, J. "Hal"–Old word, new task. *Soc. Sci. Med.* 9(1): 1-6, 1975.
23. Elinson, J., Mooney, A., and Siegmann, A. E., editors. *Health Goals and Health Indicators: Policy, Planning and Evaluation.* American Association for the Advancement of Science Selected Symposium 2. Westview Press, Boulder, Colorado, 1977.

CHAPTER 1

The Sickness Impact Profile: Conceptual Formulation and Methodology for the Development of a Health Status Measure

Marilyn Bergner and Ruth A. Bobbitt
with
Shirley Kressel, William E. Pollard,
Betty S. Gilson, and Joanne R. Morris

The evaluation of health care in terms of the outcome of such care, that is, the health status of the person cared for, has increased in importance with the expansion of the government's role in financing health care. The results of such evaluations are expected to provide information on the efficacy of programs for decisions regarding the appropriate allocation of resources. From the perspective of those assigned the task of evaluating health programs, the greatest impediments to effective evaluation are the lack of professional consensus as to what constitutes an appropriate outcome measure and the concern that cultural differences among individuals and groups may yield problematic results when a single measure is used with a diverse population.

It is toward the solution of these two problems that the development of the Sickness Impact Profile (SIP) is directed. Though its development is also aimed at providing a fiscally and logistically practical measure of health status, the following discussion will emphasize the issues surrounding the conceptual problems in the development of an outcome measure and their methodological resolution. The administrative feasibility of such a tool will be considered only tangentially.

This investigation was supported by the Health Maintenance Organization Service of the Health Services and Mental Health Administration, Contract No. HSM 110-HMO-63(2), and the National Center for Health Services Research, Health Resources Administration, Grant No. HS 01769-01. Portions of this paper were presented at the Workshop on Measurement of Outcomes, the University of Rochester School of Medicine and Dentistry, November 26-27, 1973.

OUTCOME, PROCESS, AND STRUCTURE MEASURES

Measures used for evaluation of health care are commonly grouped into three broad categories: measures of outcome, measures of process, and measures of structure. "Outcome" measures relate to "that which results from something; the consequence or issue" (1). Process evaluation may be considered as measurement of procedural end points; structure evaluation as measurement of the settings and instrumentalities in which the care takes place (2).

The measure chosen to evaluate health care in a particular setting is often dependent on the presumed general health level of the group to be measured. Mortality and morbidity measures are deemed appropriate where the bulk of health problems are acute, and outcome *seems* to be directly related to health care programs. For example, in developing countries, such outcome measures are used to assess both the health status of the general population and specific health care programs. Under such circumstances both the efficacy and effectiveness of programs are easily and quickly determined by morbidity and/or mortality rates.

For developed countries, measures of the process or structure of medical care are used to assess the quality of health care programs. In this case, process or structure measures tend to be used as proxy measures of outcome where health problems are chronic and morbidity and mortality are insensitive and seemingly unrelated to health care changes in the short run. Under such conditions the determination of the efficacy or effectiveness of a health care program is problematic since process or structure measures are used even though the relationship between the process or structure and outcome may not be known (3). This situation is often tolerated because there exists no agreed-upon or practical measure of outcome (i.e. health status) and because the task of developing such a measure appears formidable.

PROGRAM EVALUATION

The need for an outcome-based health status measure is underscored by the results of the few well-designed studies of health care that have used outcome measures to evaluate programs. It is not clear whether these results reflect problems with the outcome measure used or accurately describe the effect of the program.

Many find no difference between control and experimental groups or report inconclusive or contradictory results (4). Such results may have serious implications for the efficacy of health care. Yet they rarely provoke changes in the program to which they relate. Criticism of the findings of health care evaluation studies has undermined their usefulness. Criticism is most often centered around the measures used to evaluate change. Often there is no agreement as to the expected change to be reflected by the measure under the conditions of the study. And, even when there is agreement on this, it is difficult to obtain agreement on the extent to which the measure could be expected to discern change over a relatively short time span.

The inadequacies found in the design of many health care evaluations fall into three broad groups. First, the program goal may not be stated appropriately. Though a program may state that improved health status is its primary goal, secondary goals such as increased community participation or improved educational opportunities may in fact be the main focus of attention. Second, the measure used to evaluate the program may be inappropriate. For example, a measure such as disease-free days may be unlikely to exhibit change in a specific population even with a new health care program. Third, the measure used to evaluate the program may be insensitive. It may differentiate the very sick from the very well, but not allow the determination of levels of health on a continuum from very sick to very well.

If progress is to be made in the area of health measurement, the second and third problems must be solved. The first must be left to those who choose and apply measurement techniques.

CULTURAL CONSIDERATION IN MEASUREMENT

The applicability and appropriateness of a measure is often dependent on the culture of the group to which the measure is applied. Even universally held values such as long life or good health may generate conflicting and contradictory measures when operationalized (5). Debates concerning the validity of measures of intelligence or mental health are common in both the popular and scientific press. Much of this debate centers around the applicability of measures developed, tested, and standardized on one cultural group, to other groups with presumably different values and behavior. Measures of *physical* health appear, at first glance, to be outside this debate. The supposed objectivity of physical findings is thought to nullify the influence of cultural values. However, closer scrutiny reveals that both the recognition and treatment of disease is dependent on social and cultural factors. Within a relatively small and homogeneous town in the United States, social class differences determine the threshold of recognition and definition of pain as sickness (6). Within the physician's lexicon of diseases and conditions, a symptom such as jaundice may be assessed as a mild and frequent discomfort of no consequence, or as a symptom of a severe disease of the liver, depending on the cultural background and milieu of the physician (7).

When such differences in values exist, data collected on different groups of individuals are often not comparable. The use of *either* self-reports or clinician reports of morbidity is subject to values bias in addition to distortion attributable to memory or poor record keeping. The use of more "objective" data such as that based on laboratory or radiological examination presupposes the existence of standardized methods of testing and clearly defined limits of normalcy. Without these conditions, interpretation of results is arbitrary, that is, value dependent.

POPULATION ASSESSMENT

The need for culturally unbiased estimates of health is underscored by the demand for a measure that permits assessment of population groups. Ideally, a health status measure should be appropriate and sensitive enough to be applicable to the assessment of health status of population groups, and specific enough to permit evaluation of a specific health program directed toward a circumscribed subgroup.

Though not the prime concern of this paper, it should be mentioned here that the form of the instrument is crucial if this standard is to be met. It must be simple, require no special equipment, and be relatively inexpensive to administer. In addition, it must satisfy criteria that allow interpretation of results in the population survey setting as well as the treatment program setting. In the former, a single score or index may be most important. In the latter, detailed descriptive data in a specific area of living may be essential. But the population survey setting may also benefit from descriptive data or subscores. Such detailed information may be essential to program planning or program assessment for general populations. On the other hand, an index or overall score may be useful to the program evaluator who is comparing experimental groups in different treatment programs.

Therefore, a health status measure should provide scores and it should consist of subunits that permit the disaggregation of the scores into subscores and into descriptive statements. For the methodologist, these criteria readily provide evidence for face validity; for the planner and administrator, they allow transfer of numbers into descriptions and thence into programs.

THE BASIS FOR A MEASURE OF SICKNESS-RELATED BEHAVIOR

The development of the Sickness Impact Profile begins at this point and with this question: What can be done to change existing measures of health or to devise new measures of health which would be acceptable, appropriate, able to measure change in the short run, and universally applicable?

Baumann (8) describes three broad conceptions of health on which individuals base their appraisal of their own health status. These are a feeling-state conception, a clinical conception, and a performance conception. The feeling-state conception depends upon how healthy or sick the individual *feels.* Phrases such as "I feel good" or "I don't feel well today" are characteristic of the way subjects who base their self-perceived health status on their feeling-state describe themselves. The clinical conception depends upon symptoms to describe the individual's state of health. "My back hurts," "I am nauseated," are characteristic of phrases used by those who view their health status in terms of the clinical conception. The performance conception depends upon behavior to describe health. Individuals who base their self-perception of health on this conception tend to describe themselves as "not walking," "staying indoors," "eating less."

The feeling-state conception is extremely difficult to measure since it is subject to frequent changes from many sources and inaccessible to external validation because of its inherent subjectivity. The clinical conception, which is based on notions of disease and symptoms, limits the measure to individuals under medical care or requires the medical interpretation of symptoms reported by those under study. Thus the definitions used are those of the physician or other appropriate professionals.

The performance conception has several attributes that make it potentially useful as a basis for development of an outcome measure of health care. First, performance or behavior may be reported directly by the individual under consideration. Second, performance may also be observed and reported by another respondent about the individual under consideration. Third, performance may be affected by medical treatment even though the disease itself may be unaffected. Fourth, performance can be measured whether or not the individual is receiving medical care. And fifth, a measure based on performance or behavior permits relating diverse definitions of disease and sickness by uncovering universal patterns of behavioral dysfunction (9).

THE DYSFUNCTION CONTINUUM

Health-related behavioral dysfunction is a concept both familiar and relevant to the individual. As the basis for health status assessment, it assures measurement of significant events from the societal, individual, and health care points of view. Behaviors characteristic of individuals in societal settings are often defined within the context of fulfillment of social role (10, 11). One's importance to society may be considered in relation to one's level of function within a social role. Many factors may influence function level, including amount of sleep, parental training, personal habits and expectations, and societal habits and expectations. Health and sickness undoubtedly affect behavior and role performance. An injury as insignificant as a sprained finger may impair functioning in one's role as parent (feeding, playing), student (writing), musician (piano playing), lover (sexual relations), and so forth.

The healthy individual may be thought of as behaving without limitation and, therefore, functioning optimally. The sick individual may be thought of as behaving with limitation and, therefore, exhibiting dysfunction. Health-sickness and function-dysfunction can each be conceived of as a single continuum parallel to one another. Presumably there are levels of positive health ranging from maximally healthy to minimally healthy, just as there are levels of positive function ranging from maximally functional to minimally functional. At some point, however, the continuum moves toward the negative side–not healthy or sick, not functional or dysfunctional. The medical care process is usually concerned with this negative side. Rarely does it promulgate new programs, develop new techniques, or plan new health systems in order to maximize the health or functioning of an individual or group. Even so-called preventive programs, aimed at examining the well, are often directed toward detection and treatment of sickness. Thus, the behaviorally based measure of health status should measure sickness or dysfunctional behavior since it is most relevant to the process being assessed.

A MODEL OF SICKNESS BEHAVIOR

A model for measuring sickness-related behavior should be independent of the conception of health, the health care system, or care-seeking behavior. Such a model should be universally applicable and, in conjunction with the concepts of health, it forms the basis for the *development* of a useful measure of health outcome.

An individual, within social, cultural, or societal bounds, learns to associate certain signs with sickness. When he perceives these signs as related to himself, he begins to move through stages in a career of sickness (12). If the symptoms (e.g. signs) are mild and transitory, the individual may consider himself sick for only a very short time span.

Duration and severity of symptoms change the self-perception of sickness and the associated sickness-related behavior.

Symptom definition, severity, and duration determine whether the individual will seek help (e.g. medical care) from an outside source. If he does not and his sickness persists, he experiences the effect (impact) of sickness, nonetheless. If he does seek help, he may seek the advice of neighbors, friends, relatives, pharmacists, folk healers, physicians, nurses, etc. When he finally comes under the care of that professional designated by his culture as the "curer," he enters the medical care process.

At this point, his heretofore self-defined sickness may be redefined by the professional as disease, and the results of care may eventually be measured in terms of morbidity or mortality (13). For those who do seek advice from others when they are sick, the combination of their own sickness perception, the redefinition in terms of disease provided by professionals, and the medical care process itself influence the effect (impact) the illness has.

Effects or impacts, whether they derive from untreated sickness or from sickness under professional care, may be manifested in changes in performance, feelings, attitudes, or symptoms. A diagrammatic representation of this model is presented in Figure 1.

In transforming this model into the framework for developing an outcome measure of health, sickness impacts were conceptualized as changes in behavior associated with the carrying out of one's daily life activities. These changes in behavior were considered dysfunctions since they represent deviations from the way an individual usually behaves. Though these changes in behavior may be functional in accelerating the return to good health, they are dysfunctional in the sense that they represent impaired or ineffective role performance. It is in this latter sense that the term dysfunction is used here.

The transformation of the model into a set of working definitions is shown in Figure 2. Signs and symptoms are defined as those found in oral reports and/or written records of individuals, patients, doctors, folk healers, nurses, etc. Sickness is defined

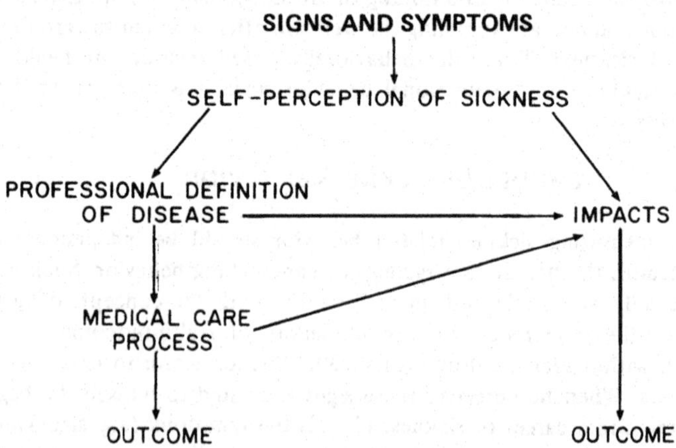

Figure 1. Diagrammatic representation of a model of sickness behavior.

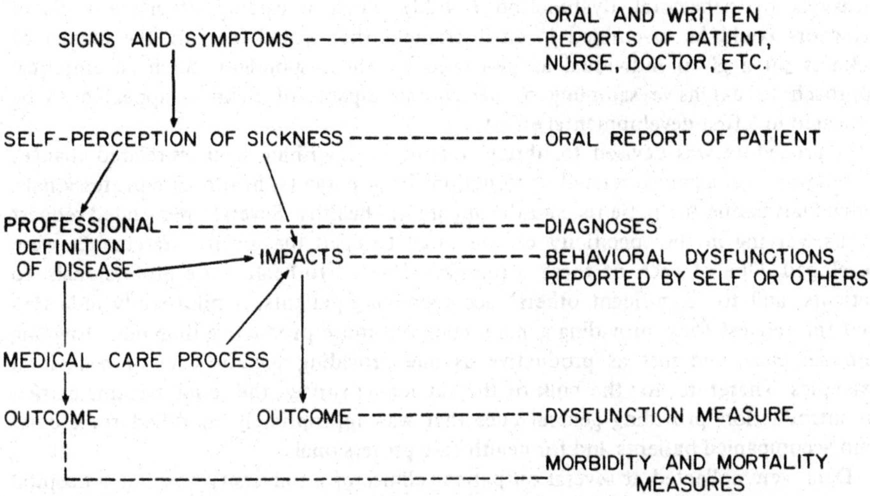

Figure 2. Transformation of a model of sickness behavior into a set of working definitions.

as an individual's own perception of his health. Disease measures are defined as different diagnoses and their severity. Sickness impact is defined as self-reports of dysfunction, clinical reports of dysfunction, others' reports of dysfunction, and tests of dysfunction using other instruments.

These working definitions are converted into measures with the expectation that they will individually and collectively relate to the dysfunction measure so as to permit a series of validation studies. Such studies are essential to determine both the specificity and sensitivity of the measure and must occur prior to its generalized use. This assumes, of course, that in addition to assessing the sensitivity of the measure to change, its reliability in terms of reproducibility has also been determined.

INSTRUMENT DEVELOPMENT

Catalog of Behavioral Impacts

The intent to develop a behavior-based instrument for measuring the impact of sickness that is comprehensive in scope and applicability, and that is sensitive in detailing the kind and degree of impact, raises the question of what sources to tap to assure a representative catalog of sickness impacts.

Most function assessment instruments are based on statements of dysfunction devised by experts and are principally concerned with the extremely dysfunctional individual. Ideally, the instrument should be based on an all-inclusive, though nonduplicative, list of health-related dysfunctions that would cover the range from minimal to maximal dysfunction. Such data could be obtained from self-reports, from reports based on clinical observation or observation by other trained observers, from reports of "significant others" such as family members, and from existing measures of behavioral dysfunction (14-23). Such a catalog of sickness-related behaviors could be assembled in an instrument that would measure the impact of sickness on a given individual as perceived by the respondent. Such an empirical approach to extensive sampling of behavioral impacts of sickness appeared to be indicated in a first developmental effort.

A procedure was devised to obtain statements describing sickness-related changes in behavior, i.e. sickness-related dysfunction, from patients, health care professionals, individuals caring for patients, and the apparently healthy. Several open-ended request forms, varying in the specificity of cues used to elicit the specific statements, were developed. One of each of these forms was directed to health care professionals, to patients, and to "significant others" accompanying patients. A pilot study indicated that the request form providing general cues was more productive than one providing minimal cues, and just as productive as one providing specific cues or behavioral examples. Therefore, for the bulk of the cataloging survey, the request forms carried an introduction providing general cues that was appropriately modified for escorts who accompanied patients and for health care professionals.

Data were collected at several outpatient clinics of a university hospital, a hospital walk-in clinic, a private partnership practice, and a prepaid group practice. The prepaid group practice enrollees provided a particularly appropriate population since it was known to be demographically equivalent to the population of the region from which it was drawn. These enrollees completed the bulk of the request forms. A sampling scheme was devised which ensured that the respondents represented all the relevant demographic and illness-related variables. This scheme focused on securing a universe of behaviors, not a universe of individuals.

Over 1100 completed request forms were collected. Sampling continued until the yield of new and usable statements diminished markedly. As a final step in the empirical search, existing catalogs of behavioral dysfunction related to illness were reviewed and statements were added to the empirically obtained catalog.

Processing the Raw Data

Data obtained in the search were subjected to the following set of criteria to provide a basic catalog of statements to be used in the prototype Sickness Impact Profile:

> Each statement must (a) describe the behavior, and (b) specify the nature of the dysfunction. Dysfunction was defined as including modification or impairment in degree or manner of carrying on an activity, cessation of an activity, or initiation of a new activity that interferes with or substitutes for a usual activity.

Statements obtained from the entire sample of subjects and from the literature were processed according to these criteria into a set of potential *items* for inclusion in the prototype instrument. The first 500 statements obtained were examined by five staff members. Working independently and then together, they eliminated or rephrased statements that were ambiguous or were not expressed in sufficiently explicit behavioral terms. During this process, statements considered virtual duplicates were eliminated. Statements that were similar but in which there were significant shades of difference were rewritten to make the differences clear. An item to be used in the SIP had to be unique in terms of at least one of the following criteria: (a) in the behavior it described, (b) in the nature of the dysfunction described, or (c) in the degree of dysfunction specified.

On completion of this process, the 500 statements had been reduced to 180 unique items. A preliminary sort of the 180 items was performed independently by each of the five staff members. Items were grouped together if they seemed to refer to a common type of activity. Agreement among staff members on the grouping of items was analyzed. The minimum criterion for retaining a pair of items in the same group was agreement by at least three of the five staff members. Grouping all pairs of items linked by three or more agreements produced 18 categories of activity.

The remaining 600 statements were then sorted independently by each staff member using the framework provided by the items included in these preliminary categories, but having freedom to alter or add categories. As a part of this process, statements were discarded that did not meet the criterion for a unique item (including statements regarded as duplicating each other or one of the 180 items already accepted). An analysis of agreement among staff was again performed, using three agreements as a minimum criterion. On the basis of this analysis, the SIP instrument was reduced to 312 items in 14 categories. Three of the original 18 categories became amalgamated into other categories as the second group of items was added to the sort. One of the original categories of items containing behavioral statements relating to the use of health services or medical care was discarded. Such statements were considered evidence of the utilization and/or availability of health care and not necessarily statements of dysfunctional behavior. Thus, they could be regarded as artifacts of the health care system itself that might confound results obtained across cultures or across health care systems. Table 1 shows the descriptive titles subsequently applied to the categories of items and examples of items included in each.

Though the data gathering, and sorting and grouping process were aimed at collecting and retaining any statements that might be useful, relevant, unique, or discriminative, the completeness of the SIP catalog was uncertain at this point. However, continuing review of the literature has not revealed major areas of behavior or specific dysfunctions omitted from the SIP and obviously appropriate for inclusion. Furthermore, two field trials of approximately 250 subjects each which solicited additional statements, and an intensive review of the SIP by 17 clinicians, yielded no useful new behavioral statements.

Construction of the Sickness Impact Profile Instrument

The SIP was conceptualized as an instrument which would provide a descriptive profile of the responses of a given individual in terms of the specific behavioral impacts of sickness. It was intended that these impacts should be capable of being summarized within specific areas of living as well as in some form of overall assessment. Though the respondent to the SIP can be someone other than the subject, the primary focus,

Table 1

Categories and selected items of the Sickness Impact Profile

Category	Items Describing Behaviors Involved in or Related to	Selected Items
A	Social interaction	I make many demands, for example, insist that people do things for me, tell them how to do things I am going out less to visit people
B	Ambulation or locomotion activity	I am walking shorter distances I do not walk at all
C	Sleep and rest activity	I lie down to rest more often during the day I sit around half-asleep
D	Taking nutrition	I am eating no food at all; nutrition is taken through tubes or intravenous fluids I am eating special or different food, for example, soft food, bland diet, low-salt, low-fat foods
E	Usual daily work	I often act irritable toward my work associates, for example, snap at them, give sharp answers, criticize easily I am not working at all
F	Household management	I have given up taking care of personal or household business affairs, for example, paying bills, banking, working on budget I am doing *less* of the regular daily work around the house that I usually do
G	Mobility and confinement	I stay within one room I stop often when traveling because of health problems
H	Movement of the body	I am in a restricted position all the time I sit down, lie down, or get up only with someone's help
I	Communication activity	I communicate only by gestures, for example, moving head, pointing, sign language I often lose control of my voice when I talk, for example, my voice gets louder, starts trembling, changes pitch

Table 1 (Continued)

Category	Items Describing Behaviors Involved in or Related to	Selected Items
J	Leisure pastimes and recreation	I am doing more physically inactive pastimes instead of my other usual activities
		I am going out for entertainment less often
K	Intellectual functioning	I have difficulty reasoning and solving problems, for example, making plans, making decisions, learning new things
		I sometimes behave as if I were confused or disoriented in place or time, for example, where I am, who is around, directions, what day it is
L	Interaction with family members	I isolate myself as much as I can from the rest of the family
		I am not doing the things I usually do to take care of my children or family
M	Emotions, feelings, and sensations	I act irritable and impatient with myself, for example, talk badly about myself, swear at myself, blame myself for things that happen
		I laugh and cry suddenly for no reason
N	Personal hygiene	I dress myself, but do so very slowly
		I do not have control of my bowels

and indeed the usual respondent, is the subject himself. Thus, the items in the instrument were retained as first-person statements rather than formulated into questions. In addition, the 312 items were phrased in the present tense; in simple, clear, and direct sentences; and ambiguities such as the use of double negatives and abstract or value-loaded terms were avoided. Thus, the items conform to informal criteria appearing in the literature on the construction of attitude scales (24).

The 312 items in various random orders were grouped within their appropriate categories and incorporated into a standardized and structured interview schedule. Since little is known about the effect of order of presentation on response rates to items concerning sickness-related behavior, the items and categories were randomly ordered for each subject. Thus, in the first test of the instrument, there could be no systematic bias in response due to the order of presentation of items.

The entire instrument is administered by a trained interviewer who reads the instructions and each item. The respondent is asked to respond *only* to items which: (a) he is *sure* describe him on this day, and (b) are related to his health. This approach uses the concept of health as a condition defined or perceived by the individual against which he evaluates his own behavior on the day of the interview. So as to ensure the reliability of response and to err in the direction of omitting descriptions of dysfunction that the respondent might regard as questionable, the respondent is instructed *not* to respond to an item unless he is *sure* that it describes his behavior.

Scaling: Methodological Considerations

It is to be expected that the relative impact of sickness on the behavior of two individuals would be expressed to some extent by a simple comparison of the number of items each selected as descriptive of himself. However, this measure may lack sensitivity in an instrument designed to cover a broad range of behavioral impacts in various areas of living. It is quite possible that an individual suffering minor impacts expressed, for example, in a slight slowing down in usual activities, might check as many SIP items as an individual who describes himself as not performing certain usual functions at all. In other words, a weighting of the various behavioral impacts, according to some social norm or consensus, might provide a more sensitive and discriminative measure of the relative severity of dysfunction describing the two individuals.

Torgerson (25), and later Shinn (26), have discussed "subject-centered" and "stimulus-centered" scales. Using a subject-centered method, a group of judges might be asked to rate a number of stimuli in order to draw conclusions about certain characteristics of the judges. Using a stimulus-centered method, a group of judges might be asked to rate a number of items in order to secure a consensus as to the relative value of the items. For example, in securing ratings of SIP items in terms of severity of dysfunction, the primary purpose would be to secure information about the items; information about the judges would be used only to evaluate the reliability or generalizability of the item ratings. As Shinn suggests, two different groups of judges, perhaps from two subcultures, might be asked to rate the items with the interest of comparing the ratings to illuminate differences between the two groups of judges' perceptions on the scaling continuum. But it would still be the items that would be placed on the continuum of severity of dysfunction.

In a stimulus-centered approach, some form of either magnitude or ratio scaling, or of category or equal-interval scaling, is usually selected. Category scaling has predominated in the social sciences primarily because of the simplicity of the procedures and their adaptability to almost any individual involved in the judging task.

Considering that the prototype SIP consisted of a large number of statements about behavior, and that it was proposed that the scaling should ultimately reflect the judgments of health care consumers covering a broad range of sophistication, education, and cultural background, it appeared that equal-interval scaling provided the most dependable and appropriate approach. Researchers have observed the tendency to a logarithmic relationship between interval and ratio scaling on a set of stimuli. Therefore, to assure equal-interval measures, Edwards (24, pp. 120-148) suggests a method of successive-interval scaling to assure equal-interval measures from ordered category data. This method was employed recently (27) on a health status instrument (28). Reliable category scaling appeared possible of attainment and capable of correction by the successive-intervals technique. A scaling procedure was therefore developed and tested.

Scaling: Procedures

The judging group of 25 persons included seven nursing students (all with clinical experience), eight medical students (three with clinical experience), four physicians, and six health administration students.

The sorting and grouping of SIP items into areas of activity or categories provided a manageable framework for item scaling. Recall that it was proposed that the SIP should be capable of providing discriminative dysfunction scores ranging from an overall index, through subscores in meaningful descriptive areas of activity, to specific profile or pattern scores reflective of diagnostic or treatment groups. This implies that all items ultimately be related to each other on a single scale. And yet the number of items made this a most formidable task unless some modification of Thurstone scaling was employed.

As has been reported previously, the scaling consisted of two steps. "In the first step, the judges rated each item within each category on an 11-point scale, ranging from minimally dysfunctional to severely dysfunctional. Judges were asked to rate the severity of the dysfunction described by an item without regard for what might be causing it, i.e., without regard for any specific health condition, prognosis, or personal characteristics, in the context of which the behavior might seem more or less dysfunctional" (29). As discussed below, the mean scale values of the items were stable, and there was high agreement among judges. This result and the fact that each item in each category had been rated in terms of the same concept of severity of dysfunction suggested that the items could be rated in terms of dysfunction, across categories (29).

In the second step of item scaling, the judges were asked to place those items that had been judged on the average to be the most dysfunctional and the least dysfunctional within each category on a single 15-point scale. Use of the larger scale provided for stretching out or discriminating the extreme items among categories. Assuming that continued agreement among the judges was obtained, the average scale value for each of these extreme items could be calculated and could provide a set of commonly scaled end points within which the 15-point scale value for each of the remaining items in each cateogry could be mathematically assigned. The high agreement in scaling within the 11-point scale would thus be retained.

Scaling: Reliability

As has been reported elsewhere (29), there was high agreement among the judges in discriminating among the items with respect to severity of dysfunction. First, the correlation of each judge's ratings of the 312 items with the mean of the 25 judges' ratings of these items was generally high and indicated that this "itemistic" approach produced reliable scale values from this group of judges. Second, the agreement among the judges on each item scaled was generally high; that is, items were scaled with a mean standard deviation of 1.99 scale points, and with a standard deviation of the standard deviations of 0.446. This means that the largest 95 percent confidence interval for the mean scale value of a given item was approximately two scale points. Twenty-nine of the 312 items were omitted from the prototype instrument because they were scaled with 95 percent confidence intervals greater than two scale points. Results of the scaling of the end point items of each category were comparable.

In general, the more circumscribed the scaling task, the less culturally biased the resultant scale values appear to be. The results of the scaling provide support for this statement. Differences in sophistication in health matters among the judges appeared not to effect the scale values assigned to items in terms of relative severity of dysfunction. T-tests showed no significant difference between the clinically sophisticated and unsophisticated types of judges with respect to the mean scale values assigned to items. Edwards' method of successive-interval scaling was applied to the 11-point category scaling data for the 284 reliably scaled items. The item scale values obtained by the equal-interval category scaling method were comparable throughout the 11-point scale to the transformed 11-point scale values obtained by the method of successive-interval scaling. Regressing the SIP scale values on the successive-interval scale values, $r = 0.99$, slope = 1.1, intercept = −0.93.

Although this scaling of the items in the SIP will be validated by a large and broad group of health care consumers, the preliminary scale values obtained provided the basis for testing various scoring approaches.

Scoring the SIP

Four scoring systems were selected for testing the extent to which each would reflect the item scale values and the interactive pattern of dysfunction portrayed by a given subject. Each scoring method permitted calculation of a profile of scores across categories and for the overall SIP. In defining each of these scores, the relative weight assigned to number of items checked and the item checked with the highest scale value are specified. The methods selected for testing were:

- A *mean* of the scale values of the items checked. A mean score represents an average of the dysfunction weights of the items checked in an SIP.
- A *mean* of the *squared* scale values of items checked. This represents an average of the dysfunction weights of items checked, but increases the relative weights of items that have high scale values.
- A *percent* of total possible dysfunction, which is the sum of the scale values of items checked, divided by the sum of the scale values for all items, multiplied by 100. This method of scoring provides a relative frequency that is weighted by the magnitude of the scale values as well as by the number of items checked.
- A *profile,* indicating the number of items checked within one of four scale-point groupings. The determination of scale-point groupings is based on the distribu-

tion of items scaled across 15 points, 15-11, 10-7, 6-5, 4-1. For example, the profile score for two different protocols, each with 8 items checked, might be 1430 or 0044 depending on the scale values of the items checked. While the profile describes a frequency distribution, its size as an integer may also relate in some systematic way to the scale value pattern of items checked, as well as reflecting the number of items checked.

Field Testing the SIP

A limited field trial was conducted as part of the initial development of the SIP to provide (a) scaling, scoring, and, indirectly, construct validation; (b) preliminary data about administrative feasibility; (c) a preliminary analysis of reliability and validity; and (d) a set of completed SIPs in which items would be checked a sufficient number of times to provide data for item analysis and revision.

In the field trial, 246 group practice enrollees were interviewed. To secure respondents from within a broad range of states of health, nonpatients, outpatients, "walk-in clinic" patients, inpatients, and home care patients were sampled. Six interviewers were trained intensively through the use of demonstration and practice interviews conducted according to a set of instructions provided by a training manual. As part of the training, pairs of interviewers interviewed a given respondent within a period of twenty-four hours. This permitted an estimate of the reliability of all possible pairings of interviewers. Procedures were standardized and interviewers were required to report problems encountered in contacting and interviewing subjects, subject reactions, evidence of confusion regarding meaning or applicability of items, and any other information which might be useful in interpreting data and in revision of the questionnaire.

Results: Validation of Scaling and Scoring and Dysfunction Construct

The SIP items were scaled individually in relation to each other. It is possible, of course, that there are pattern or interaction effects among dysfunction items that might be checked by a given subject that should be reflected in the scoring. To test the scoring methods and to validate the construct of dysfunction, a second severity of dysfunction scaling procedure was employed using data obtained from the field trial SIPs.

Four groups of 25 judges, none of whom had been involved in the item scaling procedure, each rated 50 SIPs obtained from field trial subjects. This provided 25 ratings each of 200 SIPs. As in the item scaling, this rating was also done in two steps. In the first step, the judges were asked to make a global rating of dysfunction of each subject's protocol of responses in each category of the SIP. The points on the scale ranged, as for item scaling, from 1, "minimally dysfunctional," to 11, "maximally dysfunctional." Also, as in item scaling, judges were asked to make their ratings without regard to the cause of the dysfunction. The mean scale value assigned to subject SIPs was stable, and again there was high agreement among the judges. Therefore, in the second step, the judges were asked to rate each subject's complete SIP on a 15-point scale, having as reference his previous ratings of dysfunction for each subject on each category of dysfunction. This information was provided to him by a computer printout of his category ratings attached to each subject's SIP protocol.

The results of scaling by each of the four groups of judges were analyzed in two ways (29). First, the correlations of each judge's ratings with the mean ratings of subject protocols were high for each of the groups of judges. Second, the agreement among judges on each SIP scaled was consistently high for each of the four groups of judges. The mean standard deviation for the four groups of judges ranged from 1.6 to 1.7 in judging subjects' protocols by category on the 11-point scale, and from 1.9 to 2.0 in judging overall protocols on the 15-point scale.

For readers with a technical interest, it should be noted that a unique method for assessing agreement among judges was employed. In all of the judging tasks for item and SIP subject scaling, it was important to determine if certain items or subjects were unusually difficult to rate. If an item or subject was difficult to rate, little agreement would be expected among judges regarding the scale value assigned to it. Thus, the standard deviation of the values assigned by the judges to an item or to a subject was used as an index of this difficulty, since it is a measure of the spread of judgments around the mean judgment. For each group of judges, the mean of the standard deviations for all items or subjects and the standard deviations of the distribution of judges' ratings for each individual item or subject were computed. The individual item or subject's standard deviation was converted to a z-score, which indicates how many standard deviations the individual standard deviation of judgments is from the mean or average standard deviation. For example, a z-score of −1.5 means that the standard deviation of that item or subject was 1.5 standard deviations less than the mean standard deviation, while a z-score of +1.0 means that the item or subject had a standard deviation 1.0 standard deviation larger than the mean standard deviation. Any item or subject with a z-score equal to or greater than +1.0 was said to be difficult to judge in comparison with the rest of the group. By this criterion, the largest standard deviation acceptable in any of the judging tasks for any of the groups of judges was 2.78 scale points. The standard error of the mean of items or subjects with a standard deviation of this maximum size is 0.55. Confidence limits were computed using this standard error, and they indicate that we can be 95 percent confident that the population means for even those items or subjects lie within plus or minus 1.15 scale points of our obtained sample means. Thus, the values we obtained in our scaling procedures are quite stable. The mean values derived for items or subjects with standard deviations of less than 2.78 are, of course, even more stable.

The field trial SIPs were scored according to each of the scoring methods outlined above. It was anticipated that comparisons among pairs of these scoring methods and of each scoring method with the judges' scaling of the same SIP protocol would permit the determination of whether interaction effects among items were most appropriately represented by a specific scoring method. The comparison between each scoring method and the judges' evaluations would give some insight into the factors that were important to those judging the individual SIPs. The intent of these comparisons was to determine the degree to which the SIP ratings could be predicted by one of these item scoring methods, or some combination of them.

Initially, correlation coefficients were analyzed to compare scoring methods with each other and with the SIP ratings. The results of this comparison indicate that all of the scoring methods relate sufficiently well to ratings of the SIPs to give evidence of the validity of the values derived in item scaling. Each scoring method correlates to about the same extent with each of the others except percent with mean squared scores. Percent score gives considerable weight to number of items checked, while mean squared score gives greatest weight to items that have high scale values. The highest correlations are between profile and mean squared scores and next, between profile and percent scores. This suggests that the profile score, considered as an integer, incorporates the increased weight to items of high scale value as does the mean squared score, but also takes into account the number of items checked, as does the percent score.

Looking at the correlations between the scoring methods and the protocol ratings of the field trial SIPs, it was seen that profile and percent correlate very closely with ratings ($r \geqslant 0.85$) but profile correlations are somewhat higher across categories. Though protocol judges did not know the item scale values, it appears that, in making their ratings, they attended to both number of items checked and the item checked with the highest scale value. Therefore, partial correlations of each scoring method were calculated with the ratings, holding constant number of items and maximum item value, first singly and then together. The amount of variance left unexplained suggests that judges assigned differential weights to an item when it was seen in different patterns of items. The profile score appears to be the most reflective, however, of all facets involved in the ratings of the SIPs. As noted above, the profile score describes a distribution. It should be observed, however, that if it is regarded as an integer, it increases exponentially in the direction of the higher scale value items. The profile and the percent of maximum scoring methods were retained after the pilot field trial for further examination through multiple regression and interaction detection techniques.

The analysis of scaling and scoring gave evidence of the validity of the values derived in item scaling and of the construct of dysfunction as a basis for scaling.

Results: Feasibility, Reliability, and Validity

The 246 interviews with group practice enrollees permitted an assessment of the administrative feasibility of the SIP. As has been reported elsewhere (29), respondents found the instrument and the interviewing procedure acceptable. Preliminary assessment of reliability and validity made during this field trial warranted further and more systematic tests of reliability and validity. These were undertaken, using a revised instrument, during a second field trial. In general, the results were positive and have already been reported (30, 31).

Refinement and Revision Based on Item Analysis

Items to be retained in the SIP or any measurement instrument should be discriminative and reliable. This determination can only be based upon data provided by field trial. Caution must be exercised in omitting items until there has been sufficient sampling to provide representative SIP and criterion data from the general health care population. Criterion data for item analysis within areas of activity or categories are particularly difficult to obtain except in a few instances (17-21) where there are other function assessment measures available. In general, data are analyzed to determine:

1. The interrelationships among items;
2. The relationship of items to category and overall scores;
3. The relationship of category scores to overall scores;
4. The relationship of items to various criterion measures;
5. The reliability of items;
6. The reliability in terms of internal consistency of categories and overall SIP;
7. The discriminative capacity of the items in accounting for variance among subjects; and
8. The clarity of items.

The SIP revision process involves a data gathering field trial, a statistical and content analysis, the development of a revised form(s) of the instrument, a pretest of the revision(s) by a reanalysis of previously obtained data, and finally, a validation of the revision(s) in another field trial.

Although at the time of this writing, the SIP has been revised twice to a long form of 189 items and a short form of 138 items (30, 31), the first revision will be described here. In order to refine and revise the prototype SIP, the pilot field trial data were item analyzed using the judges' ratings of SIP protocols and SIP scores for categories and overall. Since profile and percent scores were highly correlated, percent scores were used in item analysis, at this stage, to permit application of parametric statistics. This assessment and revision process involved four phases:

1. Statistical and content analysis of items;
2. Rewording and subsequent rescaling of some items;
3. Development of a revised SIP;
4. Pretesting the revised SIP by reanalyzing the pilot study data according to the revisions.

Statistical and Content Analysis

The *statistical analysis* of SIP items was performed on the SIP item data, SIP scores, and the judges' ratings of SIP protocols collected during the field trial.

Specifically, multiple regression analyses and interaction detection analyses (32) were carried out to examine the relationships among items describing subjects, and the ratings of dysfunction and the scores of those subjects in each of the 14 categories. In looking at the relationship between items and category ratings of dysfunction, the items in a category are the predictor variables and the category rating is the criterion. In looking at the relationship between items and category scores, the items in a category are the predictor variables and the category score is the criterion. The analyses showed which items in each category were most highly related to each other and to the criterion, and which items were relatively independent and accounted for most of the variance. Based on these analyses the SIP items were tentatively sorted into four mutually exclusive groups:

Group I: Items which were responded to by more than 10 subjects and accounted for more than 1 percent of the variance in the multiple regression analysis.

Group II: Items which were responded to by more than 10 subjects and accounted for less than 1 percent of the variance in the multiple regression analysis, and were predictors in the interaction detection analysis or were otherwise considered substantively important by the SIP staff.

Group III: Items which were responded to by 10 or fewer subjects irrespective of variance accounted for.

Group IV: Items which were responded to by more than 10 subjects and accounted for less than 1 percent of the variance in the multiple regression analysis.

Additional regression analyses were conducted to assess the contribution of the items in each of the four groups in accounting for variance among subjects. These groups of items were entered in different stepwise orders in the multiple regression to examine the relative contribution of each group in accounting for the variance among subjects.

Regression analyses were also carried out separately in each category for two groups of subjects, those whose SIPs were rated or scored as "high dysfunction" and those whose SIPs were rated or scored as "low dysfunction." These analyses were made to ensure that items which were useful predictors for severely or minimally dysfunctional subjects, but which were not useful predictors for the sample as a whole, were retained in the revised SIP.

Content analysis at this point was especially important since the pilot field trial sample was not random and it was not considered representative of the possible range of dysfunctional behavior. The content of each item was reviewed by the staff and outside professionals.

Items which were marginally significant on the basis of the statistical analysis (Group II) were retained if the behavior described by the item appeared substantively important enough to the staff to warrant further testing.

Items in Groups II, III, and IV were reviewed by staff in an effort to minimize redundancy and to cover the entire range of dysfunction both in terms of item content and item scale value. After review, no Group IV items were retained in the revised SIP.

During the pilot field trial, interviewers noted comments about unclear items.

These items and items regarded as unclear by staff were reviewed and some were reworded.

Finally, the four groups of items, including the reworded items, were submitted to 17 clinicians (11 MDs, 3 PhDs or MPHs in health care, 2 RNs, and 1 speech therapist) for review. This part of the content analysis was undertaken to determine which items clinicians believed to be important in differentiating patients. The clinicians were specifically asked to consider the items to be retained, retested, or omitted, and items that were reworded according to the item analysis. They were asked to make any comments, revisions, or additions they considered important. The results of their review were then analyzed and incorporated into the revised SIP.

Rewording and Rescaling

The content analysis described above resulted in the rewording and rescaling of 49 items. No new items were added. These 49 items were scaled by 25 judges, similar in background to those who scaled the original SIP items. The scaling procedures were the same as those used for the prototype SIP. All of the items were reliably scaled and were, therefore, retained in the revised SIP.

Revised Forms of the SIP

Since it is considered important to develop an instrument that will provide maximum information with minimal administrative cost, length and level of detail are important factors in instrument development. Therefore, two forms of the SIP were developed.

- A short form was derived, containing 146 items (only those items shown to be most discriminative in the statistical analysis, i.e. Group I items plus those items in Group III that accounted for more than 5 percent of the variance).
- A long form was derived, containing 235 items, i.e. those items included in the short form plus items which were considered by staff and clinicians to be substantively important or which deserved further testing (Groups I, II and III).

Statistical Pretest of Revised SIP– Rescoring 1973 Pilot Data

The revised SIP can of course only be tested and validated in a further field trial. Nevertheless, it is possible to make some preliminary assessment of the extent to which the revised instrument reflects the same information about subjects that is provided by the prototype. All pilot field trial SIPs were rescored, using the items and scale values of the revised SIP, both long and short forms, to examine the effect of the proposed revisions on original SIP scores. The relationship between the pilot study SIP scores and those scores using the revised forms was analyzed. Though not an independent measure, profile and percent scores for both revised forms correlated highly with scores on the prototype SIP and with SIP protocol ratings. These correlations were as high as those between prototype SIP scores and protocol ratings across categories and overall. Since these data were obtained on a nonrandom sample of subjects, the correlations between the short form revised SIP and the prototype SIP may be unique to this sample.

In summary, pretesting of the SIP revisions suggested that the shortening and rescaling provided as efficient and sensitive an instrument as was the prototype.

CONCLUSION

The development, testing, and revision of a prototype health status measure, the Sickness Impact Profile, is based on considerations of health planning and administration needs, health-related behavior, and measurement methodology. This development and preliminary testing demonstrate that such a measure is feasible and worthy of further refinement. The SIP's potential is enhanced by the fact that it deals with a concept, health-related dysfunction, that is familiar and relevant to the individual. In addition, it assures measurement of significant events from the societal and health care points of view.

Two important aspects require detailed assessment: validation of the SIP in relation to clinical criteria, and validation of the catalog of behaviors and of the item scale values in diverse cultural settings. The use of a multifaceted approach to the study of the validity of the SIP, showing its relationship to the many indicators of health status, is necessary (33). Research now under way will provide data on the relationship of SIP responses to clinician assessments of dysfunction. Also under way is an effort to estimate the relationship between SIP scores and quantitative measures of clinical severity in three specific diagnostic categories (e.g. total hip replacement). Translation of the SIP into the language of a Spanish speaking subculture and rescaling of the items by members of the subculture will be carried out. This, plus a rescaling of SIP items by a random sample of group practice enrollees, will provide an estimate of the universality of the scale values.

Though these data may provide necessary evidence to permit development of finalized forms of the SIP, continuing studies of validity will enable specification appropriate for certain populations and services. Such specification could yield different forms of the SIP, each relevant to and efficient in a particular situation or with a particular group of individuals.

An assessment of the Sickness Impact Profile as has been described should make it possible to delineate its usefulness as a health status measure. Though developed as an outcome measure of health care, it cannot be regarded as a sole criterion for either evaluating health programs or assessing population health levels. The SIP should provide a valuable extension in measurement of health status beyond that provided by mortality, morbidity, utilization, and consumer satisfaction which constitute the armamentarium of multiple health indicators currently appropriate for health care evaluation.

REFERENCES

1. *The American College Dictionary*. Random House, New York, 1966.
2. Donabedian, A. Evaluating the quality of medical care. *Milbank Mem. Fund Q.* 44(3): 166-206, 1966.
3. Starfield, B. Measurement of outcome: A proposed scheme. *MMFQ/Health and Society* 52(1): 39-50, 1974.
4. Elinson, J. Effectiveness of social action programs in health and welfare. In Report of the Fifty-sixth Ross Conference on Pediatric Research: Assessing the Effectiveness of Child Health Services, pp. 77-88, 1967.
5. Machlauchlan, J. M. Cultural factors in health and disease. In *Patients, Physicians, and Illness*, edited by E. Gartly Jaco, pp. 94-105. Free Press, New York, 1958.
6. Koos, E. L. *The Health of Regionville*. Hafner Publishing Company, New York, 1967.
7. Trussell, R. E., and Elinson, J. *Chronic Illness in a Rural Area: The Hunterdon Study*. Harvard University Press, Cambridge, 1959.
8. Baumann, B. Diversities in conceptions of health and physical fitness. *Journal of Health and Human Behavior* 2(1): 39-46, 1961.
9. Fabrega, H., Jr. The need for an ethnomedical science. *Science* 189(4207): 969-975, 1975.
10. Sigerist, H. E. In *On the Sociology of Medicine*, edited by M. I. Roemer, pp. 20-21. MD Publications, Inc., New York, 1960.
11. Parsons, T. Definition of health and illness in the light of American values and social structure. In *Patients, Physicians, and Illness*, edited by E. Gartly Jaco, pp. 165-187. Free Press, New York, 1958.
12. Suchman, E. A. Stages of illness and medical care. *Journal of Health and Human Behavior* 6(3): 114-128, 1965.
13. Mechanic, D. *Medical Sociology*, pp. 16-17. Free Press, New York, 1968.
14. Beck, A. T., Ward, C. H., Medelson, M., Mock, J., and Erbaugh, J. An inventory for measuring depression. *Arch. Gen. Psychiatry* 4(6): 561-571, 1961.
15. Brown, M. E. Daily activity inventory and progress record for those with atypical movement. *Am. J. Occup. Ther.* 4(5): 195-204, 1950.
16. Buchwald, E. *Physical Rehabilitation for Daily Living*. McGraw-Hill, New York, 1952.
17. Dinnerstein, A. J., Lowenthal, M., and Dexter, M. Evaluation of a rating scale of ability in activities in daily living. *Arch. Phys. Med. Rehabil.* 46(5): 579-584, 1965.
18. Haber, L. D. The epidemiology of disability: The measure of functional capacity limitations. Social Security Survey of the Disabled. U.S. Department of Health, Education, and Welfare, July 1970.
19. Katz, S., Ford, A. B., Moskowitz, R. W., Jackson, B. A., and Jaffe, M. W. Studies of illness in the aged: The index of A.D.L.: A standardized measure of biological and psychosocial function. *JAMA* 185(12): 914-919, 1963.
20. Malamud, W., and Sands, S. L. A revision of the psychiatric rating scale. *Am. J. Psychiatry* 104(4): 231-237, 1947.
21. McReynolds, P., and Ferguson, J. T. *Clinical Manual for the Hospital Adjustment Scale*. Consulting Psychologists Press, Inc., Palo Alto, Cal., 1953.
22. Shatin, L., and Freed, E. X. A behavioral rating scale for mental patients. *Journal of Mental Science* 101(424): 644-653, 1955.
23. Shontz, F. C., and Fink, S. L. A method for evaluating psychosocial adjustment of the chronically ill. *Am. J. Phys. Med.* 40(2): 63-69, 1961.
24. Edwards, A. L. *Techniques of Attitude Scale Construction*, p. 13. Appleton-Century-Crofts, Inc., New York, 1957.
25. Torgerson, W. S. *Theory and Methods of Scaling*, pp. 45-48. Wiley, New York, 1958.
26. Shinn, A. M., Jr. Relations between scales. In *Measurement in the Social Sciences: Theory and Strategies*, edited by H. M. Blalock, Jr., Ch. 4, pp. 121-158. Aldine Publishing Company, Chicago, 1974.
27. Blischke, W. R., Bush, J. W., and Kaplan, R. M. A successive intervals analysis of social preference measures for a health status index. Presented to the Social Science Section of the American Statistical Association, St. Louis, August 1974.
28. Patrick, D. L., Bush, J. W., and Chen, M. M. Toward an operational definition of health. *J. Health Soc. Beh.* 14(1): 6-23, 1973.

29. Gilson, B. S., Gilson, J. S., Bergner, M., Bobbitt, R. A., Kressel, S., Pollard, W. E., and Vesselago, M. The Sickness Impact Profile: Development of an outcome measure of health care. *Am. J. Public Health* 65(12): 1304-1310, 1975.
30. Pollard, W. E., Bobbitt, R. A., Bergner, M., Martin, D. P., and Gilson, B. S. The Sickness Impact Profile: Reliability of a health status measure. *Med. Care* 14(2): 146-155, 1976.
31. Bergner, M., Bobbitt, R. A., Pollard, W. E., Martin, D. P., and Gilson, B. S. The Sickness Impact Profile: Validation of a health status measure. *Med. Care* 14(1): 57-67, 1976.
32. Gillo, M. W., and Shelly, M. W. Predictive modeling of multivariable and multivariate data. *Journal of the American Statistical Association* 69(347): 646-653, 1974.
33. Campbell, D. T., and Fiske, D. W. Convergent and discriminant validation by the multi-trait multi-method matrix. *Psychol. Bull.* 56(2): 81-105, 1959.

CHAPTER 2

Unmet Needs as Sociomedical Indicators

Willine Carr
Samuel Wolfe

Flook and Sanazaro (1) have stated that the broad purpose of health services research "... is to produce knowledge that will contribute to improvement in the delivery of health care. Health services research is concerned with problems of organization, staffing, financing, utilization and evaluation of health services." Health services research is contrasted with biomedical research and could well be termed "sociomedical" research.

Sociomedical research is conducted at the Center for Health Care Research of Meharry Medical College (2), where one particular focus is the evaluation of different ways of delivering care by examining their effects over time on changes in community-wide levels of unmet needs. Through a two-part Study of Unmet Needs, funded by the National Center for Health Services Research, three forms of care are being evaluated:

- a neighborhood-based health center designed to provide a broad range of in-center services which are linked to a broad range of outreach services that emanate from the center;

The research reported in this paper is supported by research grants HS-00620 and HS-01710 from the National Center for Health Services Research, Health Resources Administration, Public Health Service, Department of Health, Education, and Welfare.

- a hospital-based center designed to provide a broad range of in-center services but which, because of fiscal constraints, offers only limited outreach services; and
- the traditional system of care which includes, in particular, hospital outpatient clinic services, care by private physicians, emergency room services, and public health clinic services.

These forms of care are available to three geographical communities in Nashville, Tennessee, which are substantially similar along multiple demographic parameters. The Study of Unmet Needs will examine the effectiveness of these three presumably different kinds of health care services, and it will measure the extent of adequate care for defined health problems found among persons in the three geographical areas.

Operationally, "unmet needs" are defined as the differences, if any, between those services judged necessary to deal appropriately with defined health problems and those services actually being received. The existence of a problem or problems where health care services or certain health-related welfare services are required or are judged necessary represents a situation where there is need. An unmet need is the absence of any, or of sufficient, or of appropriate care and services.

The study has been conducted at two points in time, in 1972-1973, and again in 1975-1976, to determine if there are differences in "program-related changes" in levels of unmet needs. A longer period of time between the two sets of observations would have been preferred, but this was judged unrealistic for staff stability and fiscal reasons. The central hypothesis of this study, designed to measure differences at two points in time, is that health programs with a broad, comprehensive range of services, for reasons that relate to the structure, organization, and staffing arrangements, will be more effective in reducing unmet needs than traditional care, and that such broad-scope programs with broad outreach services will reduce unmet needs more than those with limited outreach. The ability to relate levels of unmet needs to health services will depend in part, of course, on the ability to monitor satisfactorily the content of the health services alternatives.

Changes in unmet needs, in our view, are measures of the outcome of health services and, as such, are one of several types of sociomedical indicators. Sociomedical indicators attempt to use factors other than biomedical or biological states as measures of program outcome. The development of sociomedical indicators has been encouraged in view of the apparent inadequacies of traditional morbidity, mortality, and other biomedical data as indicators of the levels of health of a population or as indicators of the effectiveness of health services programs (3).

VARIOUS WAYS TO MEASURE UNMET NEEDS

Over the years various approaches have been developed to measure unmet needs. One such approach is called the "symptoms approach" and is typified by the work in the 1940s in North Carolina and Michigan by Hoffer and Schuler (4, 5) and by Schuler, Mayo, and Makover (6). This approach involved the use of a list of nontechnical questions about the presence of symptoms and about the medical care received as a result of treatment of the symptoms. Each listed symptom was regarded as representing a health danger signal and, in the opinion of a panel of physicians, required medical attention.

The symptoms list was presented to respondents by lay interviewers in a household survey. The occurrence of one or more symptoms denoted need, and the nonreceipt of professional attention for these symptoms was used as an indication of unmet needs for medical care. A fivefold classification relating needs and unmet needs was derived. The classification ranged from "no positive symptoms" to "all symptoms untreated or treated by home remedy only." In Michigan, this approach was validated by follow-up of some of the interviews with medical examinations and limited laboratory testing; for 80 percent of individuals there was agreement between interview data and medical examination data regarding the need to see a doctor (4). In the North Carolina studies it was noted that this approach tended to record unmet needs for medical care for chronic ailments and impairments and, as such, it might be used as an addition to traditional morbidity rate estimates of need (6).

A second approach to measuring unmet needs is exemplified by the work of Rosenfeld, Donabedian, and Katz (7) in the 1950s which attempted to explore the use of fairly simple restricted indexes that might reflect the degree of unmet needs for medical care and demonstrate the correspondence or correlation between indexes. Indexes were developed by looking at perinatal mortality, adequacy of prenatal care, neglect of important symptoms, and neglect of dental care, using a combination of data from official sources, questionnaires to postpartum mothers, and household interviews. For the latter, the researchers drew on the symptoms approach developed by Schuler and his colleagues. When the indexes were related to socioeconomic status by census tracts, it was found that for all indexes unmet needs were greater in the lowest socioeconomic group. The authors suggested that the indexes could identify groups with high and low levels of unmet needs, and that clinical and epidemiological studies on these groups could then focus on the nature, extent, and cause of need and unmet needs.

Wallace, Eisner, and Dooley (8) in the 1960s combined health and social indexes and compared two techniques–factor analysis and map plotting–in order to determine the usefulness of these indexes. They concluded that the most useful health indexes pointing to unmet needs were inadequate prenatal care, fetal mortality, incidence of prematurity, and incidence of tuberculosis. The most useful socioeconomic indexes were found to be low income, inadequate education, unemployment, overcrowding, parental composition, and school-age illegitimacy. It was felt that these indexes could be used by health planners in developing programs for specific census tracts and that, since some of the indexes are available in postcensus years, they could be useful in areas of rapid population change during intercensal years.

These studies have generally indicated that high unmet needs in one indicator area are related to high unmet needs in other indicator areas. If this is true, then it should be reasonable to expect that a limited number of well-chosen indexes may provide a useful profile of the needs in a community (7).

The more recent work of David Kessner (9) of the Institute of Medicine of the National Academy of Sciences suggests a similar approach to measuring unmet needs. Kessner has developed the "tracer methodology" as a means of evaluating ambulatory programs. Although it is not specifically labelled as an unmet needs approach, the tracer methodology leads directly to conclusions about unmet needs for care and services. As an evaluation tool, this methodology proposes the examination of the management of specific health conditions, or tracers, to identify the strengths and weaknesses of specific forms of ambulatory practices. Underlying the tracer method is the assumption that how professionals routinely administer care for common ailments and what happens to the patients that receive that care will be an indication of the quality of care delivered in a medical practice.

Criteria for selecting tracers and a set of six tracer conditions have been proposed. The six tracers are middle-ear infections and associated hearing loss, visual disorders, iron-deficiency anemia, hypertension, urinary tract infection, and cervical cancer. These tracer conditions were selected because of their prevalence among a variety of age and sex groups, because they have a significant functional impact and are relatively easy to diagnose, because there is a degree of consensus about medical management and the natural history which should vary with the utilization and effectiveness of medical care, and because the effects of nonmedical factors on the tracers are understood.

The tracer methodology has been applied in a Washington, D.C., study of the health status of some 2000 children (10). The study consisted of randomly selecting families from selected census tracts, interviewing parents, examining children, questioning sources of care, and, in some cases, reviewing medical records. It was found that regardless of social class, the prevalence rates for three tracer conditions—anemia, visual problems, and middle-ear infections—were very high, and in a large proportion of the children, and regardless of source of care, inappropriate, incomplete or ineffective management for the specific tracer conditions was received.

The bench mark study of unmet needs in the area of chronic disease which used home interviews and physical examinations is the work of the Commission of Chronic Illness of the 1950s, and, in particular, the Hunterdon County study for which Ray Trussell and Jack Elinson (11) were responsible. Basic to this study of *Chronic Illness in a Rural Area* was the evaluation, by a professional health team, of the needs for various types of health and social services in the twelve months before and after the clinical evaluation. The clinical evaluees were drawn, based on complex stratification procedures, from among 14,315 persons within the households contacted for interview.

The study revealed major deficiencies in the quantity and quality of health care received by this representative sample of the population of an entire county in the state of New Jersey. Part of the creativity of this work was demonstrated by the fact that the estimates were based on a clinical evaluation which could be compared with household survey reports. The focus was on the *kinds* of care needed, *where* the care might best be given, and *who* should give the needed care. Judgments were made by a well trained team consisting of a physician, public health nurse, and social worker, with certain other health professionals involved in the judgments in special instances. There were no follow-up reassessments in order to determine the extent to which needed care was later received. A companion to this rural study is one of *Chronic Illness in a Large City* (12).

Assessments of unmet needs based on physical examination and interview findings have been made in other studies. In 1966 Pearman undertook a "Survey of Unmet Medical Needs of Children in Six Counties in Florida" (13). This study of children in the Florida Head Start Program utilized two study methods. The first was a review of the medical examination records of the Head Start children. The second was an interview with the families of the children. The interview focused on the presence of health problems and the receipt of medical and dental care during the prior twelve-month period. The interview schedule was adapted from the work of Hoffer and his colleagues in Michigan. Based on this study, unmet needs findings, such as "33 percent of the Head Start children had not been vaccinated against smallpox," were reported (13). Methodological problems, such as incompleteness of the existing Head Start medical records, the currency of census data, and the accuracy of the respondent reports, were encountered.

A study by Salisbury and Berg (14) also examined unmet needs among Head Start participants. This 1966 study was conducted in Boston, Massachusetts. Physical examinations of 618 children aged 14 to 16 were carried out, and historical, demographic, and other interview data were obtained. Based on examination and interview data, the examining physician developed subjective conclusions about the past and current management of existing problems, and judged the need for further care and follow-up. The researchers concluded that obtaining information on the prevalence of medical and dental abnormalities among the children studied was not sufficient, by itself, to describe the health status of these children. The needed additional dimension, they concluded, was supplied by examining the number of abnormalities judged to require further evaluation and treatment, that is, by examining levels of unmet needs. Further, Salisbury and Berg concluded that the magnitude of the requirements for follow-up and treatment resources can be estimated from studies of this kind (14).

The relevancy and usefulness of unmet needs indicators may be attested to by the fact that an evaluation of unmet health care needs has been incorporated as a component of the current cycle of the Health and Nutrition Examination Survey (HANES) conducted by the Division of Health Examination Statistics, National Center for Health Statistics. This component of the HANES project is obtaining data on the current and unmet health care needs of persons in the age group 25-74.

> It was considered that these data could best be obtained by ascertaining the health needs as self-perceived by the individuals examined, and as professionally and scientifically determined by the survey's examination and tests. Information obtained through the use of questionnaires would include data on what health care has been received (15).

The unmet needs component of the HANES project is not intended to cover all aspects of an individual's health. Instead it focuses on unmet needs that relate to a limited number of index conditions. These index conditions include chronic pulmonary disease; chronic disabling arthritis of the hip, knee, and other joints; specific dermatological disease; dental and oral conditions; cardiovascular disease (including peripheral vascular disease); thyroid abnormality; auditory acuity; correctable level of visual acuity; and ocular hypertension and other ocular conditions.

Unmet needs as revealed in the HANES examination are to be related to the "self-perceived" needs of the examinees. This aspect of the HANES project is seen as providing an enormous amount of information, heretofore unavailable, that will relate to the health care that had been, is being, or should be received. "It would not, however, provide any total systems-analysis-type assessment of the present overall functioning of the medical care system" (15).

The application of the unmet needs concept is not limited to the medical care field, per se. The application of index conditions for examining the relationship between care needed and care received has been frequently used in the social work field (16).

This review of approaches to examining unmet needs has revealed that unmet needs have been measured in a variety of settings and in a variety of ways. Basic to most of these approaches to measuring unmet needs is the fact that they are deliberately "limited" in their focus. They look, for example, only at medical or specific category needs, or at chronic illness needs, or at a limited number of indicator conditions.

THE MEHARRY MEDICAL COLLEGE APPROACH TO MEASURING UNMET NEEDS

The Meharry Medical College Study of Unmet Needs may be more ambitious, global, and comprehensive in its approach than other studies. As such, it may have advantages, but also many limitations that relate to methods, study costs, and interpretations of findings. First of all, this study may be the first attempt to look at unmet needs in similar population groups at two points in time, in order to assess not only the current levels of unmet needs but also changes in unmet needs through time. It is one of few attempts to relate unmet needs outcomes to particular models of care. The Meharry approach is comprehensive in that it looks at numerous spheres of potential needs, including medical, dental, nursing, and social needs, as well as the quality of life of individuals in the home and community setting. Further, a comprehensive view of the individuals being assessed is taken by looking for "all" problem conditions within each of the medical, dental, nursing, and social spheres. This contrasts with approaches which focus only on indicators or tracer conditions. After "complete" problem lists have been developed, judgments of levels of unmet needs are made about each problem individually and then, within each of the medical, dental, nursing, and social areas, about "overall" or aggregate unmet needs.

Study Design and Methods

The Study of Unmet Needs is evaluating the relative success or failure of comprehensive care with broad outreach, comprehensive care with limited outreach, and traditional care in reducing levels of unmet needs.

Each of the two comprehensive care programs under study serves a defined geographical population in Nashville which is predominantly black and poor. Persons within these areas have access to one or the other of the comprehensive care programs, but not to both. All, of course, are free to continue using the traditional care services.

For purposes of the study a third geographical area was delineated, similar in demographic characteristics to the two comprehensive care service areas. Persons in this third area do not have access to use of the new programs; they are users or potential users of traditional care.

Data collection for Phase I (T_1) of the study was carried out between February 1972 and April 1973, and Phase II (T_2) data will be collected between September 1975 and September 1976. The final study reports and findings will be completed no later than December 31, 1977.

For Phase I and Phase II, the study design calls for independent, cross-sectional samples to be drawn. Both an equi-probability sample of households and an equi-probability sample of individuals, representative of the households and of the individuals in the three study areas, are required. From a universe of approximately 24,000 households and approximately 85,000 individuals, samples of 1,350 households for interview and 1,350 individuals for clinical evaluation were selected for observation during T_1. Because of fiscal constraints, a smaller sample of households but a similar sample of individuals will be drawn for observation at T_2. The methods used in acquiring these samples have been described elsewhere (17,18).

Two primary methods of data collection are being utilized. These methods include (a) household interviews to obtain information about the family unit, and (b) detailed clinical evaluations which provide information on selected individuals. Household interviews are conducted at every sample household. An average of one person per sample household is randomly selected to take part in a detailed health examination during which a physician, dentist, nurse, and social worker examine and interview the clinical evaluees. Selected persons are paid a small amount of money to take part in the clinical evaluations. Following the examinations the health professionals make judgments about problems and unmet needs for care or services. Also, during the household interview and clinical evaluation, individuals are asked, to a limited extent, to express their own judgments about unmet needs.

Instruments and Sources of Information

Through *household interviews,* neighborhood residents trained as interviewers obtain demographic data, data on housing and neighborhood problems, information on employment, economic security and food costs, information about the health of each family member, and a limited amount of information on self-perceived needs.

Medical judgments are made by an internist or pediatrician and are based on information from automated multitest screening (adults), systematic laboratory testing and screening (children), a detailed health history, and a careful physical examination. Individual medical problems are recorded, as are the services currently being received; the appropriateness of services being received is evaluated; and a judgment is made about the services and care needed from primary physicians and specialists, and the need for drugs, aids, and appliances. These judgments are made for each problem and overall, for all problems. Primarily because of logistical and financial considerations the physician-judges do not have access to previous medical records of the evaluees, or to follow-up information on abnormal or doubtful findings discovered during the clinical evaluation. In this respect the study differs in the basis for judgments from the Hunterdon County study.

Dental judgments made by a dentist are based on a dental history, and on clinical assessment of oral hygiene, caries conduciveness, occlusion and alignment, periodontal status, oral lesions, and of decayed, missing, and filled teeth. Judgments are made about needs for extractions, fillings, bridges, dentures, dental specialist services, and dental health education. Overall unmet needs judgments are made.

Nursing judgments are made by a nurse based on interviews in the home and review of the study medical records, but not of other medical records. The nurse determines whether there are problems requiring nursing services to permit the evaluee (a) to maintain physical independence, (b) to carry out necessary treatments (therapeutic competence), (c) to have knowledge and understanding of existent medical conditions, and (d) to carry out health maintenance practices. Ability to cope is taken into account in judging unmet needs for nursing services for direct patient care, and for nursing services relating to instruction, counseling, and other supportive help.

Social judgments are made by a social worker based on an interview in the home and information drawn from the earlier household interview. Problems are defined and judgments are made of needs relating to neighborhood and home environment, employment and income, life style (clothes, recreation, community and religious activity), family relationships, education, evaluee's estimates of life's satisfactions, emotional problems, critical incidents of the past twelve months, and social role.

The professional who makes judgments in the medical, dental, nursing, and social areas tries to take a broad view of the individual in the context of his or her family unit and larger environment. Each professional looks for "all" need conditions (within his area of expertise) existing for the individual, and expresses each one of these by labeling from problem lists created for use in the study components. A judgment is made about the care that should have been received for these problems, details are obtained about the care actually being received, and the adequacy or appropriateness of this care is assessed. A professional judgment is then made about the individual's unmet needs for care and services for each problem. Finally, the professional looks at all the problems combined and makes a judgment about the individual's "overall" unmet needs; that is, "aggregate" unmet needs are assessed. Unmet needs judgments for individual problems and for all problems combined are expressed on ordinal scales. In making judgments about unmet needs the professionals take into account problem severity and the intensity and urgency of needs.

The MONSAQ Unmet Needs Scales

From the data gathered in this way, the Meharry MONSAQ scales are derived. This is a series of numeric ratings of unmet needs for care and services for medical (*M*), oral-dental (*O*), nursing (*N*), and social (*S*) services, and for aids, appliances, and drugs (*A*). There is a separate scale (and rating) for each component. The ratings for the separate components are not combined in any manner, nor do we think they can be. The scales range from zero, indicating no unmet needs, to four, five, or nine (for the nursing, social and dental, and medical components, respectively), indicating great or urgent unmet needs. Collectively the Meharry scales are labeled MONSAQ. The *Q* indicates the "quality of life" of the individual. The quality of life index is derived by combining and scaling twenty indicators of social well-being based on reports of health, housing, neighborhood, education, income, job, and adequacy of insurance contained in the household interview schedule.

The unmet needs judgments which follow from the examination and interview data are made by persons normally practicing in the study area. The "standards" and "criteria" applied to the judgment process are those normally applied to practice settings, as opposed to special, limited standards established for study purposes. In effect clinicians have been asked to do what they routinely do with regard to assessment of problems and needs, but to do this in a more structured, systematized way and to record these assessments systematically. Then they go beyond what they usually do by scaling or quantitating unmet needs. Judgments of professionals seem reasonable bases for evaluating the health system where professional decisions dominate. For the medical components judgments are made by a team of physicians working together in order to provide a degree of "consensus validity" to the findings.

At T_2 *all* of the judgments will be made again for all components of the study and for both the 1972-1973 and 1975-1976 sets of data. This will be done, in part, to reduce some of the possible biases relating to knowledge of T_1 and T_2 time frames and to increase judgment comparability.

For all study components, a mechanism has been established in order to get a quantitative measure of the reliability of the judgments. In a sample of cases the data base from which the original judgments are made is given to a second judge or team of judges. Without having access to the original judgments, these persons use the historical, examination, and interview data to create the problem lists and to produce their own independent judgments of unmet needs. The degree of match between the original judgments and these subsequent judgments gives an indication of the degree of interjudge reliability.

Consumer Judgments

The individual clinical evaluee's self-perceptions regarding health problems and unmet needs are being obtained in less detail than are the professional assessments, and these consumer judgments are not scaled. One example of the consumer judgment information obtained follows. In the medical area the individuals are asked to name any problems they have which they feel require medical attention. The individuals are then asked if these perceived medical problems are under care and, if they are not, reasons for this lack of care are sought. If care is received, the name of the source of care is sought, and the individual is asked to rate the care received. Other general information regarding perceived needs for dental care, nursing services, and social services is obtained through the household interview and through interviews in the clinical setting.

Data Analysis and Findings

Following T_1, analysis of data has been primarily descriptive of problems and unmet needs levels in the population studied. Frequency distribution and a wide array of contingency tables have been obtained. Further, Automatic Interaction Detector (AID) analysis has been performed to reveal "predictors" of unmet needs. For example, the number of medical problems was the best predictor of unmet medical needs, while age was the best predictor of unmet dental needs.

Factor analysis has also been done to determine whether the dimensionality of the five unmet needs scales can be reduced to fewer than five. We have found that the scales cannot be reduced to fewer than five by factor analysis. In other words, evaluees with high levels of unmet needs for dental care do not necessarily have high levels of unmet needs for social services or for medical care.

Following T_2, in addition to descriptive analysis, T_1-T_2 differences in unmet needs will be tested in the following ways, among others: (a) computation of Chi-square tests on the distributions of overall unmet needs at T_1 and T_2; (b) comparison of means (and standard errors) in the three areas at T_1 and T_2; (c) computation of Goodman-Kruskal correlation coefficients between time periods and overall unmet needs for each of the three areas; (d) computation of rank correlation coefficients between geographical area and overall unmet needs scores at T_1 and T_2; and (e) determination of the directionality of change at T_2, if any, for each of forty hypotheses relating to the presumptive effects of the three alternative kinds of health care services.

In addition to these analyses, the programmatic characteristics, similarities, and differences of the three alternative kinds of health care will be monitored. These data analyses and monitoring activities taken together should enable us, during the final year of our work, 1977, to make statements about changes within each of the three geographical areas and about interarea differences that may then be attributed to the intervention of the alternative kinds of health care services.

During Phase I of the study, 1266 household interviews and 586 clinical evaluations were completed. Some of the pertinent findings of this phase of the study are summarized briefly in the following. Household interview data indicate widespread economic poverty, with 65 percent of the families reporting annual incomes of less than $5000. The families had numerous complaints about neighborhood and housing conditions. The social data show that social services were quite available for environmental, income, employment, and educational problems, but because of harsh regulations and criteria of agencies, seldom did these services fully meet the basic needs. Social services were seldom received for interpersonal and emotional problems.

Nursing services were needed by 88 percent of the persons because of lack of awareness of or understanding of a health condition and by 97 percent of persons because of poor health maintenance and preventive practices. Referrals, counseling, and health education services were virtually never received for these problems. Nursing services requiring laying on of hands were, of course, far less frequently needed. Ninety-five percent of persons examined by the dentist had unmet needs for dental services. In the medical component of the study, an average of 3.9 medical conditions or problems were found per clinical evaluee. In only 13 percent was appropriate care being received. Even if one subtracts the new conditions or *possible* abnormalities found from the clinical evaluations, the level of adequacy of care for confirmed current conditions was very poor indeed. Strikingly low utilization of dental and medical services was reported.

In looking at overall unmet needs levels across the three study areas, it was found that, with the exception of the social component, unmet needs were not statistically significantly different in the three areas at T_1. This has been a favorable finding in that it represents a common baseline from which changes can be measured, and has been a major justification for proceeding with the second phase of the study.

Significance and Applications of This Approach

Why was such a global unmet needs approach chosen for the evaluation of alternative delivery systems? First of all, it was assumed, as Donabedian (19) has said, that an ". . . appropriate objective of medical [health] care programs may be said to be the delivery of appropriate medical care services according to need. . . ." Unmet needs, then, can be used to evaluate the performance of different programs in achieving the objective of meeting needs. Secondly, unmet needs measures, which link health problems to health services, are measures which are expected to change in the relative short run.

Thirdly, a global assessment of unmet needs was chosen because this kind of evaluation seemed closely related to the stated objectives of the new Meharry models of care. These new models were designed to provide a broad range of services to affect more than the usual medical needs. By reaching into the homes and encouraging use of the new services, they could reasonably be expected to have a community impact. For these reasons a community-based study with a broad focus was needed.

Finally, a comprehensive unmet needs approach was chosen because this seemed more relevant to program evaluation than just comparing traditional morbidity and mortality statistics (20). As Elinson (3) has noted, the inadequacy of traditional morbidity and mortality rates is "due in part to the stagnation of total mortality rates over long periods of time . . . to the increase of chronic, non-infective disease . . . and to difficulties in determining the relationship of mortality and morbidity."

Unmet needs ratings are one of several types of "sociomedical" indicators which attempt to use factors other than biological states as measures of outcome. In addition to unmet needs indicators, the variety of sociomedical indicators includes (a) measures of social disability, that is, the inability to perform a social role; however, social role performance may depend upon other variables besides health; (b) typologies of presenting symptoms, classified along the two dimensions of seriousness of symptoms and prognosis, which have been used to estimate probable needs or demands for care; (c) measures such as the "Sickness Impact Profile," which focus not on professionally defined disease entities but on behavioral expressions of sickness; and (d) measures developed from operational definitions of "positive mental health," including so-called "Happiness Research" and efforts to develop measures of perceived quality of life (3). Most of these indicators have been labeled "health status" indicators.

Unmet needs indicators, however, are not health status indicators, and to designate them as such is, in our view, an error. Assessments of met and unmet needs for health care are not measurements of the level of health of an individual or a population, but rather of the social capacity of the society to care for the sick. They measure the extent to which our present state of knowledge is being applied in a given population, and they direct attention away from preoccupation with the biomedical aspects of disease in a population and toward the discharge of social responsibility for the organization and delivery of appropriate health care (3). The quantification of unmet needs may be more helpful in many instances than preoccupation with health status. Thus, for example, in a population of the aged, or of patients with hip fractures, or of patients with malignancy, surely unmet needs indicators are more relevant than health status indicators in determining the extent of application of those measures which are possible in the present state of our knowledge.

Unmet needs indicators and health status indicators, though not the same, are related. One implicit assumption underlying the unmet needs concept, as applied in this study, is that the provision of appropriate health services according to need is an intermediate outcome of a health system whose ultimate goal may be to improve the health status of a population. Unmet needs indicators relate to appropriate services and resources which may be the inputs necessary to maintain or improve health status.

The particular methodology used in the study for examining unmet needs has both advantages and limitations. It is an extremely complex methodology which, in its entirety, cannot and should not be frequently replicated. This involved study was undertaken by Meharry Medical College because of the unique opportunity presented by the nearly simultaneous development of two new comprehensive care programs which differed from one another in certain essential respects. There was also the opening of an automated health testing service and a computer center which enabled Meharry to pull together resources for a multidimensional evaluation of various forms of care. As well, since only part of the poverty community could be provided with these new services, it was known that another part would continue to be primarily at risk of use of what we have referred to operationally as the traditional health services.

Although the study may not be replicable in its entirety, it is feasible for this method of unmet needs assessment to be used in an ongoing clinical medical practice to focus on a broad-based view of overall unmet needs for care along multiple dimensions, without bypassing assessments of unmet needs for specific problems or diagnostic entities. Similarly the application of unmet needs assessments to randomly selected patients of prepaid group practices or of fee-for-service practices may provide an ongoing way of evaluating these forms of practice. The unmet needs approach may also be an appropriate means of assessing problems and needs in middle-class communities, as well as in poverty communities. It is encouraging to see that the National Center for Health Statistics has introduced unmet needs indicators into the national Health and Nutrition Examination Survey since this approach goes a step beyond the counting and reporting of problems toward a look at the use and allocation of health care resources in relation to needs.

A strength of this approach is its multidimensionality. Unmet needs are examined for medical, dental, nursing, and social services, and "quality of life" is assessed because health is viewed broadly and in the context of the individual's home and community environment. No attempt is used in this methodology to come up with a single index or composite of unmet health needs by aggregating unmet needs for the multiple components in any way. In fact, as we have noted above, factor analysis of the T_1 unmet needs data suggests that unmet needs levels in one component are not necessarily correlated with unmet needs in another, and that the five unmet needs scores (medical, drugs and appliances, dental, nursing, and social) cannot meaningfully be reduced.

Although the unmet needs scales as sociomedical indicators focus attention on factors other than biomedical factors, a wealth of biomedical, historical, and social information is obtained as the basis for making unmet needs judgments. As a result, detailed biomedical information, such as prevalence rates for specific diseases and conditions, can be examined. Further, since unmet needs indicators look at deficits in care received for defined problems, it may be possible to use unmet needs data to estimate how services can be allocated and distributed and organized, as well as the manpower and other resources required to meet these needs.

There are major limitations and biases in this unmet needs study, and the question has been repeatedly raised: "How good are the data and judgments in this type of study? " Some of the limitations include reliance on evaluee reports of care received and actions taken as opposed to use of previous records or documents, and the "intuitive" or "subjective" element involved in reaching a professional judgment of unmet needs. There is, however, a great degree of face and consensus validity built into the study design. We have also found a relatively high degree of agreement between independent judges regarding problems and unmet needs, though much less in the case of the medical component where the number of conditions could be very great and the number of service alternatives from which to choose are great.

Meharry's work on unmet needs represents a single, specific application of the concept and has contributed to advancement in research methodology and findings in this area. Further, the Meharry work should give direction to future work on unmet needs, especially as regards the usefulness of unmet needs indicators in program evaluation, the multidimensionality of unmet needs, the comparative measurements of unmet needs in unlike populations, and the relationship between unmet needs and health status. Another area of possible exploration relates to the development of different kinds of unmet needs indicators or indexes, some based on professional judgments and others based on defined equations which combine and weight data variables in specific ways. This look at unmet needs suggests that the concept of unmet needs, however operationally examined and applied, is a useful addition to the battery of sociomedical indicators which merits further exploration, development, and refinement.

REFERENCES

1. Flook, E. E., and Sanazaro, P. J., editors. *Health Services Research and R & D in Perspective.* Health Administration Press, University of Michigan, Ann Arbor, 1973.
2. Wolfe, S. The Meharry Medical College Center for Health Care Research. *J. Natl. Med. Assoc.* 65(4): 293-295, 1973.
3. Elinson, J. Toward sociomedical health indicators. *Social Indicators Research* 1(1): 59-71, 1974.
4. Hoffer, C. R., and Schuler, E. A. Measurement of health needs and health care. *Am. Sociol. Rev.* 13(6): 719-724, 1948.
5. Hoffer, C. R., and Schuler, E. A. Determination of unmet needs for medical attention among Michigan farm families. *Journal of the Michigan State Medical Society* 46: 443-446, 1947.
6. Schuler, E. A., Mayo, S. C., and Makover, H. B. Measuring unmet needs for medical care: An experiment in method. *Rural Sociology* 11(2): 152-158, 1946.
7. Rosenfeld, L. S., Donabedian, A., and Katz, J. Unmet need for medical care. *N. Engl. J. Med.* 258: 369-376, 1958.
8. Wallace, H. M., Eisner, V., and Dooley, S. Availability and usefulness of selected health and socioeconomic data for community planning. *Am. J. Public Health* 57(5): 1762-1771, 1967.
9. Kessner, D. M., and Kalk, E. *Contrasts in Health Status.* Vol. 2, *A Strategy for Evaluating Health Services.* Institute of Medicine, National Academy of Sciences, Washington, D. C., 1973.
10. *Contrasts in Health Status.* Vol. 3, *Assessment of Medical Care for Children.* Institute of Medicine, National Academy of Sciences, Washington, D. C., 1973.
11. Trussell, R. E., and Elinson, J. *Chronic Illness in the United States.* Vol. 3, *Chronic Illness in a Rural Area. The Hunterdon Study.* Harvard University Press, Cambridge, Mass., 1959.
12. *Chronic Illness in the United States.* Vol. IV, *Chronic Illness in a Large City.* Commission on Chronic Illness, Harvard University Press, Cambridge, Mass., 1957.
13. Pearman, J. R. Survey of unmet medical needs of children in six counties in Florida. *Public Health Rep.* 85: 189-196, March 1970.
14. Salisbury, A. J., and Berg, R. Health defects and need for treatment of adolescents in low income families. *Public Health Rep.* 84: 705-711, August 1969.
15. National Center for Health Statistics. *Vital and Health Statistics,* Series 1, No. 10a and No. 10b, Plan and Operation of the Health and Nutrition Examination Survey, United States–1971-1973. U. S. Department of Health, Education and Welfare, Washington, D. C., February 1973.
16. Carter, G. Measurements of need. In *Social Work Research,* edited by Norman Polansky, pp. 201-222. University of Chicago, Chicago, 1960.
17. Center for Health Care Research, Meharry Medical College. Report of Contract HSM 110-69-199, Evaluation of Health Services in a Largely Black City Slum. Submitted to the National Center for Health Services Research and Development, July 1971.
18. Wolfe, S., Carr, W., Revo, L. T., Neser, W. B., Edwards, M., Martin, J., Penn, B., and Lefkowitz, L. The Meharry Medical College Study of Unmet Needs for Health and Welfare Services. Paper presented at 102nd Annual Meeting of the American Public Health Association, New Orleans, La., October 1974 (mimeographed).
19. Donabedian, A. The evaluation of medical care programs. *Bull. N. Y. Acad. Med.* 44(2): 118, 1968.
20. Veney, J. Health status indicators. *Inquiry* 10: 3-4, December 1973.

CHAPTER 3

Propositions on Social Disability

Joseph Greenblum

INTRODUCTION

The series of propositions presented in this report has a dual purpose. It is of course intended as a contribution to knowledge about disability (1, 2). But we hope that it will also prove to be relevant to current concerns about sociomedical health indicators. Social disability has been considered as a central concept in the discussion of such indicators (3).

Propositions are inferences or generalizations from the findings of numerous empirical studies and attempt to state stable associations among variables (4). Such statements about a concept, based on an examination and analysis of studies conducted by various methods in diverse populations, have implications in respect to attempts to develop social indicators (5, 6, 7). While these studies may utilize reliable indices or scales to define variables, the propositions themselves suggest the possi-

No official support or endorsement by the Social Security Administration or the Department of Health, Education, and Welfare is intended or should be inferred. Work for this report was done while the author was Research Associate at the Columbia University School of Public Health, Division of Sociomedical Sciences, and with the aid of the Carnegie Foundation Grant to the Section on Medical Sociology of the American Sociological Association, Subcommittee on Sociomedical Health Indicators. Special acknowledgement is due to Jack Elinson, Head of the Division and Chairman of the Subcommittee, for initiating and stimulating the propositional inventory project on sociomedical health concepts.

bility of a comprehensive valid indicator latent in the various measures of the concept. Furthermore they point to the ability of such an indicator to predict relationships with other variables. The propositions in this report that have emerged from our review of the literature may therefore encourage efforts to develop indicators of social disability as well as of other kinds of sociomedical health concepts.

In our search of the literature and in the formulation of propositions we have been guided by the concept of social disability as an incapacity to perform social roles due to illness. We have assumed the community's normative standards governing role behavior; an inability to perform one's usual roles in the community because of ill health defines one as disabled. This definition embraces individuals residing in health institutions as well as persons incapacitated in work, family and other community roles.

Our review of the huge body of literature on disability (8, 9) was selective. We emphasize health surveys of populations rather than studies of patients in treatment settings. We have focussed particularly on two national surveys in the last decade sponsored by agencies of the U.S. government: The National Health Interview Survey (NHIS) conducted periodically by the National Center for Health Statistics (10) and the Social Security Survey of the Disabled (SSSD) conducted in 1966 by the Social Security Administration (11). The Appendix briefly describes the measures of disability used in these surveys.

PROPOSITIONS

Validity and Reliability of Disability Measures

Disability is a state of heath perceived by self and others and can be validly observed and reported by the affected individual.

- Self-reports on health status are more valid measures of self-perceived health than of clinical disease.
  - Health conditions reported by individuals are likely to be matched or "confirmed" by clinical examination. But fewer of the conditions identified in a clinical examination are reported by the individual.
- Disabling conditions and the resulting state of role incapacity are salient to the individual; they are experiences that disrupt normal role functioning. Hence they are more likely to be perceived by self and reported to physicians and to non-medical persons in health interviews or questionnaires.
  - Health conditions thought to be disabling, unusual or serious are more likely to be "confirmed" by medical examination or reported than are other conditions.

Several community health surveys published during the 1950s employed both a household interview and a medical examination but found the interview survey an unsatisfactory method of estimating clinical chronic disease. In the Pittsburgh & Butler County (Pa.) household survey respondents were found to report "fairly accurately" the diagnosis of the physician they had consulted for a condition, but such reports did not necessarily match the actual amount of clinical disease known by the physician (12). In the same survey a subsample was interviewed for ascertaining self-reports on heart disease and a subsample of these repsondents was given a physical exam for evidence of heart disease. An 80 percent agreement was found among the different measures. The investigators concluded that a physical examination was necessary to measure clinical heart disease (13). The twin surveys of the Commission on Chronic Illness confirmed in a thorough manner the disjunction between the household interview and clinical methods. The Baltimore study discovered that about seven-tenths of household-reported conditions could be detected in a diagnostic examination, while only two-tenths of diagnosed conditions were matched in the interview (14). The Hunterdon County (N.J.) study found that one-half of chronic conditions reported for the family in the household interview were "confirmed" by clinical examination, while only one-fifth of diagnoses were matched in the interview. However, it was also found that between two-thirds and almost all of the disabling or handicapping conditions reported in the interview were identified in the diagnostic examination (15, 16, 17). In a sample study of men aged 65 and over who were given both a medical examination and a self-administered questionnaire, the findings from the two methods were conceptually distinguished. Observing that self-ratings of health status were more favorable than physician ratings the investigator suggested that the self-ratings measured "perceived" health rather than "actual" health. Self-ratings, it was concluded, had low validity as a substitute for medical examinations (18).

A series of methodological studies sponsored by the National Center for Health Statistics were designed to test the degree of match between physicians' records and their patients' interview reports of their chronic conditions. While these studies generally demonstrated that patients' reports were inadequate indicators of their medically recorded conditions, they also showed that conditions affecting a person's life style or self-image produced a relatively high match between reports and records. A study of a sample of Health Insurance Plan of New York subscribers found that they reported in an interview less than one-half of the chronic conditions recorded in the preceding year by their Plan physicians. But it was also found that more than four-fifths of the recorded conditions resulting in an unusual experience, such as hospitalization or as many as ten physician contacts, were reported (19). An interview study of members enrolled in the Kaiser-Permanente health group found that they reported about half of the chronic conditions recorded by their group physician in the preceding year. Higher percentages were found for recorded conditions that appeared to be important to the respondent, i.e., they were more severe, serious or had an impact on his activities. Thus they reported 86 percent of the conditions that required many (six or more) visits to the physician, 70 percent of the conditions if they perceived themselves in poor or fair health, and from 60 to 75 percent of the conditions that affected their way of life, for example in work limitations, in pain or worry, or in changes in food and beverage consumption (20). Another study, complementing the previous one, interviewed a sample of members who had contacted physicians only at Kaiser-Permanente in order to determine the degree to which reported conditions were recorded by the physician. It was found that reported conditions resulting in a greater number of physician visits were more often recorded than those leading to one or a few visits. Greater physician contacts may have provided more opportunity for the patient to communicate his complaint or for the physician to diagnose and confirm the condition (21). In a similar type of study conducted under different auspices, it was found that more than half of chronic conditions reported by Kaiser Plan members in self-administered questionnaires used in a county survey had been noted in clinical records; other types of complaints were recorded less often (22).

Disability can be reliably identified and measured in the population. The 1966 Social Security Survey of the Disabled developed reliable techniques for screening the national population aged 18-64 for disabled people. Various methods were tested to identify people who had been classified as disabled in the National Health Interview Survey. Mail questionnaires were found to be more effective than personal interviews, simple-choice questions more than multiple-choice questions; questions about chronic conditions did not improve agreement with NHIS and caused confusion among respondents. High rates of agreement with NHIS were found therefore by using a schedule with simple-choice questions, no questions on chronic conditions, and in the form of a mail questionnaire. It also resulted in a prevalence rate twice as high as that of NHIS. These methods yielded results that were more consistent with data from disability benefit and compensation programs than were NHIS procedures; but they were viewed essentially as extensions of such procedures. The techniques were used in the first stage of the Survey to identify disabled people for further study in the second stage (11).

Social Disability, Physical Limitations, Illness

Social disability and physical (functional) limitations are two distinct dimensions of disability.

- Social disability and physical limitations are related in individuals, but many physically disabled are not socially disabled while many socially disabled are not physically disabled.

In an analysis of data based on a national survey of the disabled in Great Britain, it was found that the results of specially designed tests of physical impairment were related to self-reported social dependency. However one could not be used to predict the other, and it was concluded that they measured two indicative dimensions (23, 24, 25).

Data gathered in the period, July 1965 to June 1967, in the NHIS yielded a relationship between self-reported limitation of physical mobility and self-reported limitation of activity in one's major social role (in work, housework, school or play). However as many as one-third of those with extreme mobility limitations (confined to house) were able to carry on their major activity with or without limitations, while one-fifth of those with moderate mobility limitations (able to get around alone though with trouble) are unable to carry on their major activity at all. Table 1 shows the detailed relationship (26).

The SSSD examined several components of self-reported functional physical capacity. Most (three-quarters) persons disabled from work have one or more limitations of physical activity while only one-tenth are limited in mobility or self-care.

Table 1

Percent distribution of persons in mobility limitation categories by degree of chronic activity limitation, 1965-1967[a]

	Mobility Limitation		
Activity Limitation	Trouble Getting Around Alone	Needs Help in Getting Around	Confined to House
Unable to carry on major activity	21.3	45.4	66.8
Limitation in kind or amount of major activity	53.4	39.6	27.4
Limited but not in major activity	20.4	9.1	4.1
Not limited	5.0	5.8	–

[a]Source, reference no. 26, NCHS, *Chronic Conditions and Limitations of Activity and Mobility, July 1965-June 1967,* 1971.

However the rate of severe work disability is high among those with mobility or self-care limitations. It was found that these components, separately, as well as an index of functional limitations that summarized them were related to the severity of work disability. The index was also related to the same factors as work disability: age, sex, less-skilled work, heavy labor, low education. But it was shown to be related to disability even when these factors were controlled (27, 28). The index of functional limitations is also related to disability severity independent of type of chronic illness, and even more than is chronic condition. However, it is not more predictive of work disability than are various social factors (29).

A study of selected samples of disabled patients in rehabilitation and other outpatient treatment agencies found that they underestimated their general physical capacities in relation to their physicians' assessment but overestimated their general work capacities relative to the physicians' reports. Patients and physicians responded to identically worded scales in separate interviews (30).

Type of chronic illness has a weak relationship to social disability. Studies have noted a wide variety of conditions associated with disability. Among selected samples of men, women and Chinese professionals it was found that the amount of sickness disability in work was related to a large variety of illnesses of different etiologies and body systems (31). More recently the NHIS has found eight leading conditions causing activity limitation in 1969-70 and in 1965-67. Heart conditions and arthritis/rheumatism were the two leading causes in both periods, especially among middle-age and old-age persons (26, 32). The same two conditions were found to be the most frequent illnesses reported among persons with work limitations in the SSSD (33).

However, type of self-reported disabling condition in the latter study was not strongly related to work disability—neither to the prevalence nor to the severity of disability. Functional limitations and certain social factors were stronger factors in disability. Nor could reported chronic conditions account for the effects of these factors (27, 29, 33). A similar finding was reported in a national survey sponsored by the Office of Economic Opportunity among men aged 25-64 who were identified as disabled. Type of chronic condition was an insufficient predictor of severity of work disability when various social and demographic factors were controlled (9).

Social Factors in Disability: Age

Age is strongly related to social disability.

- Age effects on disability are independent of all associated factors examined, not only of other social and demographic factors but also of illness characteristics and of functional physical limitations.
- The relationship of age and social disability results from societal devaluation of the residual capacities of older people.

Sullivan comprehensively summarized and aggregated data on length of disability (disability days) during the mid-1960s gathered by the National Health Survey (NHS) (including the NHIS as well as the survey of resident health institutions), and grouped them into three types: long-term institutional, long-term noninstitutional and short-term. Advancing age resulted in a steep rise in both forms of long-term disability and a more gradual rise in short-term disability; the curve for the latter type however drops after age 75. Under age 45 the great majority of disability days are of the short-term type but after age 65 long-term noninstitutional disability predominates. Because of the decrease in short-term disability after age 75, we find in this age segment that even long-term institutional disability days become more numerous than short-term (34). A similar pattern of age change in these categories of disability occurs in the 1969 data of the NHS as presented in a more recent study using aggregated measures (35). The percent of the population with long-term disability multiplies in each successive age category, sometimes by factors of four and five, as seen in Table 2.

The acceleration of disability rates with age is found in NHIS data for every year between 1960 and 1971. This is reflected in a review of the data on the percent of persons reporting activity limitations due to a chronic condition. The age trend appears regardless of the category of degree of activity limitation considered: unable at all to carry on major activity, any limitation in major activity, or limitation in other activity (35, 36). The data for 1971 in Table 3 gives an indication of the age pattern. NHIS data gathered in 1957-1958 on person-years of "restricted activity" and "bed disability" show a similar pattern by age (37). Long-term forms of chronic limitations of major activity also vary with age: among those reporting any restriction of their principal activity, the percent with a limitation lasting five years or longer increases with age. The NHIS of 1969-1970 found that the percent unable to carry on their major activity at all for at least five years rose from 30 percent among children under age 17 to 49 percent among those 65 years or older. (The major activity of children is either school, for ages 6-16, or play, for ages below 6) (32). Disability due to acute conditions—or "short-term" limitations—rises with age regardless of the measure of disability. Thus in 1970-1971 the average number of days of restricted activity rose from 3 for adolescents to 10 among those over 65; bed-disability days increased from about 1.5 for adolescents to 4 after age 65 (38).

Table 2

Percent of persons with two types of long-term disability, by age, 1969[a]

	Age				
	Under 15	15-44	45-64	65-74	75 & Over
Long-term institutional	0.1	0.2	0.6	1.8	8.3
Long-term noninstitutional	0.2	0.8	4.4	12.4	20.5

[a]Source, reference no. 35, OMB, *Social Indicators, 1973,* 1973.

Table 3

Percent of persons with limitations of major activity, by age, 1971[a]

	Age			
	Under 17	17-44	45-64	65 & Over
Percent unable to carry on major activity	0.2	0.9	4.5	16.9
Percent any limitation in major activity	1.5	4.9	16.0	38.7

[a]Source, reference no. 35, OMB, *Social Indicators, 1973,* 1973.

There is some indication that disability varies with age among those in resident health institutions. The data cited above on institutionalized disability assume that persons in health institutions are equally disabled. Measures of variations in activity limitations among such persons do not seem to have been used in those studies. However a sample of nursing home patients included in the National Health Survey were specially studied with respect to possible variations in "debility," a Guttman-type scale based on measures of performance of activities of daily living (ADL). Although such a measure can be considered more appropriately as an index of functional limitations, it is of interest to note that it was found to be related to age among the patients (39).

The SSSD also found a steep age gradient in the prevalence of chronic disability for work and in the severity of work disability. The rate of disability was twice as high for those aged 35-44 as for those 18-34 years old; it was three times higher among those 45-54 years and five times higher for the 55-64 year-old group. The percent severely disabled was twice as high among those aged 35-44, four times higher for the 45-54 year-old group, and ten times more among those 55-64 years old (29, 40, 41).

There is sufficient evidence to indicate that the diminished participation of older people in work and other activities is not simply a function of the more severe illnesses that beset them or of the physical restrictions imposed by their diseases. Nor is it entirely explained by other social circumstances associated often with the aged, such as reduced income or lower education. Thus a multiple regression analysis of data from a household interview survey of low income areas in Nashville found that age (along with present activity: home or work) was the largest single predictor of a measure of illness severity based on duration of disabling condition (42). Age effects occur for both sexes: data from the 1968 NHIS show that both restricted activity days and bed-disability days increase with age for both males and females. The rising curve for the former becomes defined and steep only after about age 40, while for women it continues gradually from adolescence and turns sharply upward only after age 60 (43). Sullivan's findings on the relation of age to long-term and short-term disability emerged even when sex and race were simultaneously controlled (34). Data from the 1971 NHIS show that the percent of persons limited in their major activity increases with age in every income stratum (from "under $3000" to "$15,000 and over") (35). A larger variety of social and demographic factors were controlled separately in an analysis of NHIS data from a 1968-1969 survey. Age was consistently related to both the number of days of restricted activity and the percent with a chronic activity limitation regardless of sex, color, income, region, area of residence (metropolitan vs. other urban vs. farm), and living arrangements (living alone vs. with nonrelatives vs. with relatives) (44).

The relationship between age and social disability independent of biological and physical condition emerges clearly in an analysis of SSSD data. These effects occur even in a population with a limited age range of 18-64. Age was found to affect severity of work disability among men when functional physical limitations and disease classification were controlled. The relationship also occurred when social variables (education, occupation) were held constant (29, 33, 40). These findings strongly suggest that age norms devaluate the residual capacities of older people and result in increased withdrawal from activities.

The disabling effects of age occur in activities prescribed by sex role norms. Data from SSSD also appear to indicate that the devaluation of older persons' capacities is shaped by sex-role norms and that it occurs also for activities other than work. Age effects operate particularly in activity areas prescribed by such norms. This may help further to interpret the above finding on work disability among men. It may also help understand the additional finding that withdrawal from home and social participation increases with age among women disabled from work due to a chronic condition and even when severity of work disability is controlled. Among men, age does not affect social participation independent of degree of work disability. Although functional limitations and disease were not held constant, the strong association of these factors with severity of work disability leads one to suspect that they too would not entirely explain the relationship of age and non-work social disability among women (40).

The disabling effects of age are more pronounced among less industrialized, poor populations. An analysis of NHIS data gathered in 1968-1969 found that age differences in the number of days of restricted activity and in the percent with chronic limitation of activity were greater among low (vs. higher) income persons, among nonwhite (vs. white) individuals, in the southern states of the U.S. (vs. other regions), and in localities outside the metropolitan areas, both farm and city (vs. SMSA localities) (44). This combination of factors reflects the industrially underdeveloped sector of the United States and suggests similar effects on social disability in other societies sharing these elements.

Sex

Men generally are more socially disabled than women with long-term conditions, while women are generally more disabled than men with short-term conditions. In a summary analysis of NHS data from the mid-1960s, Sullivan computed the total volume of disability (number of disability days times persons) of all types, short-term and long-term, and for the latter, institutional as well as noninstitutional forms. He found that the total burden of disability was greater among men than women and that the disparity increased with age, especially after age 45, and decreased after age 75. Long-term disability was greater among men, but women experienced more short-term disability than men. The pattern of sex differences by age for all disability was reflected only in the long-term noninstitutional type. For long-term institutional and short-term types, the differences decline with age; the difference is even reversed in long-term institutional disability past age 75 (34). However, in another type of analysis of NHS data, based on life-table methods, Sullivan found little sex difference in the expectation of total disability of all types, although there were noticeable differences in bed-disability expectation favorable to males (45).

Annual NHIS data on chronic activity limitation generally support the proposition. Data for 1971, 1969-1970, 1968-1969, and 1965-1967 consistently show that within all age groups above 17 a greater percent of men than of women are chronically limited, especially in respect to the proportion unable to carry on their major activity (26,32,35,44).

Female vulnerability to short-term disability is demonstrated in a number of NHS studies. In such studies short-term disability is generally measured by several indicators of the number of days of disability. Data from 1970-1971 and 1969-1970 agree that females have higher rates of restricted activity and bed-disability days. In the latter period a similar difference was found in days lost from work among employed persons (46, 38). Analysis of 1971 and 1968-1969 data show that the sex difference holds within all age groups above 17 years; in the later study the finding occurred for all three measures of disability days: restricted activity, bed-disability, and work-loss (36, 44). An analysis of 1968 data found, however, that two age groups largely accounted for the differences in restricted activity and bed-disability: the child-bearing years of ages 15-45 and the most advanced age group of 75 years and over. The same study also found that the sex difference was consistent in a variety of other situations: in both urban (metropolitan or other) and rural areas, within each region of the country, and within income strata (43).

One type of short-term condition was consistently found to be an exception to the general finding: disability due to injury. Data from both the 1965-1967 and 1957-1961 periods show that men have higher rates of restricted activity and bed-disability than women (47).

Sex role norms discourage exemption from prescribed activity sought through claims to disability but sanction disability in nonprescribed activity. An illness condition does not permit men more often than women to be exempt from work, nor women as often as men from home and social activities: disabled men more readily withdraw from family and social participation, women from work.

- This proposition may be linked to the above proposition on the age effects on disability in sex role activities: only with increasing age do the norms permit exemption from activity prescribed by sex roles and such exemption may be granted by legitimizing claims to disability.

Differential participation in work by disabled men and women was found in the SSSD. While the proportion who had been limited in some way in their work by a health condition for at least three months was no greater among men than women, disabled women were more likely not to be working at all; men were more likely to work part-time, to shift to another line of work or to accept limitations in the amount or kind of their usual work (48, 49). Furthermore women participated less often in the labor force and in full-time employment at the time of the survey than did men who had been disabled from work. This occurred among those who had been employed at the time of onset of their disability and even among those with similar degrees of work disability (40).

Differential participation in family and social activities was also found in SSSD. Among those who had reported any limitation in work due to a chronic condition, men participated less in home and social activity than women. Furthermore, this finding emerged even when age and degree of work disability were held constant (40). While the SSSD focussed only on those who had reported some work disability, the NHIS in an analysis of 1968 data studied withdrawal from home vs. work activity among all women affected by a health condition. It classified women according to whether their usual activity in the past year was keeping house or working, and found a difference in the rate of disability between these two groups depending upon age. Below age 40, housekeepers reported no greater number of days restricted activity or bed disability due to illness than did workers despite the greater opportunity for self-exemption from major activities and the greater access to alternative pursuits at home. (These female workers are probably disproportionately young and unmarried in relation to the housekeepers and therefore have a lower risk of experiencing a disabling condition. If these factors were controlled, housekeepers' disability rates might be lower than those of workers.) However both types of disability days occurred more often among the housekeepers in all groups above age 40 (43). Below age 40, during the major period of child-rearing responsibilities, the home role is more obligatory than the work role and exemption from the housekeeping role through disability is severely restricted. In later years however home responsibilities diminish and the work role may become more important; thus claims to disability in the home role can more readily be legitimated.

Race

Nonwhites have higher rates of disability than whites, but this is largely a function of their lower socioeconomic status.

- Differences between racial groups are reduced or disappear within the same socioeconomic status.

A number of studies employing NHS data have reported more disability among nonwhites than whites. Nonwhites were found in a recent analysis of 1971 data to have a slightly higher percent with limitation of major activity (35) and, in a summary analysis aggregating the various forms of disability in the 1960s, to have less favorable lifetime expectation of disability (45). The difference between racial groups is more stable when age and sex are controlled and persists when the various types of disability are analyzed separately: short-term, long-term institutional and noninstitutional, chronic limitation of activity, restricted activity, bed-disability and work-loss days. Furthermore the difference increases with age, although it tends to diminish after age 75 (34, 50). In the latter study, based on 1965-1967 data, it was also found, when controlling for age, that nonwhites reported chronic conditions less, or no more often, than whites leading to the inference that chronic illness results in disability more often among nonwhites, and that this tendency increases with age.

When other factors are held constant, however, differences between racial groups are less reliable. Thus there are only slight differences in chronic activity limitation when family size is controlled, no differences within metropolitan areas in restricted activity, bed-disability or work-loss days even when sex is controlled (although differences do appear among those outside the metropolis), and an inconsistent pattern of differences in these forms of disability within regions of the U.S. controlled by sex and age (50).

When income is controlled racial group differences in disability are consistently reduced or even reversed in some cases. Age-adjusted rates of chronic activity limitation (in 1965-1967 data) are similar among nonwhite and whites within three income levels. Among those of similar income and family size nonwhites' rates are lower if not the same as those of whites. Furthermore, with income and sex controlled, nonwhites are most often found to have lower frequencies of disability days, whatever measure is employed (restricted activity, bed-disability, work-loss) (50). In a recent analysis of 1969-1970 data age-adjusted rates of chronic activity limitation are almost identical in the two racial groups within each of two family income strata, as shown in Table 4 (32).

Table 4

Percent distribution of persons in family income-race categories by degree of chronic activity limitation, 1969-1970, age-adjusted[a]

	No Limitations	Limitations, but Not Major Activity	Limitations in Major Activity	Unable to Carry on Major Activity
Under $5000				
Whites	82.5	3.3	9.0	5.2
Nonwhites	81.9	2.7	9.0	6.5
$5000 and over				
Whites	90.2	2.6	5.2	2.0
Nonwhites	90.1	1.6	4.9	3.3

[a] Source, reference no. 32, NCHS, *Limitation of Activity Due to Chronic Conditions, U.S., 1969 and 1970*, 1973.

Socioeconomic Status

Social disability is inversely associated with socioeconomic status independent of other factors, but cause-and-effect relationships are not clear.

- Socioeconomic status differences in disability generally widen with age.

All the studies examined are consistent in demonstrating this relationship. Low SES may result in greater disability but it may also be a product of incapacity due to health conditions. Each may mutually affect the other but the degree of mutual impact, if any, is not clear from these studies. The evidence however clearly establishes a relationship with social disability rather than with reported physical disability or disease. A study of NHIS data in 1965-1967 finds consistent and sizeable differences among income levels in age-adjusted percents with chronic activity limitations. However differences in limitations of physical mobility are less consistent and small, and there is no consistent pattern of differences in the percent with one or more chronic conditions (26).

Several other studies have also found income differences in disability with age adjusted or controlled. Thus the higher rates of disability and poverty of older people do not account for the greater disability of the lower strata. A study of 1971 NHIS data found that the percent limited in major activity increases as family income decreases in each age group. The greatest differences occurred within the 45-64 years category where the percentage was six times greater at the lowest income level (under $3000) than in the highest stratum ($15,000 and over). In the groups above age 64 differences were found only between strata above and below the $5000 level (35). An analysis of age-adjusted data in 1969-1970 found that the relationship was most pronounced in respect to the most severe activity-limitation category, "unable to carry on major activity" (32). A study of 1968-1969 data found family income to vary inversely with number of restricted activity days as well as with chronic activity limitation regardless of age (44). Differences are small among children (below age 17) but expand with age and contract in the age 65-and-older group, although they still remain wide. Differences between extreme income levels in Table 5 show the general pattern.

SES differences in disability persist when other factors are held constant. Income differences are found in 1968 data in restricted activity, bed-disability and school-loss days when age and sex are controlled, in 1965-1967 data in restricted activity, bed-disability and work-loss days when age, sex and color are simultaneously controlled, in the same data for chronic activity limitation when color and family size are held constant, and in 1969-1970 data for chronic activity limitation when age and color are controlled (32,43,50). Another SES measure, education, was also found to be related to disability: the individual's education varies inversely with limitation of major activity, age-adjusted, although differences between the high-school graduate and higher achievement levels are small (32). Earnings and education were also found to be important factors in a national survey of work disability among working-age men sponsored by the Office of Economic Opportunity (9).

Educational achievement, more than family income, may be considered an antecedent variable and perhaps provides a firmer clue to the causal role of SES in

Table 5

Two measures of disability, by age and family income, 1968-1969[a]

	Percent Activity Limitation				No. Restricted Activity Days			
Income	Below 17	17-44	45-64	65 & Over	Below 17	17-44	45-64	65 & Over
Under $3000	3.2	13.6	40.9	50.4	11.5	18.5	42.8	43.0
$15,000 and over	2.0	5.1	11.2	32.9	9.9	9.4	12.7	23.4

[a]Source, reference no. 44, NCHS, *Age Patterns in Medical Care, Illness and Disability, U.S., 1968-1969,* 1972.

disability. The studies thus far reviewed however have generally failed to distinguish cause and effect in the relationship between the two variables. A clearer picture may be obtained in data of the SSSD that give evidence of the impact of work disability on SES. The study distinguished disabled breadwinners from other disabled adults (by identifying married men and married women who were disabled) and compared the respective family incomes. While severity of disability was found generally to be inversely related to family income (the median income of the severly disabled was half of that of the general population), the family income of severely disabled married men was lower than that of severely disabled married women. Furthermore three-fifths of those married men who had children were below the poverty level compared to less than one-third of those with no children (51). Other SSSD data show that severe disability results in loss of earnings and in increasing dependency on public or family support. Nonmarried individuals who are severely disabled, especially younger persons, are most affected, public income maintenance becoming their major source of financial support. Among severely disabled working-age men earnings generally are their major income source, but more than two-fifths received no public support although they no longer had earnings; the latter depended upon family and other sources of support although one-sixth had no income from any source (52).

APPENDIX

Since this inventory is largely based on the findings of two major national surveys of disability, a brief word on some of their respective methods of measuring and classifying disability is in order. Further information is available in the relevant reports by NCHS (53) and Haber (11). This discussion is principally concerned with chronic rather than short-term disability.

The National Health Interview Survey, focussing on the total population, attempted to measure "chronic activity limitation" in any of four major areas: work, housework, school and play. The latter two were reserved respectively for ages 6-16 and ages below 6. Other respondents selected one of the other two areas as their major activity. Until 1967, respondents were first given a check list of chronic conditions and impairments ("conditions approach"). Those who selected at least one of these conditions, or who stated, in answer to another general question, that they had a condition lasting more than three months, were then given a card with the following choices, which represent, in order, the varying degrees of limitation used for the classification system of the survey:

1. Not able to work (do housework, go to school, play) at all.
2. Able to work, etc., but limited in amount or kind of work.
3. Able to work, etc., but limited in kind or amount of other activities.
4. Not limited in any of these ways.

Since 1968, respondents are no longer screened for conditions but instead are questioned about long-term disability or activity limitations as well as recent medical care ("person approach").

The Social Security Survey of the Disabled sampled a limited population, ages 18-64, and attempted to measure disability principally in work but also included housework in one of the categories in the classification system. Respondents were asked directly, without a screening question for chronic conditions, whether they had various limitations in kind or amount of work due to a health condition or impairment. Information was also obtained about the duration of the limitation. The survey developed the following classification system for limitations that lasted more than three months.

1. Severely disabled: unable to work altogether or regularly.
2. Occupationally disabled: able to work regularly, but unable to do the same work as before onset of disability, or unable to work full-time.
3. Secondary limitations: able to work full-time, regularly and at same work, but with limitations in kind or amount of work. (Includes women with limitations in keeping house but not in work.)
4. Not limited in work.

In some reports data are presented for disability lasing more than six months. An analysis of two groups according to duration of disability, 4-6 months vs. over 6 months, shows that they are basically similar. Only a few characteristics differentiate them: the shorter-term disabled group is younger, less severely disabled and more likely to receive rehabilitation services (49).

REFERENCES

1. Safilios-Rothschild, C. *The Sociology and Social Psychology of Disability and Rehabilitation.* Random House, New York, 1970.
2. Nagi, S. Z. *R & D in Disability Policies and Programs: An Analysis of Organizations, Clients and Decision-Making.* Mershon Center, Ohio State University, Columbus, Ohio, 1973 (mimeographed).
3. Elinson, J. Toward sociomedical health indicators. *Social Indicators Research* 1: 59-71, 1974.
4. Berelson, B., and Steiner, G. *Human Behavior: An Inventory of Scientific Findings.* Harcourt Brace and World, New York, 1964.
5. Bauer, R., editor. *Social Indicators.* MIT Press, Cambridge, 1966.
6. Sheldon, E. B., and Moore, W. E. *Indicators of Social Change.* Russell Sage, New York, 1968.

7. U.S. Department of Health, Education, and Welfare. *Toward a Social Report.* U.S. Government Printing Office, Washington, D.C., 1969.
8. Riley, L. E., Spreitzer, E. A., and Nagi, S. Z., editors. *Disability and Rehabilitation: A Selected Bibliography.* Forum Associates, Columbus, Ohio, 1971.
9. Wan, T. T. H. *Correlates and Consequences of Chronic Disability.* A Research Report prepared for the Social Security Administration, 1973 (mimeographed).
10. National Center for Health Statistics, U.S. Department of Health, Education, and Welfare. *Origin, Program and Operation of the United States National Health Survey.* No. 1000, Series 1, No. 1. U.S. Government Printing Office, Washington, D.C., April 1965.
11. Haber, L. D. Identifying the Disabled: Concepts and Methods in the Measurement of Disability. Report No. 1. *Social Security Survey of the Disabled: 1966.* Social Security Administration, Office of Research and Statistics, December 1967.
12. Ciocco, A., Graham, S., and Thompson, D. J. Illness and receipt of medical services in Pittsburgh (Arsenal) and Butler County. *Pennsylvania's Health* 17: 2-9, October-December 1956.
13. Thompson, D. J. and Tauber, J. Household survey, individual interview and clinical examination to determine prevalence of heart disease. *American Journal of Public Health* 47(9): 1131-1140, September 1957.
14. Commission on Chronic Illness. *Chronic Illness in a Large City.* Volume IV of Chronic Illness in the United States. Harvard University Press, Cambridge, Massachusetts, 1957.
15. Trussell, R. E.,and Elinson, J. *Chronic Illness in a Rural Area.* Volume III of Chronic Illness in the United States. Harvard University Press, Cambridge, Massachusetts, 1959.
16. Trussell, R. E., Elinson, J., and Levin, M. L. Comparisons of the various methods of estimating the prevalence of chronic disease in a community–the Hunterdon County Study. *American Journal of Public Health* 46: 173-182, February 1956.
17. Elinson, J. and Trussel, R. E. Some factors relating to degree of correspondence for diagnostic information as obtained by household interviews and clinical examinations. *American Journal of Public Health* 47: 311-321, March 1957.
18. Suchman, E. A., Phillips, B. S., and Streib, G. F. An analysis of the validity of health questionnaires. *Social Forces* 36: 223-232, March 1958.
19. National Center for Health Statistics, U.S. Department of Health, Education, and Welfare. *Health Interview Responses Compared with Medical Records.* No. 1000, Series 2, No. 7. U.S. Government Printing Office, Washington, D.C., 1965.
20. National Center for Health Statistics, U.S. Department of Health, Education, and Welfare. *Interview Data on Chronic Conditions Compared with Information Derived from Medical Records.* No. 1000, Series 2, No. 23. U.S. Government Printing Office, Washington, D.C., 1967.
21. National Center for Health Statistics, U.S. Department of Health, Education, and Welfare. *Net Differences in Interview Data on Chronic Conditions and Information Derived from Medical Records.* Series 2, No. 57. U.S. Government Printing Office, Washington, D.C., 1973.
22. Meltzer, J. W., and Hochstim, J. R. Reliability and validity of survey data on physical health. *Public Health Reports* 85: 1075-1086, December 1970.
23. Jeffreys, M., Millard, J. B., Hyman, M., Warren, M. D. A set of tests for measuring motor impairment in prevalence studies. *Journal of Chronic Diseases* 22: 303-319, November 1969.
24. Harris, A. *Handicapped and Impaired in Great Britain.* Her Majesty's Stationery Office, London, 1971.
25. Jeffreys, M. Presentation before Seminar on Sociomedical Health Indicators, Columbia University, April 27, 1973.
26. National Center for Health Statistics, U.S. Department of Health, Education, and Welfare. *Chronic Conditions and Limitations of Activity and Mobility, July 1965-June 1967.* No. 1000, Series 10, No. 61. U.S. Government Printing Office, Washington, D.C., 1971.
27. Haber, L. D. The Epidemiology of Disability–II: The Measurement of Functional Capacity Limitations. Report No. 10. *Social Security Survey of the Disabled: 1966.* Social Security Administration, Office of Research and Statistics, 1970.
28. Haber, L. D. Some parameters for social policy in disability: a cross-national comparison. *Milbank Memorial Fund Quarterly,* Summer: 319-340, 1973.
29. Haber, L. D. Disabling effects of chronic disease and impairment. *Journal of Chronic Diseases* 24: 469-487, 1971.
30. Nagi, S. Z. Congruency in medical and self-assessment of disability. *Industrial Medicine* 38: 27-36, March 1969.

31. Hinkle, L. E., et al. Studies in human ecology. *Amer. J. Psychiatry* 114: 212-220, September 1957.
32. National Center for Health Statistics, U.S. Department of Health, Education, and Welfare. *Limitation of Activity Due to Chronic Conditions, U.S., 1969 and 1970.* No. 1000, Series 10, No. 80. U.S. Government Printing Office, Washington, D.C., 1973.
33. Haber, L. D. Epidemiological Factors in Disability–I: Major Disability Conditions. Report No. 6. *Social Security Survey of the Disabled: 1966.* Social Security Administration, Office of Research and Statistics, 1969.
34. National Center for Health Statistics, U.S. Department of Health, Education, and Welfare. *Disability Components for an Index of Health.* No. 1000, Series 2, No. 42. U.S. Government Printing Office, Washington, D.C., July 1971.
35. Office of Management and Budget, Executive Office of the President. *Social Indicators, 1973.* U.S. Government Printing Office, Washington, D.C., 1973.
36. National Center for Health Statistics, U.S. Department of Health, Education, and Welfare. *Current Estimates from the Health Interview Survey, U.S., 1971.* No. 1000, Series 10, No. 79. U.S. Government Printing Office, Washington, D.C., 1973.
37. Linder, F. E. Health as a Demographic Variable. International Population Conference, Vienna, 1959.
38. National Center for Health Statistics, U.S. Department of Health, Education, and Welfare. *Acute Conditions: Incidence and Associated Disability, U.S. July 1970-June 1971.* No. 1000, Series 10, No. 82. U.S. Government Printing Office, Washington, D.C., 1973.
39. Skinner, D. E., and Yett, D. E. Debility index for long-term-care patients. In *Health Status Indexes,* edited by R. L. Berg. Hospital Research and Educational Trust, Chicago, Illinois, 1973.
40. Haber, L. D. Age and capacity devaluation. *Journal of Health and Social Behavior* 11: 167-182, 1970.
41. Haber, L. D. The Effect of Age and Disability on Access to Public Income-Maintenance Programs. Report No. 3. *Social Security Survey of the Disabled: 1966.* Social Security Administration, July 1968.
42. May, J. T. *Health Status, Health Action and Psychosocial Indicators.* Evaluation, Survey, and Health Research Corporation, Nashville, Tennessee, 1973.
43. National Center for Health Statistics, U.S. Department of Health, Education, and Welfare. *Disability Days, U.S.–1968.* No. 1000, Series 10, No. 67. U.S. Government Printing Office, Washington, D.C., 1972.
44. National Center for Health Statistics, U.S. Department of Health, Education, and Welfare. *Age Patterns in Medical Care, Illness and Disability, U.S., 1968-1969.* No. 1000, Series 10, No. 70. U.S. Government Printing Office, Washington, D.C., 1972.
45. Sullivan, D. F. A single index of mortality and morbidity. *HSMHA Health Reports* 86: 347-354, April 1971.
46. National Center for Health Statistics, U.S. Department of Health, Education, and Welfare. *Acute Conditions: Incidence and Associated Disability, July 1969-June 1970.* No. 1000, Series 10, No. 77. U.S. Government Printing Office, Washington, D.C., 1972.
47. National Center for Health Statistics, U.S. Department of Health, Education, and Welfare. *Types of Injuries: Incidence and Associated Disability, U.S., July 1965-June 1967.* No. 1000, Series 10, No. 57. U.S. Government Printing Office, Washington, D.C., 1969.
48. Haber, L. D. Disability, Work and Income Maintenance: Prevalence of Disability, 1966. Report No. 2. *Social Security Survey of the Disabled: 1966.* Social Security Administration, 1968; also in *Social Security Bulletin* 31: 14-23, May 1968.
49. Allan, K. H., and Cinsky, M. E. General Characteristics of the Disabled Population. Report No. 19. *Social Security Survey of the Disabled: 1966.* Social Security Administration, July 1972; also in *Social Security Bulletin* 35: 1-14, August 1972.
50. National Center for Health Statistics, U.S. Department of Health, Education, and Welfare. *Differentials in Health Characteristics by Color, U.S., July 1965-June 1967.* No. 1000, Series No. 10, No. 56. U.S. Government Printing Office, Washington, D.C., 1969.
51. Swisher, I. G. Family Income of the Disabled. Report No. 13. *Social Security Survey of the Disabled: 1966.* Social Security Administration, October 1970.
52. Swisher, I. G. Sources and Size of Income of the Disabled. Report No. 16. *Social Security Survey of the Disabled: 1966.* Social Security Administration, April 1971.
53. National Center for Health Statistics, U.S. Department of Health, Education, and Welfare. *Health Survey Procedures: Concepts, Questionnaire Development and Definitions in the Health Interview Survey.* No. 1000, Series 1, No. 2. U.S. Government Printing Office, Washington, D.C., May 1964.

CHAPTER 4

Evaluation of Health Care Quality by Consumers

Howard R. Kelman

The involvement of the "consumer" in health services planning, organization and delivery has in recent years gained increasing, although perhaps grudging, acceptance by health planners and providers, and by legislative and other groups concerned with health affairs, as a necessary and important concomitant of efforts designed to refashion our "crisis-ridden" health care system (1, 2). Recent legislation indeed mandates consumer representation on comprehensive health planning bodies and as members of advisory boards of health care institutions and neighborhood health centers, and some legislative proposals concerned with national health insurance envisage even wider roles for consumers.

Despite the wide acceptance of the principle of consumer involvement, it has also been observed that the application of this concept has not proceeded without difficulty and in some instances has led to open conflict with providers and other groups (3-5). It is not yet clear what eventual form or forms consumer participation will take, although there is a consensus that the more or less exclusive prerogative that the provider group enjoyed in decision making in health is to be shared, to a greater or lesser degree, with consumers, their representatives, or persons acting on their behalf (3, 6).

This article is based on a paper presented at the Annual Meeting of the American Sociological Association, Medical Sociology Section, at Montreal, Canada, on August 29, 1974.

THE LEGITIMACY OF CONSUMER ASSESSMENT OF HEALTH CARE QUALITY

One of the areas of health care effort which, until recently, has been "unchallenged" as being the exclusive domain of providers of health care has been that of the evaluation or assessment of health care quality. Since society has vested these professional groups with the legal and social responsibility for health care provision, it has also looked to these groups for standards and procedures whereby the interests of the public in receiving quality care would be protected and assured (7, 8).

As a consequence, the involvement and participation of consumers in health care quality evaluation have to date been restricted despite acceptance of the legitimacy of consumer participation in other areas of health decision making. However, various spokesmen for consumer interests and consumer health groups have begun to question the validity and even the objectivity of these provider-dominated and controlled procedures, and have called for some measure of participation in, and contribution by, consumers in these hitherto "nonpublic" operations (9, 10).

The articulation of what is essentially a new role in health care provision for consumers is likely to provoke even greater controversy and conflict in this area of health activity than it has in other domains since it strikes more directly into the heart of what has traditionally been defined as health professionalism–namely, the power and authority of the health professions to define and to judge the merits of their own activities.

If, as has been suggested, there is value to be gained from the involvement of consumers in health care quality assessment, then it becomes important to identify and clarify certain of the issues that such efforts raise and which now loom as barriers to further development.

Undoubtedly, the most significant and potentially controversial issue, or set of issues, is the ideological one, namely, the legitimacy (in a moral, legal, and technical sense) of consumer or lay assessment of health care quality. Such activities on the part of consumers can be viewed as illegitimate intrusion into professional prerogatives not only to define the content of their activities but to determine their efficacy as well. However, it is precisely because professional groups have failed to monitor aggressively the professional activities of their constituents–to police their ranks, so to speak–that public confidence that its interests are being guarded has eroded. While some measure of scapegoating may be involved, spokesmen for consumer interests have come to believe that professional groups have not fully addressed themselves to the public interest in exchange for the special social status and rewards that have been conferred upon them by society.

Closely tied to the "professional infringement" aspect of the legitimacy issue is the question of the continuing mystique of health care assessment. In the realm of assessment of quality, it takes the form of relegating the recipient of care to little or no role in the judgment of quality of care, or, even further, to not even defining its parameters.

PROVIDER PERSPECTIVES ON HEALTH CARE QUALITY

The traditional provider perspective on health care quality and its assessment views quality care essentially as technically competent performance on the part of the physician and, by extension, other professional providers of health care. This performance may be recognized by its approximation to recognized and accepted normative or empirically derived practice standards. Assumed or demonstrated correlates of competent performance are given levels of training and experience and necessary facilities and equipment (11). Judgments of performance are deemed possible by knowledgeable peers or are measured against more objective standards, both based usually on data recording performance behavior to be found in patient care records (12-14). The methodological extension of this orientation finds its most developed expression in the form of "audits," a procedure whereby provider performance (or capacity to perform adequately, in the case of facility accreditation or auditing) is assessed by peers within the system (internal audits) or outside the system (external audits) (15).

The logic of this perspective therefore excludes all but peers of the provider from participation in quality care assessment because of technical incompetence. Such a perspective leaves little or no room for consumers, or even nonpeer providers, to even suggest parameters of quality care of concern to them. This perspective also assumes that demonstration of competent performance or its proxy measures—structural standards—produces effective care, that is to say, care that is beneficial to the patient. (Such assumptions, of course, are increasingly being subjected to empirical test.)

Other health care researchers have sought to modify this traditional definition of health care quality, and its assessment, to include elements of the delivery process as well as outcome measures of health care benefit (16, 17). This orientation has resulted in efforts to judge the quality of care in terms of its benefits to patients and recipients of care, and to relate the processes of care delivered to health benefits (18-21). This broader view of health care quality also encompasses dimensions of care believed salient to patients and consumers, namely, measures of accessibility, acceptability, compliance, communication, and satisfaction (22, 23).

However, these modifications have not significantly altered nor greatly expanded the role and participation of consumers in health care quality determination or assessment. Typically, consumers or, more usually, "recipients" of care are viewed by these providers essentially as data sources for information on the worthwhileness or effectiveness of one or another health care program or benefit plan. Their views and behavior have been studied along with other parameters of health care provision as "measures" of health care quality.

It is also not entirely clear, aside from the obvious saliency of these issues to program administrators and providers, why these particular parameters have been chosen as measures of quality. Such information is certainly significant to those providing care or administering services or benefit plan programs. However, these parameters of quality are not necessarily the *dimensions* of major concern to consumers.

What is clear from the above analysis is that although the traditional and the mere "enlightened" provider perspectives on quality care and its assessment may differ with respect to the importance or relevance of the consumer as a data source, neither viewpoint provides opportunity for the consumer to participate in the definition of quality, that is, in specifying the criteria of health care quality or the elements of health care provision that are of importance to the users or potential users of such services. To justify this exclusion or constraint on the grounds of ignorance or incompetence is essentially an ideological denial of legitimacy.

Similar if not the same arguments were put forward nearly a decade ago concerning the "legitimacy" of consumer or community involvement in health care organization and planning. However, the thrust of political forces favoring such developments has now overcome professional objections, and consumer participation in a wide range of such activities has now been legally sanctioned. Similarly, the passage of the Bennett Amendment to the Social Security Act in 1972, the activities of consumer and public interest groups in and around hospital accreditation review procedures, and the attempts to obtain relevant information on available physician services all suggest that consumer-oriented forces are likely, over time, to prevail in these areas as well.

CONSUMER CRITERIA OF HEALTH CARE QUALITY

It is one thing to mandate, legally, the participation of consumers in health care quality assessment, but it is another matter to structure participation in ways that are acceptable and contributory to the interests of both health care providers and consumers. This process will require modification of the perspective of providers' exclusive rights to define the ingredients of quality and the roles of the participants in its determination. It will also require that increased attention be given to efforts designed to determine, from the perspective of the consumer, those attributes of health care organization and delivery which *they* regard as desirable and salient to their needs, that is, their definition of health care quality, and again from their perspective, how quality health care can be assessed and monitored.

In this regard, an overview of the relevant literature, although numerically extensive, suggests certain crucial limitations in current knowledge of consumer definitions of health care quality. There is an extensive series of reports, stemming mainly from the middle 1960s, in the general area of community and/or consumer involvement in health. These reports are of several types. Some are philosophical or political statements regarding the role and importance of the participation of the "community" or "consumer" in health care policy, administration, and other roles (2, 24). Other reports describe problems and processes observed in such endeavors (5, 25), and suggest how professional roles are affected and modified (26, 27). Such reports are valuable in documenting or asserting the positive values for health care planning and organization of consumer involvement, and for suggesting certain special concerns of particular communities or consumers (low-income or minority groups, mostly) concerning health care availability and accessibility.

Another group of reports emanates largely from spokesmen for consumer groups who purchase care such as trade unions, civic, and fraternal organizations; from "consumer advocate" groups, public figures, and legislators; and from providers speaking on behalf of consumers (3, 24, 28). These materials, usually but not exclusively polemical in style, suggest a wide range of consumer complaints and dissatisfactions with health care costs, delivery, availability, accessibility, facilities, personnel, policies, coordination, administration, and planning. These materials, although useful in suggesting the rather wide range of potential or actual concerns of consumers, are of limited value because:

- The extent to which the views of these spokesmen accurately reflect consumers, or even their constituencies, is not known since no empirical evidence other than an occasional group of selected "dramatic" case histories is presented.
- The parameters of consumer concern are usually stated in global terms so that the variations and extent of concern and dissatisfaction and the priorities of concern cannot be gauged.
- Finally, the representativeness of these "spokesmen" and their views is not known.

Another set of relevant materials is the series of national health surveys begun in the middle 1950s conducted under the aegis of the Health Information Foundation in New York and, more recently, by the Center for Health Administration Studies of the University of Chicago. Although their main focus has been on developing information on the costs and utilization of medical and hospital services, and with public attitudes concerning these, the studies also contain information and data bearing on the issue of identifying the concerns and interests of consumers with elements of health care quality (29, 30). One such report, for example, revealed the "reasons" why the "public" rated hospital facilities as being "excellent" or "poor," what they liked and disliked about hospital care and treatment, and reasons for not complying or following up on their physician's care recommendations (31). A more recent study reported on the extent of public dissatisfaction with health care and how it varies among different subgroups in the national population (32).

Against the background of these national surveys is a fairly extensive body of materials which reports on the behavioral and attitudinal responses of groups of patients or their families to specific, and usually local, hospital- or community-based treatment programs or health benefit plans. These studies, for the most part, were undertaken by providers of care in an attempt to evaluate the effectiveness of such care, to identify and rectify "unsatisfactory" program elements, to better understand differential utilization among "target" groups, and to uncover reasons for choice of alternate health benefit programs among eligible groups (8, 33-41).

As with the national surveys of the "public" cited above, these studies have not focused specifically on identifying consumer standards or criteria of health care quality. Rather, their aims were to identify program components or elements that different groups of recipients of hospital, clinic, or physician services "complain" about, are satisfied or dissatisfied with, or otherwise affect their utilization of or response to specific health care programs (22, 42-52).

Although generalization to "well" populations or to other programs of a similar genre is hazardous because such reports are either program- or site-specific and based on selected groups of patients or other population subgroups,[1] it is possible to infer from such studies that:

- Providers and researchers do *not* regard consumers as competent to judge accurately or knowledgeably the technical aspects of medical and related health care quality.
- Recipients of care are more concerned or dissatisfied with the manner and means of the processes of health care delivery, the way in which they are regarded and dealt with by health care personnel, and by certain structural characteristics of these programs, both physical and administrative, than with the outcome of care or the competencies of the health care personnel providing care.
- Different clusters of health care program characteristics causing dissatisfaction can be identified for different care sites and auspices (hospitals, clinics, health centers, private office practitioners), while some dimensions of care appear to be non-site-specific (reasonable charges, communication with staff, privacy, personal interest shown, and responsiveness to community needs).
- Differences among recipient groups in social and demographic background (age, sex, income, family composition, and ethnic group), health circumstances (type and seriousness of condition, benefit coverage, having "own" doctor, prior experience in obtaining care), and social circumstances (distance from facility, related social problems, knowledge and experience in obtaining health services) lead to different designations of program elements as being either unsatisfactory or helpful.

The importance of these studies of recipient groups, the national sample surveys cited earlier, and other studies of unselected populations of well and sick persons (54-57) lies again in their potential contribution of parameters of consumer health interests, the identification of important population subgroups that may hold different views, and the necessity to tap populations unselected from the point of view of enrollment in a specific health care program, benefit program, or perceived sickness status, if a generalizable consumer-salient definition of health care quality criteria is to be determined.

A final group of materials reviewed for their potential contribution might be classified under the rubric of "provider-derived quality care assessment methodology." The materials in this field have accumulated at a very rapid rate in the past decade or more, as interest in and demand for objective assessment of health service quality and effectiveness have grown (12, 17, 58-60). It is evident that despite rather impressive advances, serious substantive and methodological problems remain, centering on such issues as the definition of quality (61, 62), measurement methods and criteria (12, 63, 64), and the relationships between the structure, process, and end results of quality measures (20, 21, 65).

These materials suggest that the dominant provider views of health care quality, its standards and assessments, are matters which continue to be viewed as the exclusive prerogative of the practitioner-provider group in which nonpeers and the consuming

[1] A recent critical review of consumer assessment methods by Lebow (53) suggests other reasons which limit the utility of the findings of such studies.

"lay" public have no expertise. It is also apparent that although the traditional provider view and definition of quality still prevail, a broader, multifactoral view of health care quality embodying variables believed more important to consumer interests has emerged and appears to be gaining increasing acceptance. Methodologically, this orientation or "definition" of quality does include the recipient or consumer of care, but only as a source of information or data on those dimensions of care quality determined a priori by the providers, or planners, as was earlier discussed.

SUGGESTIONS FOR NEEDED RESEARCH

This overview of the related literature has revealed considerable rhetoric but sparse empirical data which speak directly to the question of what consumers regard as the quality characteristics of health care. Numerous spokesmen, groups, and professionals represent consumer views with an unknown degree of accuracy, or decide on an a priori basis what they should desire or should value in health care. Population sample surveys and studies of different recipient groups suggest a wide range of elements of care that are defined as being "causes" of dissatisfaction or of other complaints. Although these materials may be helpful in suggesting parameters of health care quality of importance to consumers, the primary purposes for their a priori selection by providers appear related more to providers' needs for evaluation of particular programs.

The evolution of standards and procedures for the assessment of health care quality has reflected essentially the concerns, values, and interests of the health care provider, administrator, or planner. Despite a broadening definition of health care quality which now includes concern for the processes of delivery and outcome, in addition to traditional concerns for technical competence and performance, quality care attributes believed salient to consumers are still viewed largely through the spectrum and perspective of the provider. It is not at all certain that those aspects of health care which providers *believe* are salient to the recipients or "targets" of their programs are, in fact, the attributes of importance to the actual or potential recipients of care. Nor can one be certain that those attributes which are *believed* to be of importance to a particular patient group "selected" along a variety of dimensions (e.g. health status, location, age) can be generalized to larger or more diverse populations in different sociomedical circumstances and locales.

Against this background, there rests an inadequate base of empirically derived information on what consumers, sick or well, do regard as being of importance to them in decision making in health care. Given the social desirability of the involvement of consumers in a variety of roles related to resolving problems of health care policy, delivery, and assessment, empirical investigations of health care quality attributes—derived from the mouths and perspective of actual and potential consumers of health care—as a basis for the further development of criteria and standards appears called for.

Particularly useful would be population-based, rather than program- or facility-based, studies of consumers' views (sick and well) and their perceptions of the attributes of quality care. The hazards of bias resulting from either self-selected or "captured" or sick populations, or groups dependent for care on particular programs, or survivors of programs of care are too well known to be disregarded in this as in other areas of research. This identification of these attributes of health care quality should be obtained against the background of the individual's experience, preferences, and desires with respect to health care provision rather than "requiring" the individual to justify or to rationalize his or her present health care arrangements (or lack of them) or choice of alternate programs, as has been the case in many available studies.

Efforts might also be made to rank order quality attributes with respect to their importance for the individual. It is likely that some aspects of care quality may be considered absolutely essential, others important but not necessarily critical, and still others desirable but not crucial. Additionally, it would be important to identify variability within the population by health and social circumstances, by locale, by type of health care arrangement, and by type of facility.

Especially strategic for learning more about consumer criteria or decision making would be studies of "special" consumer groups. Such studies might include investigation of persons newly resident in areas whose social networks, including health care patterns, have been disrupted and need to be recreated, and studies of the health behavior of health professionals. It is of some interest to note in this regard, that there is evidence which suggests that when physicians are viewed as consumers in decision making regarding their personal health care, their behavior concerning their own choice of a physician contradicts that which is advocated for the public by physicians (66, 67). This suggests that more knowledgeable or "sophisticated" consumers are likely to be able to suggest parameters of health care quality (for consumers) which arise out of their particular areas of health expertise, and that these parameters of quality *may* contradict standards or "rules" for health care behavior that are publicly advocated.

The extent to which the views and perspectives of providers and consumers are congruent or discordant on what health care quality criteria are has not been extensively studied, nor has there been systematic investigation of differences between different groups of providers. Gaps between providers and consumers in perceived health care needs and action priorities at the local community level continued to be documented (68, 69) as anticipated, and discordant ratings of quality between physicians and recipients were obtained in the 1961 Teamster study (70). (In the latter study the physicians' definition and rating of quality was considered to be the "objective" measure.) Smith's recent finding (71), in an institutional setting, of considerable agreement among patients and staff groups on the importance of both technical and personal aspects of care suggests the possibility, however, of considerable overlap in the specifics, if not on broad or more general dimensions, of health care quality attributes or perspectives of both groups. Additional studies of this genre in which the quality criteria of providers and consumers are viewed as perhaps different or even complementary, rather than using the former as the more valid or objective measures, would also contribute greatly to current knowledge.

Finally, investigation of the impact of consumer involvement in quality or accreditation review procedures on health provider behavior or health services organization would also be useful. Have such encounters proved fruitful in upgrading care? Is this a socially desirable format for generating change in health care provision? Perhaps it is too early or occurrences are too sporadic to tell, but it is not too early to consider ways and opportunities to enlarge our base of knowledge of consumer impact.

In summary then, ideological as well as methodological issues arising out of the involvement of consumers in health care quality assessment and review have been identified.

From the perspective of health care providers, the definition and determination of quality remain as areas requiring professional expertise and control in which legal, moral, and technical qualifications restrict the consumer role either to one of non-participation or to that of a potentially useful data source.

The development and articulation of a consumer role in quality determination will require both a modification of this perspective and more vigorous and systematic efforts to enlarge our current knowledge base concerning quality criteria derived from the perspective of the consumer. These two perspectives, which are assumed to be both homogeneous within each group and antagonistic to one another, may, in fact, not be so. Reliable information on this and related issues is lacking and necessary if sound social policy in this regard is to result in public benefit.

REFERENCES

1. Anderson, D. M., and Kerr, M. Citizen influence in health service programs. *Am. J. Public Health* 6: 1518-1523, 1971.
2. Community Participation for Equity and Excellence in Health Care. *Proceedings,* New York Academy of Medicine, Annual Health Conference, New York, 1970.
3. Glasser, M. Consumer expectation of health services. *Medicine in a Changing Society,* edited by L. Corey, S. E. Saltman, and M. E. Epstein, pp. 29-39. C. V. Mosby, St. Louis, 1972.
4. Huntly, R. R. Improving the health services system through research and development. *Inquiry* 1: 15-21, 1970.
5. A hospital meets with its neighbors, but it isn't easy for either of them (editorial). *Modern Hospital,* 1970.
6. White, K. L. Organization and delivery of personal health services: Public policy issues. In Dimensions and Determinants of Health Policy, edited by W. L. Kissick. *Milbank Mem. Fund Q.* 46 (part II): 225-258, 1968.
7. Freidson, E. *Professional Dominance.* Atherton Press, New York, 1970.
8. Mechanic, D. *Public Expectations and Health Care: Essays on the Changing Organization of Health Services.* John Wiley & Sons, New York, 1972.
9. Rubin, D., and Gluckman, E. Consumers organize to check health services. *Pension and Welfare News,* p. 60, April 1973.
10. Solomon, J. Health care: A buyer's market. *The Sciences* 13: p. 21, 1973.
11. Donabedian, A. Evaluation of the quality of medical care. Health Services Research I. *Milbank Mem. Fund Q.* 44(part 2): 166-203, 1966.
12. Donabedian, A. *Medical Care Appraisal Quality and Utilization.* Vol. II, *A Guide To Medical Care Administration.* American Public Health Association, New York, 1969.
13. Flashner, B. A., Reed, S., Coburn, R., and Fine, P. R. Professional standards review organizations–analysis of their development and implementation. Based on a preliminary review of the hospital admission and surveillance program in Illinois. *JAMA* 233: 1473-1484, 1973.
14. Sheps, M. Approaches to the quality of hospital care. *Public Health Rep.* 70 (9): 877-886, 1955.
15. Richardson, F. Methodological development of a system of medical audit. *Med. Care.* 10(6): 451-462, 1973.
16. Berg, R. L. *Health Status Indexes.* Hospital Research and Education Trust, Chicago, 1973.
17. Hopkins, C., editor. Methodology of identifying, measuring and evaluating outcomes of health service programs, systems or subsystems. *Outcomes Conference I, II, Proceedings.* United States Department of Health, Education, and Welfare, Public Health Service, Health Services and Mental Health Administration, Washington, D. C., 1969.

18. Hulka, B. S., and Cassel, J. C. The AATP-UNC study of the organization, utilization and assessment of primary medical care. *Am. J. Public Health* 63: 494-501, 1973.
19. Kessner, D. M., Kalk, C. E., and Singer, J. Assessing health quality–the case for tracers. *N. Engl. J. Med.* 288: 189-194, 1973.
20. Shapiro, S. End results measurements of quality of medical care. *Milbank Mem. Fund Q.* 45: 4-30, 1967.
21. Williamson, J. W. Evaluating quality of patient care: A strategy relating outcome and process assessment. *JAMA* 218: 564-569, 1971.
22. Davis, M. S. Predicting non-compliance behavior. *J. Health Soc. Behav.* 8: 265-271, 1967.
23. Korsch, B. M., Gozzi, E. K., and Francis, V. Gaps in doctor-patient communication. *Pediatrics* 42: 855-870, 1968.
24. Haynes, A. M. Professionals and the community confronting change. *Am. J. Public Health* 60(3): 519-523, 1970.
25. Geiger, J. H. Hidden professional roles: The physician as reactionary, reformer, revolutionary. *Social Policy* 1(6): 24-33, 1971.
26. King, M. Can the medical profession share power with the community? In *Medicine in the Ghetto,* edited by J. D. Norman, pp. 55-57. Appleton-Crofts, New York, 1969.
27. Reeder, L. The patient-client as a consumer: Some observations on the changing professional client relationship. *J. Health Soc. Behav.* 13(4): 406-413, 1972.
28. Sheps, C. M. The influence of consumer sponsorships on medical services. *Milbank Mem. Fund Q.* 50: 41-73, 1972.
29. Anderson, R., and Anderson, O. W. *A Decade of Health Services: Social Survey Trends in Use and Expenditure.* University of Chicago Press, Chicago, 1967.
30. Anderson, O. W., Collette, P., and Feldman, J. *Family Expenditure Patterns for Personal Health Services, 1953 and 1958.* Research Series 14. Health Information Foundation, New York, 1960.
31. Freidson, E., and Feldman, J. J. *The Public Looks at Hospitals.* Health Information Foundation Research Series 4, 1958.
32. Anderson, R., Kravits, J., and Anderson, O. The public's view of the crisis on medical care: An impetus for changing delivery systems. *Economic and Business Bulletin* 24: 44-52, 1971.
33. Colver, A., Tave, R. T., and Spearce, M. C. Factors influencing the use of maternal health services. *Soc. Sci. Med.* 1: 293-308, 1967.
34. Brooks, C. H. Associations among distance, patient satisfaction, and utilization of two types of inner city clinics. *Med. Care* 11: 373-383, 1973.
35. Freidson, E. *Patients' Views of Medical Practice.* Russell Sage Foundation, New York, 1961.
36. Kelman, H. R., and Elinson, J. Strategy and tactics of evaluating a large-scale medical care program. *Med. Care* 7: 79-85, 1969.
37. Kelman, H. R., Camerman, E., Herr, C., Sword, K., and Perry, W. Monitoring patient care. *Med. Care* 7: 1-13, 1969.
38. Metzner, C. A., Bashur, R. L., and Shannon, G. W. Differential public acceptance of group medical practice. *Med. Care* 10(4): 279-287, 1972.
39. Metzner, C. A., and Bashur, R. L. Factors associated with choice of health care plans. *J. Health Soc. Behav.* 8: 291-299, 1967.
40. Mustafa, A. T., Hopkins, C. E., and Klein, B. Determinants of choice and change of health insurance plan. *Med. Care* 9(1): 32-41, 1971.
41. Podell, L. *Studies in the Use of Health Services by Families on Welfare: Utilization of Preventive Health Services.* Center for the Study of Urban Problems, City University of New York, 1969.
42. Clausen, J., Seindenfeld, M., and Deasy, L. Parent attitudes toward participation of their children in polio vaccine trials. *Am. J. Public Health* 44: 1526-1536, 1954.
43. Kegeles, S. A field experimental attempt to change beliefs and behavior of women in an urban ghetto. *J. Health Soc. Behav.* 10: 115-124, 1969.
44. Ludwig, E. G., and Gibson, G. Self perception of sickness and the seeking of medical care. *J. Health Soc. Behav.* 10: 125-133, 1969.
45. Martin, P. L. Detection of cervical cancer: A study of motivation for cytological screening. *California Med.* 101: 427-429, 1964.
46. Metz, A. The relationship of dental care practices to attitudes toward fluoridation. *J. Health Soc. Behav.* 8: 55-59, 1967.

47. Rosenblatt, D., and Suchman, E. A. Blue collar attitudes and information toward health and illness. In *Blue Collar World*, edited by A. B. Shostak and W. Gomberg, pp. 324-333. Prentice-Hall, New York, 1964.
48. Rosenstock, I. M., DerryBerry, M., and Carriger, B. K. Why people fail to seek poliomyelitis vaccination. *Public Health Rep.* 74: 98-103, 1959.
49. Suchman, E. A. Preventive health behavior: A model for research on community health campaigns. *J. Health Soc. Behav.* 8: 197-209, 1967.
50. Tyroler, H. A., et al. Patterns in preventive health behavior in populations. *Journal of Health and Human Behavior* 6: 128-140, 1965.
51. Francis, V., Korsch, B., and Morris, M. Gaps in doctor-patient communication. Patients' response to medical advice. *N. Engl. J. Med.* 28: 535-540, 1969.
52. Welch, S., Comer, J., and Steinman, M. Some social and attitudinal correlates of health care among Mexican Americans. *J. Health Soc. Behav.* 14: 205-213, 1973.
53. Lebow, J., Consumer assessment of the quality of medical care. *Med. Care* 12: 328-337, 1974.
54. Coe, R. M. Attitudes toward Medicare among older people. *Public Health Rep.* 85: 868-872, 1970.
55. Kane, R., and Kane, R. Determination of health care expectations among the Navajo: Consumers in the federal care system. *Med. Care* 10(5): 421-429, 1972.
56. Kane, R. L. Determination of health care priorities and expectations among rural consumers. *Health Serv. Res.* 142-151, 1969.
57. Koos, E. L. *The Health of Regionville: What the People Thought and Did About It.* Hafner Publishing Company, New York, 1954.
58. Altman, I., Anderson, A. J., and Baker, K. *Methodology in Evaluating the Quality of Medical Care: An Annotated Selected Bibliography, 1955-1968.* University of Pittsburgh Press, Pittsburgh, 1969.
59. Daily, E. F. Improving the quality of medical care. *Am. J. Public Health* 39:337-339, 1947.
60. Sanazaro, P. J., Goldstein, R. J., Roberts, J., Maglott, D. B., and McAlister, J. W. Research and development in quality assurance: The experimental medical care review organization program. *N. Engl. J. Med.* 287: 1125-1131, 1972.
61. Donabedian, A. Models for organizing the delivery of personal health services and criteria for evaluating them. *Milbank Mem. Fund Q.* 50 (part 2): 103-154, 1972.
62. Kerr, M., and Trantow, D. G. *Perspectives and a Suggested Framework for Defining, Measuring, and Assessing the Quality of Health Services.* United States Department of Health, Education, and Welfare, Health Services and Mental Health Administration, Washington, D. C., 1968.
63. Elinson, J. Methods of sociomedical research. In *Handbook of Medical Sociology*, Ed. 2, edited by H. Freeman, S. Levine, and L. G. Reeder, pp. 483-501. Prentice-Hall, Englewood Cliffs, N. J., 1972.
64. Lewis, C. The state of the art of quality assessment. *Med. Care* 12: 799-806, 1974.
65. Brook, R. W., Appel, F. A., Avery, C., Arman, M., and Stevenson, R. L. Effectiveness of in-patient follow-up care. *N. Engl. J. Med.* 285: 1509-1514, 1971.
66. Bynder, H. Doctors as patients: A study of the medical care of physicians and their families. *Med. Care* 6: 157-167, 1968.
67. Mahoney, M., Trussell, R., and Elinson, J. Physicians choose medical care: A sociometric approach to quality appraisal. *Am. J. Public Health* 50: 1678-1686, 1960.
68. Kurtz, R. A., Chalfaut, H. P., and Kaplan, K. Inner city residents and health decision makers: Perceptions of health problems and solutions. *Am. J. Public Health* 64: 612-613, 1974.
69. Richardson, J. D., and Scutchfield, F. D. Priorities in health care: The consumer's viewpoint in an Appalachian community. *Am. J. Public Health* 63: 79-82, 1973.
70. Ehrlich, J., Morehead, M. T., and Trussel, R. E. *The Quantity, Quality, and Costs of Medical and Hospital Care Secured by a Sample of Teamster Families in the New York Area.* Columbia University School of Public Health and Administrative Medicine, New York, 1961.
71. Smith, D. B. The measurement of health care quality: A problem in psychological scaling and social decision theory. *Soc. Sci. Med.* 6: 145-153, 1972.

CHAPTER 5

Constructing Social Metrics for Health Status Indexes

Donald L. Patrick

One can characterize human society as a cooperative endeavor aimed at achieving a better life for all through various social arrangements and joint labors. This cooperative venture can be further characterized as a set of individual interests, the union of which sometimes produces conflict when working toward the greatest good. Sociopolitical philosophers, from Locke and John Stuart Mill to John Rawls and Robert Nozick, have argued over concepts of social justice or that set of principles for choosing between the social arrangements which determine the division of benefits and for underwriting a consensus as to the proper distributive shares (1, 2).

Efforts to improve the delivery of health services, and thereby the health status of the population, must confront the two principles of justice as delineated by Rawls (1, pp. 302-303):

> *First Principle.* Each person is to have an equal right to the most extensive total system of equal basic liberties compatible with a similar system of liberty for all.
> *Second Principle.* Social and economic inequalities are to be arranged so that they are both: (a) to the greatest benefit of the least advantaged, consistent with the just savings principle, and (b) attached to offices and positions open to all under conditions of fair equality of opportunity.

In Rawls' view, these principles of justice rest on what he labels the "General Conception," i.e. all social primary goods–liberty and opportunity, income and wealth, and the basis of self-respect–are to be distributed equally unless an unequal distribution of any or all of these goods is to the advantage of the least favored. In its simplest version, Rawls believes society should maximize the expected welfare level of the worst off person, the "maximin" rule of justice.

Health care is in the class of basic liberties along with the right to vote, speak, and assemble (political liberty), liberty of conscience, freedom to hold property, and freedom from arbitrary arrest. Assuming that the availability of health services is associated with better health, and this may be a great assumption (3, p. 16), society should attempt to achieve an equality in the distribution of health services or an equality in levels of physical, mental, and social well-being, subject to the constraint of providing the maximum possible level of well-being, i.e. the social minimum, for disadvantaged members. Thus, the question becomes how to make social arrangements that meet these fundamental rights, while satisfying the principles of equality and social minimum.

Rawls has attempted to show that a constitutional democracy can approximately satisfy the two principles of justice, provided the government regulates a free economy in a certain way (4, pp. 69-72). The principles of justice are balanced using an economic metric, most often average income per capita. The goals of economic policy–full employment, competition, price stability, appropriate rate of growth–are thus measured against income or dollars. A detailed weighting of output is thereby used as information in the political process for deciding policy and social arrangements.

Applying the same logic to social policy in the health sector, we are constantly making decisions about what is good and bad health, what is the social minimum, and how we distribute our resources. The rise in medical care costs, particularly from public sources, has become grist in the political mill prompting federal participation in the health services industry and a broad range of efforts to both regulate and improve health services. With greater federal investment and regulation has come pressure for determining average well-being per capita, one major component being health status. One direction in quality/effectiveness assessment of the health services system has been the development of health status indexes that could be used for collective decision making involving different types of social arrangements or interventions (5).

It is the thesis of this paper that, like economic indicators of worth, health status indexes used to make collective decisions satisfying the principles of equality and social minimum must incorporate a social metric for health. This social metric will be derived from methods of determining social preference or value priorities and of pooling these preferences for input into the collective decision-making process. In this paper, I shall concentrate on methods for constructing social metrics rather than the complicated question of value aggregation, a topic treated in detail by economists and decision theorists (6, 7).

PREVIOUS APPROACHES TO HEALTH METRICS

Some general indicators[1] of health status have been utilized without explicit attention to the social metric problem. Traditional mortality indicators, readily

[1] I have attempted to conform to the usage of the term "indicator" as referring to a specific, single measure, while "index" is used to define a composite measure derived by combining several indicators.

defined and developed from available data, are often used to make international health comparisons. These indicators have been criticized for their low sensitivity to the illness/wellness continuum (8). This weakness can be further conceptualized as a problem in the binary or 0/1 assumption of value, i.e. it is better to be alive than dead. This assumption may have widespread agreement across the world, but the indicator begs the question of preferring life under varying conditions. How much better is life at a higher level of health?

Morbidity indexes, derived from quantified variables, approach degree of wellness in the living through classification systems based on disability, dysfunction, discomfort, or some other clinical, subjective, or behavioral categories (9). Most often, these categories contain implicit assumptions of preferences, e.g. minor morbidity such as restricted activity is less serious than major morbidity such as bed disability. These classification systems, however, are often nominal or ordinal systems used without explicit attention to the social weighting process (10).

The optimal mix of information for making judgments about total welfare and standards of well-being requires combined morbidity/mortality indicators or a general health index that incorporates preference measures on the illness/wellness continuum. Many approaches have been made toward constructing such preference metrics (11). These approaches can be loosely classified as utility modeling, psychometric scaling, and empirical social decision valuation.

Utility modeling and its application to the health field is an outgrowth of modern interest in the classical utilitarianism of the eighteenth century, a major exponent being Jeremy Bentham and *The Principles of Morals and Legislation* (1789). Many utilitarians are concerned with individual and social decision making under conditions of certainty, i.e. when the outcome is known. Such decisions require only ordinal measures of preference or indifference in evaluating alternatives. Von Neumann and Morgenstern's now classic study of individual choice under risk or uncertainty, known as the mathematical theory of games, demonstrated the possibility of obtaining cardinal (interval or ratio) scales of utility (12). Game theory, specifically the expected utility hypothesis, has been extensively investigated and extended by a number of social scientists (13, 14). In the health field, Torrance and his colleagues (15) have used a Von Neumann-Morgenstern (N-M) standard gamble and a time trade-off technique to measure health utility values of physicians for five health states in a linear interval scale. These utilities are then applied in evaluating health care programs for planning and resource allocation. Stimson (16) used the Churchman-Ackoff model, a decision theory application of the N-M method, to measure the utilities of the objectives of decision makers in a large public health agency. Berg (17) used game theory to solicit the preference of medical students and physicians for confinement to bed in comparison to full function. Vertinsky and Wong (18) have compared two N-M methods of eliciting health preferences, and Forst (19) has formulated a preference or disutility function based on optimal choices elicited through a series of hypothetical questions to be validated with choices actually made.

All these approaches confront the problem of constructing a metric using gambles or decisions based on probability for whatever factors are used to describe function status or health. The number of health states used must be small, since utility measurement is time consuming and complex. Judges often find the decisions difficult to make, because they are uncomfortable with the gambling or explicit probability nature of the methods. Everyday notions of probability, particularly when death is used as the reference state, do not seem to transfer easily to the theoretical decision-making situation, opening the possibility of inconsistent or invalid choices. If the classical axioms of utility can be followed, however, these methods have great merit, since the mathematical foundations are vigorous and well understood.

Psychometric scaling models encompass a number of indirect and direct methods for metric construction. These methods have found wide application in the social sciences, particularly for the scaling of persons with respect to psychological traits (20, 21). Indirect methods involve comparisons of alternatives with a scaling model derived from laws of comparative judgment or the discrimination between two states or conditions (22, 23). These scaling models may result in ordinal, interval, or ratio scales, depending upon the underlying mathematical functions used to derive values (24). The early work of Fanshel and Bush (25), in presenting a model for evaluating health services outcomes, advocated the use of Thurstonian paired comparison techniques to calculate social weights for health states. Only eleven health states were presented, however, since paired comparison designs with large numbers of complex stimuli are impractical to use.

Direct psychometric scaling models elicit numerical estimates of subjective feelings for stimuli, such as health conditions, without requiring judges to choose between alternatives. A large number of subjective numerical estimate models are used by social scientists, the most ardent proponent being the late S. S. Stevens (26) and his followers at the Harvard Psychophysics Laboratory. One psychometric model, often applied for determining relative values when stimuli such as crimes and life events are to be judged, is category scaling or the method of equal-appearing intervals (21, 27, 28). This method is efficient in that it requires minimal time on the part of judges or investigators, and the decision process is no more threatening than an opinion poll or household survey.

Bergner and her colleagues (29) have used the method of equal-appearing intervals to elicit preference judgments for individual items of health behavior and protocols or more global descriptions of dysfunction. Patrick, Bush, and Chen (30) used equal-appearing intervals to derive weights for case descriptions of function status that aggregate into levels of well-being. A later study compared category scaling and magnitude estimation, both direct numerical models, with the method of equivalence designed as a combined direct estimate and utility measure that approximates public health decision making (31). No significant differences were found between the category and magnitude methods or the category and equivalence methods. Although some differences were found between magnitude estimation and equivalence under different testing situations, the similarity of equivalence to category and magnitude estimation indicated the consistency of these methods with a procedure implying social choice.

Psychometric methods have been used primarily in quasi-laboratory and simulation research designs, although several efforts are being made to use category scaling in household interview surveys and with patient populations (32, 33). Substantial work is required for estimating the reliability and validity of values elicited by these methods (34). Convergent or consistency concepts of validity may be estimated using multiple judgment groups and scaling methods within a single dimension or domain of health. With such a complex theoretical construct as health, however, it is often difficult to account for nonrandom errors of measurement in an analysis of preference judgments (35). A great deal more work will be required to correctly specify the measurement models used in direct scaling experiments with various indicators of health.

Quite a different set of problems than those encountered in laboratory-type scaling experiments arise when empirical social decision valuation methods are used to construct a preference metric. Implicit values are assigned to various health conditions by a wide variety of social decisions. Health programs with alternative concerns, populations, and goals are allocated different amounts and types of resources by political leaders, health professionals, and program administrators. The health budget of the U.S., for example, is distributed among competing agencies, disease categories, target populations, and health activities. The courts compensate disability, disfigurement, and abuse at different levels. Outside the public sector, life insurance companies and other risk agents use economic valuation to assign different values to different dysfunction/disability states. These empirical decisions might be used to construct social preference weights.

Economists have long been using human capital valuation as a method of estimating the cost-benefit of social arrangements or the compensation of death and disability (36, 37). Estimates of the value of human life are usually based on future earnings or some quasi-measure of economic value, such as willingness to pay (38). Decision making based on human capital valuation has been studied by Schelling (39), who outlined how individuals might think when allocating resources to their own benefit. Public decisions and procedures for valuing lives have been examined by Zeckhauser (40), who concludes that the process of evaluation is as important as the values themselves.

Rosser and Watts (41) analyzed 500 compensation awards made by British courts to derive relative values for various health conditions. Disability and distress jointly define eight levels, the lowest being slight social disability and distress. Persons confined to bed with severe distress were awarded 158 times as much as those with the lowest level of disability/distress. Comparable studies of U.S. court compensation cases do not appear in the literature, though similar methods seem feasible.

Human capital valuation methods are often criticized for treating life as a market trade item, when life exchange is qualitatively different than the exchange of goods. For the most part, economic measures place positive value on the productive individual with earning power, denying value to the nonproducer or producers who do not trade their product in the market, e.g. housewives. Furthermore, such measures serve to maintain the status quo by failing to recognize the extent to which health care increases life satisfaction, equity, and quality regardless of productivity. Thus, the human capital approach, per se, violates the principle of equality by denying value to those outside the market. This problem has been mitigated by "shadow pricing" or imputing economic values to the nonmarket sector where monetary prices are nonexistent, e.g. housework is assigned the monetary value placed on maid's work (42).

The disability/distress awards by the courts may also overcome the market criticism in that the courts are arenas for both sympathy and monetary exchange. However, the courts are not often a social device for the redistribution of wealth, leaning heavily in favor of the status quo. Another major disadvantage with the court award approach is the unlikelihood that court awards will ever be available in sizeable numbers for constructing categories with a high level of disability without distress. The courts, perhaps as a reflection of social values, seem to presume that a sick or disabled person must suffer distress.

Though a host of practical problems would probably arise in attempting to construct social metrics from court awards or other social decisions, serious efforts should be made in this direction, since such decisions represent actual social behavior, thus eliminating the distance between theoretical construct and empirical measure and increasing validity. If the intention of public policy is to alter the status quo, however, social decisions would have to be used with utmost caution, since the measures, themselves, might violate the principles of equality and social minimum.

FUTURE DEVELOPMENT OF HEALTH METRICS

Utility modeling, psychometric scaling, and empirical social decision valuation all have advantages and disadvantages relative to the potential uses of a health status index. Indicators and indexes are currently used for assessing the health of individuals and populations, evaluating social arrangements and interventions, and allocating resources among competing alternatives. Available data for these uses vary in quality, in the time periods covered, and in the population groups to which they apply (43). Although not politically developed or widespread in practice, indexes might also be used as common measures of claims by disadvantaged groups. Evidence continues to mount that a pervasive difference exists in the health status of the disadvantaged vis-à-vis nondisadvantaged groups (44). These groups could and do claim equality in health resources, access to services, and health levels based on health indexes and the social minimum of health status.

Depending on the use for the index, it is likely that different metrics will be derived using different methods or combinations of methods. A basic need exists, however, for a health metric that adequately represents society's preference for well-being such that collective decisions concerning the equality and social minimum of health can be made. To meet this need, future efforts to construct health metrics should consider a number of desiderata or recommendations before selecting methods and designing a measurement strategy.

In the first place, we must consider that social preferences are not static; instead, subjective feelings that discriminate among alternatives change over time, sometimes radically. If we want to develop social metrics that remain valid over time, we must design finely tuned time series studies of preference. Measures in a cross section tend to concretize both investigators' and judges' notions of preference. Prospective measures, on the other hand, are a better approximation of the entire theoretical preference domain, since causal variables change over time, and measures can be tuned for increasing stability. Stinchcombe and Wendt (45) point out that prospective measures may require the specification of larger theoretical domains than cross-sectional measures. Concepts of health used in measurement studies, in other words, may have to shift as time studies draw the boundaries of the theoretical foundation. The development of unmet needs as sociomedical indicators might well represent such a broadening of conceptual domain (46).

Secondly, additional scaling efforts should be made in the context of specific decision alternatives. The desirability of a particular health state or condition is likely to depend upon the available alternatives. The act of choice is a behavior-specific measure influenced by an individual's standards of the desirable. By specifying the decision alternatives, we can more easily discern the standards implied by the preference judgments. Utility models of social preference measurement are particularly well-suited for simulation models of the decision-making process related to health status outcomes. More work should be done to simplify these measures and extend them to multiple health states.

Third, if preference judgments are scaled using specific decision alternatives, it is equally important to evaluate the context-independence of such scaling efforts. Preference, indifference, or direct estimation judgments are influenced by the number and character of the factors being scaled. Decision alternatives can be formulated in a variety of ways, e.g. the probability of death within a year, the duration of capacity or performance for a day, or choice of health condition. Various combinations of factors should be used in specifying decision alternatives so that we might learn which factors elicit stable value judgments or which factors are more highly valued relative to other factors. The decision-making context is also important. We must learn the differences among preference, indifference, or direct estimate judgments using the same set of decision alternatives.

Fourth, we need more research on ratio measures of preference with a zero origin and measurable distances from that origin. In health, the primary value dimension is level of well-being on a scale from 0 or death to 1 or optimal well-being. In order to assess equality or change in well-being, we must know the direction and magnitude of well-being, thereby requiring at least interval, if not ratio, judgments of worth. In Rawls' view, the principles of justice can be applied with only simple ordinal rankings of who is more or less disadvantaged, rather than elaborate attempts at obtaining and summing cardinal measures of well-being (1, p. 324). Moral theory in a well-ordered society, in other words, eliminates the need for ratio measures.

The matter really cannot be quite so straightforward. Rawls leans heavily on a well-ordered society in which decisions are made based on wealth and income alone (47). We need cardinal utility measures because ordinal utility is insufficient in the face of uncertainty that may not lead to decisions which minimize risk or maximize expected welfare for society's members, certainly the prevalent case in medical care. Society's need for collective decisions made under conditions of uncertainty gives impetus to scaling efforts that establish death as the natural zero origin and elicit judgments of well-being for scales with strong, invariant properties. Both the measurement philosophy and scaling operations must be highly specified in advance of certain disagreement that the obtained scales have ratio properties. We should meet such disagreement with multiple replications of scaling experiments that produce scales with different properties so that the scale properties, themselves, can be examined.

Most scaling efforts involve hypothetical, verbally elicited preferences obtained in the laboratory or in the field. The fifth recommendation is that we validate these preferences with social decisions made in practice. Disability/distress compensation research should be extended to the United States. Comparisons need to be made across different courts and different disabilities. Scales derived from the court awards should be tested in the laboratory where verbal preferences for disability/distress can be compared. Using this incremental, multisite approach to validity will give social preference metrics the empirical reality needed for collective decision making with important and sometimes controversial consequences for society or particular social groups.

Sixth, adequate representation of society's preference for well-being requires that we obtain probability samples of community values. Preference judgments attached to conditions of life have most often been preempted by physicians and other medical professionals. The use of physicians as judges has been justified on the grounds that physicians have a better understanding of the nature of health conditions than lay persons, and that the medical value system is imparted to society (14, p. 157). Professional judgment regarding the probable development of disease or the estimation of prognoses may well be legitimate, e.g. physicians are technical experts. However, strong empirical evidence would be needed before accepting that the values of physicians or other professionals represent the community's value system.

The task of deciding (a) what an equal right to health is or should be, and (b) how a just society evaluates inequality and social arrangements for the least advantaged, cannot be left to a single social group. Clearly, if social metrics are to have collective representation, the preferences of probability samples representative of socioeconomic status, race, age, geographic region, sex, and other potential inequalities must be measured. Such efforts have begun with a household interview survey representing all socioeconomic groups in a single community (32) and studies of consumer participation in health care decision making (48, 49). Additional work is needed comparing provider and consumer preferences, different social groups, and different communities. Each measurement effort should be considered an approximation to the level of satisfaction provided by the social system or social structure. With each successive approximation, we should come closer to the goal of evaluating the worth of social arrangements in terms of the satisfaction provided to society's members.

Finally, if we are to have confidence in health metrics tempered by an understanding of the difficulties in interpretation, we must begin applying preference measurements to specific social arrangements or program evaluations. Social metrics incorporated in evaluative research designs with randomly assigned treatment and control groups would give better indication of how much positive or negative effect could be attributed to treatments. Simply assigning higher scores to reflect what the investigator defines as higher functioning, the procedure used by Reynolds and his colleagues (50), complicates the interpretation of treatment effects. Not only do we lose information regarding how much the functioning of the treatment population changed, but we also end up with a measure defined, valued, applied, and interpreted by the investigator, not the most relevant, sensitive, or meaningful of "social" indicators.

The effects of different social preference scales on outcome evaluations should be examined, particularly in efforts to study the benefits of publicly financed programs. The different indicators of outcome used in evaluative efforts should be socially weighted, preferably by a representative sample of the population being evaluated. We need such efforts to find both the clearly decidable and undecidable comparisons between different populations and between different social programs. The use of social metrics in specific evaluative research programs should make these comparisons eminently more decidable, since an improvement in health status means that, all other things being equal, society can be considered better off.

TOWARD NORMATIVE SOCIAL RESEARCH

The task of constructing social metrics for health is one of applying normative social theory to empirical research such that the theory guides research design and analysis of results (51). Not all social scientists or architects of social indicators believe that normative social theory is possible or desirable (52). In the tradition of Donald Campbell (53, 54) and his work in evaluation research, I believe that an experimenting society that collectively spends a large percentage of its wealth on health and other social enterprises cannot afford to ignore or impede social mechanisms for weighing actions in advance or evaluating the consequences of action. We continually make decisions affecting the social equality and social minimum of society's members. If we take the principles of justice seriously, we must begin to formulate and apply normative theory to social actions.

Methods of preference measurement will undoubtedly multiply as pressure increases to use health indexes as justification for the health dollar. Utility models, scaling in the psychometric tradition, and social decision valuation will be combined, compared, and tailored to meet the need for social value scales. The utilization of these methods from economics, psychology, sociology, and political science in socio-medical research represents an emphasis on the common roots of social science. Here, in social decision making, we find common ground for theory and measurement.

Values are the metric for the social sciences. Using economic measures of worth, economists have participated in the decision process with a powerful tool. If the community is to participate in social decisions concerning health, measures of social preference for health and well-being must become the tool. Without these measures, we shall not be able to advance our understanding of the mysteries of social action and its consequences for society's well-being.

Acknowledgment—I would like to thank my colleague and friend, Milton Chen, for the time he spent actively listening and for his comments and criticisms.

REFERENCES

1. Rawls, J. *A Theory of Justice.* Belknap-Harvard Press, Cambridge, Mass., 1971.
2. Nozick, R. *Anarchy, State, and Utopia.* Basic Books, New York, 1974.
3. Fuchs, V. *Who Shall Live?* Basic Books, New York, 1974.
4. Rawls, J. Distributive justice. In *Philosophy, Politics, and Society,* Third Series, edited by P. Laslett and W. G. Runciman, pp. 58-82. Basil Blackwell, Oxford, 1967.
5. Balinsky, W., and Berger, R. A review of the research on general health status indexes. *Med. Care* 13(4): 283-293, 1975.
6. Arrow, K. J. *Social Choice and Individual Values.* Yale University Press, New Haven, Conn., 1963.
7. Whitmore, G. A. Health state preferences and the social choice. In *Health Status Indexes,* edited by R. Berg, pp. 135-145. Hospital Research and Educational Trust, Chicago, 1973.
8. Moriyama, I. M. Problems in the measurement of health status. In *Indicators of Social Change,* edited by E. Sheldon and W. Moore, pp. 573-600. Russell Sage Foundation, New York, 1968.
9. Sullivan, D. *Conceptual Problems in Developing an Index of Health.* National Center for Health Statistics, Vital and Health Statistics, Series 2, No. 17. U.S. Government Printing Office, Washington, D.C., 1966.
10. Sackett, D., Spitzer, W., Gent, M., and Roberts, R. The Burlington randomized trial of the nurse practitioner: Health outcomes of patients. *Ann. Intern. Med.* 80(2): 137-142, 1974.
11. Kneppreth, N., Gustafson, D., Rose, J., and Leifer, R. Techniques for the assessment of worth. In *Health Status Indexes,* edited by R. Berg, pp. 228-240. Hospital Research and Educational Trust, Chicago, 1973.
12. Von Neumann, J., and Morgenstern, O. *Theory of Games and Economic Behavior.* John Wiley, New York, 1944.
13. Luce, R. D., and Raiffa, H. *Games and Decisions.* John Wiley, New York, 1957.
14. Raiffa, H. *Decision Analysis.* Addison-Wesley, Reading, Mass., 1968.
15. Torrance, G., Sackett, D., and Thomas, W. Utility maximization model for program evaluation: A demonstration application. In *Health Status Indexes,* edited by R. Berg, pp. 156-165. Hospital Research and Educational Trust, Chicago, 1973.
16. Stimson, D. Decision-making and resource allocation in a public health agency. *Management Science* 16(2): 17-30, 1969.
17. Berg, R. Establishing the values of various conditions of life for a health status index. In *Health Status Indexes,* edited by R. Berg, pp. 120-127. Hospital Research and Educational Trust, Chicago, 1973.
18. Vertinsky, I., and Wong, E. Eliciting preferences and the construction of indifference maps: A comparative empirical evaluation of two measurement methodologies. *Socio-economic Planning Sciences* 9(1): 15-24, 1975.
19. Forst, B. Quantifying the patient's preferences. In *Health Status Indexes,* edited by R. Berg, pp. 209-221. Hospital Research and Educational Trust, Chicago, 1973.
20. Guilford, J. *Psychometric Methods.* McGraw-Hill, New York, 1954.
21. Torgerson, W. *Theory and Methods of Scaling.* John Wiley, New York, 1958.
22. Thurstone, L. *The Measurement of Value.* University of Chicago Press, Chicago, 1959.
23. Coombs, C. *A Theory of Data.* John Wiley, New York, 1967.
24. Bock, R., and Jones, L. *The Measurement and Prediction of Judgment and Choice.* Holden-Day, San Francisco, 1968.
25. Fanshel, S., and Bush, J. A health-status index and its application to health-services outcomes. *Operations Research* 18(6): 1021-1066, 1970.
26. Stevens, S. S. Ratio scales of opinion. In *Handbook of Measurement and Assessment in Behavioral Sciences,* edited by D. Whitla. Addison-Wesley, Reading, Mass., 1968.
27. Sellin, T., and Wolfgang, M. *The Measurement of Delinquency.* John Wiley, New York, 1964.
28. Rahe, R. Multi-cultural correlations of life change scaling: America, Japan, Denmark, and Sweden. *J. Psychosom. Res.* 13: 191, 1969.
29. Bergner, M., Bobbitt, R. A., Kressel, S., Pollard, W. E., Gilson, B. S., and Morris, J. R. The Sickness Impact Profile: Conceptual formulation and methodology for the development of a health status measure. *Int. J. Health Serv.* 6(3): 393-415, 1976.
30. Patrick, D., Bush, J., and Chen, M. Toward an operational definition of health. *J. Health Soc. Behav.* 14(1): 6-23, 1973.
31. Patrick, D., Bush, J., and Chen, M. Methods for measuring levels of well-being for a health status index. *Health Serv. Res.* 8(3): 228-245, 1973.

32. Berry, C., Bush, J., and Kaplan, R. Testing for Variations in Social Group Preferences for Function Levels of a Health Index. Proceedings of the Annual Meeting of the American Statistical Association, Atlanta, August 1975.
33. Bergner, M., Bobbit, R., Pollard, W., Martin, D., and Gilson, B. Sickness Impact Profile: Validation of a health status measure. *Med. Care* 14(1): 57-67, 1976.
34. Nunnally, J. *Psychometric Theory*. McGraw-Hill, New York, 1967.
35. Costner, H. The Validity of Indicators. Paper presented at Meeting of American Sociological Association, San Francisco, August 1975.
36. Dublin, L., and Lotka, A. *The Money Value of a Man*. Ronald Press, New York, 1946.
37. Weisbrod, B. The valuation of human capital. *J. Political Econ.* 64(5): 425-436, 1961.
38. Rice, D., and Cooper, B. The economic value of human life. *Am. J. Public Health* 57(11): 1954-1966, 1967.
39. Schelling, T. The life you save may be your own. In *Problems in Public Expenditure Analysis*, edited by S. Chase, pp. 127-162. Brookings Institution, Washington, D. C., 1968.
40. Zeckhauser, R. Procedure for valuing lives. *Public Policy* 23(4): 419-464, 1975.
41. Rosser, R., and Watts, V. The measurement of hospital output. *Int. J. Epidemiol.* 1(4): 361-368, 1972.
42. Becker, G. *Economic Theory*. Alfred Knopf, New York, 1971.
43. National Center for Health Statistics. *Health: 1975*. DHEW Publication No. (HRA) 76-1232. U.S. Government Printing Office, Washington, D. C., 1976.
44. Brook, R., and Williams, K. Quality of health care for the disadvantaged. *Journal of Community Health* 1(2): 132-156, 1975.
45. Stinchcombe, A., and Wendt, J. Theoretical domains and measurement in social indicator analysis. In *Social Indicator Models*, edited by K. Land and S. Spilerman, pp. 37-73. Russell Sage Foundation, New York, 1975.
46. Carr, W., and Wolfe, S. Unmet needs as sociomedical indicators. *Int. J. Health Serv.* 6(3): 417-430, 1976.
47. Barber, B. Justifying justice: Problems of psychology, politics, and measurement in Rawls. In *Reading Rawls: Critical Studies of a Theory of Justice*, edited by N. Daniels, pp. 292-318. Basic Books, New York, 1975.
48. Vertinsky, I., Thompson, W., and Uyeno, D. Measuring consumer desire for participation in clinical decision making. *Health Serv. Res.* 9(2): 121-134, 1974.
49. Parker, A. The consumer as policy maker: Issues of training. *Am. J. Public Health* 60: 2139, 1970.
50. Reynolds, W., Rushing, W., and Miles, D. The validation of a function status index. *J. Health Soc. Behav.* 15(4): 271-288, 1974.
51. Coleman, J. Social structure and a theory of action. In *Approaches to the Study of Social Structure*, edited by P. Blau, pp. 76-93. Free Press, New York, 1975.
52. Sheldon, E., and Freeman, H. Notes on social indicators: Promises and potential. *Policy Sciences* 1: 97-111, 1970.
53. Campbell, D. Reforms as experiments. In *Handbook of Evaluation*, Vol. 1, edited by E. Struning and M. Guttentag, pp. 71-100. Sage Publications, Beverly Hills. Cal., 1975.
54. Campbell, D. Methods for the Experimenting Society. Paper presented before the American Psychological Association, Washington, D. C., September 5, 1971.

PART 2
Measures Related to Life Stage

CHAPTER 6

Reproductive Efficiency as a Social Indicator

Charlotte Muller,
Frederick S. Jaffe,
Mary Grace Kovar

A social index is sound when the selection of the specific elements to be combined is based not merely on the accident of availability of certain data but on the capacity of these elements to reflect something that is really happening to people in society. In the course of a human life, there are certain universal events, such as birth and death and others that are very widely shared, such as the reaching of adulthood and the reproductive process. Human welfare is closely connected with the manner in which important nodal points in the life cycle are experienced by individuals.

The reproductive process is the aspect of human welfare and health that we have chosen to study. In so doing, we are using as our population base women in the reproductive years. We are focusing on a single event—the occurrence of a pregnancy—and the variations in the outcomes of this event among individuals. We have a particular interest in this because of our belief that health care interventions can affect

This paper was presented at the Annual Meeting of the American Statistical Association held in Atlanta, Georgia, August 25-28, 1975. The research was financed in part by Ford-Rockefeller Foundations Population Policy Research Grant 1972-73.

these outcomes, and that they can do so most effectively if cognizance is taken of the socioeconomic factors that influence availability of fertility-related care[1] and if these are compensated for in program design.

We are not studying the total reproductive career of females, but we are indeed enlarging the detailed perception of certain specific events that enter into the longer-run reproductive careers of individuals and cohorts of women. In this sense the measurements we are concerned with complement the models that reconstruct these longer-run aggregates of experiences under different assumptions about marriage rates, fertility choices, and other factors, but our measurements have a more explicit connection with health care needs and the possible impact of health care on reproductive events.

In the quest for a suitable basis for policy decisions relating to health, the reproductive process has been a major focus of attention. Pregnancy and birth were long attended by obvious risks to mother and child, and it seemed that these could be reduced, with much benefit to individuals and society, by organized programs of care, attention to nutrition and hygiene, and other social efforts. The extreme adversity involved in maternal death—in that presumably well, youthful women were wiped out in the course of a normal biological process and their children deprived of their care—provided a natural reason for identifying maternal mortality as a measure of reproductive health.

Infant mortality too was obviously tragic for families, frequent among the poor, and, like maternal mortality, unacceptable in a society with evolving humanistic obligations. Crude though community health records might be, death was, more than other measures of health, an easily marked event. Birth information, as organized medical services and vital statistics advanced, provided a reasonably accurate denominator for deriving infant death rates which could be used to identify groups most in need of basic environmental services, immunization and treatment services directed toward infectious diseases, and adequate supervision of pregnancy itself. Maternal mortality could be used to support policy decisions about the age of marriage, and provision of scientific obstetrics, fertility control, and prenatal services. These statistical measures, however, had limitations as a guide to policy that became more powerful as certain social and medical changes occurred.

Maternal mortality by and large yielded to the improved environment and practices of an advanced country and dropped so low that it no longer indicated areas in which allocation of future resources out of the gross national product could substantially influence health and well-being, even for deprived groups. Infant mortality, reflecting a number of social and environmental variables, was not an adequate index of the effective application of health services to the reproductive process. Indeed, it became a popular indicator of national and group levels of poverty and deprivation. At the same time, infant mortality failed to capture health deficits that result in children having a poor start in life as well as forms of pregnancy wastage in which a live birth does not occur.

[1] Fertility-related care includes maternity care, pediatric services in the first year of life, fertility control (conception, sterilization, and abortion), infertility treatment, and care of fetal loss. Virtually all women need one of these services in each year of the reproductive period except that sterilization obviates the need for other services (1).

Furthermore, in an environment in which fertility control was differentially available depending on social class, doctors' attitudes, hospital rules and priorities, legal constraints, and other factors, the probability that an actual conception was a wanted conception, and thus that a healthy live birth could be assumed to be a desired outcome of conception, was variable. The situation was not as gross as when infanticide was tolerated or mildly punished, but an obstruction to a concept of reproductive success nevertheless existed so long as unwanted pregnancy was a common experience. "Retrospective rationalization" certainly operated when a healthy child was born and raised in the context of a stable marriage, economic good fortune, and other positive factors, but the possibility that this context would be lacking or that the timing of births or family size was unacceptable to the parents made it impossible to ignore the factor of "wantedness." That is, the denominator for measuring reproductive success was ambiguous.

It was ambiguous for another reason. Abortion was illegal and many pregnancy outcomes were hence lost from view, along with the fact of the pregnancy itself. Hence any measures based on partitioning of a total sum of pregnancies according to outcome were biased by omissions due to the illegal state of abortions. In addition, many women who had a fetal loss never reported a pregnancy, wanted or unwanted, to the health care system. Another limitation arose from involuntary infertility and subfecundity. Absent from any measure of reproductive success was the "shadow denominator" of the number of pregnancies that would have occurred if fertility had been in the possession of all who wanted it in a given year, and the probable outcomes these pregnancies would have had.

The changing attitude of the community to population growth required consideration. With population stability as a societal goal, a certain percentage of births become "unwanted"–those exceeding generational replacement. Society is indifferent to whether some individuals have unwanted pregnancies so long as these are offset by the infertility of others; however, concern with the social (i.e. external) effects of poor child development and role socialization does imply some interest in seeing that all births that occur are wanted ones. That is, quality and not just quantity of population is a social matter, and becomes even more pressing if numbers are to be held within limits.

The possibility of developing more adequate measures of reproductive success has undoubtedly formed part of the frame of reference of the investigators who have studied various pregnancy outcomes other than infant deaths. Such work has an extensive history of refinement and differentiation, far too extensive to summarize here, but relating to the conceptualization of measurable low birth weight as distinct from temporal immaturity and the further refinement of separating out single births; the separation of congenital conditions on the basis of delivery-related, pregnancy-related, and genetic origins, severity, and the time at which observations are made; the creation of a composite predictor score for health of newborns by Dr. Virginia Apgar; and the establishment of criteria for length of gestation in measurement of fetal loss. Methods of analyzing complications and other features of abortions also contributed to the methodological toolkit. In addition, an array of familial and socioeconomic variables have been studied for correlation with individual measures of child growth and health and reproductive experience of women.

REPRODUCTIVE EFFICIENCY: CONCEPTUAL ASPECTS

The concept of reproductive efficiency (RE)[2] as an aggregate measure of pregnancy outcomes is proposed as a new measure applicable to current conditions in a developed country where infant mortality is no longer the central problem and where prolonged effects and incurred costs of substantial health deficits associated with birth can be given appropriate concern in the formation of health policy. The aggregate measure also is a means of introducing the welfare or satisfaction aspects of marriage and family life into the goals of health policy. This is consistent with the vitalization of women's aspirations and with the need for more assurance of satisfactory outcomes when fewer pregnancies are intended. The measure also lends itself to constructive use in relation to the concept of a health care subsystem—fertility-related health services viewed as a whole—through which virtually all women pass in their reproductive years. That is, the index aids in viewing reproductive health policy as a whole and in the selection of priorities so as to use fertility-related services to optimize reproductive experience. A number of conceptual and measurement issues that arise will be discussed below.

Many of the measurement difficulties can be resolved by a national effort to adapt current data systems to the prospective study of reproductive experience, health care, and outcomes, and to improve the recording of pertinent data by investment of specific resources for the purpose. Improved availability of reproductive health care, too, will increase the possibility of a more complete record of the occurrence and outcome of pregnancy. Part of our presentation in this paper concerns our effort to measure reproductive efficiency for the United States in the early 1960s.

THE IDEAL OF REPRODUCTIVE EFFICIENCY

In previous eras fertility could be catastrophic to society and the individuals because of food supply. Social factors contributed to a low or negative valuation of the individual pregnancy. In nineteenth-century Europe, for example, the sexual availability of the lower-class female servant was taken for granted, but she was given no support if pregnancy resulted (3). Infanticide was tolerated or given only moderate penalties over many centuries, especially if it occurred via exposure, overlaying (smothering in shared beds), or customary neglect by wet nurses—and if girl babies were the victims (4, 5). Widespread, even mass destruction of infants in Europe and Asia is believed to have occurred. It was not only knowledge of child hygiene, nutrition, and pediatrics and of sterile obstetrical procedures that cut down infant mortality; it was the rooting of the attitude that a child's life should be preserved. And this was linked to the rise of contraception and the freeing of large numbers of people of all classes to control family size (3).

An ideal of reproductive efficiency, in which pregnancy is a voluntary act and each pregnancy results in a healthy liveborn child, was only possible when fertility control

[2] This concept was introduced by Sir Dugald Baird (2), who gave no exact definition for the term.

became an instrument broadly available in society and at a high level of perfected technology, and when this evolution was complemented by substantial legal acceptance of birth control, abortion, and sterilization. Today society is in a position to address itself to raising the level of reproductive efficiency.

As a beginning definition, reproductive efficiency is the percentage of pregnancies that succeed in producing normal, surviving children, after taking into account the frequency of all measurable types of adverse outcomes of pregnancy. The precursor of this measure is the Shapiro-Abramowicz index of the loss-disability rate in 12,000 pregnancies among Health Insurance Plan of New York members (6), a composite of fetal loss at 12 weeks or later, neonatal deaths, low birth weight, and significant anomalies.

Pregnancy and Birth: Wanted and Planned

The concept of reproductive efficiency that is most compatible with values of a democratic society relates RE to a social goal of maximizing individual welfare in the area of fertility. The concept has two parts: (a) that only wanted births will occur, and (b) that the outcome of such births will be healthy children capable of survival.

As shown in Figure 1, the possible trajectory of individual pregnancies can be sorted out according to the following nodal points, stops, or states:

- Wanted or unwanted at the time of conception
- Remaining or not remaining wanted; remaining or not remaining unwanted
- Aborted or not aborted
- Fetal loss or completion of pregnancy by live birth
- Infant death or survival
- Normal good health or its absence (low birth weight, congenital abnormality)

It is apparent that there are a number of points where medical services are or can be involved and influence outcomes.

A birth can be wanted by only one of the expectant parents. From one point of view, it is the attitude of the woman that is crucial because she has access to means of terminating the pregnancy without spousal consent. However, the extent of parental resource investment that must occur for successful nurturance justifies defining a wanted child as one that is wanted by both parents. A pragmatic test of wanted pregnancy—the decision to carry a pregnancy to term—is provided when abortion services are fully available, making it possible to view wantedness ideally as a dichotomous variable.

Ideally, only wanted pregnancies should occur. But since unwanted ones do occur, allowance must be made for deliberate termination of unwanted pregnancies. Abortion, although superior to completion of an unwanted pregnancy, is a negative reproductive outcome because it represents a failure of the contraceptive care system, and would not occur with ideal availability and use of contraception. Occurrence of an abortion is a conservative measure of unwanted pregnancy; it does not capture an unwanted pregnancy that is not aborted.

For the first time fairly accurate measurements of the incidence of abortion are

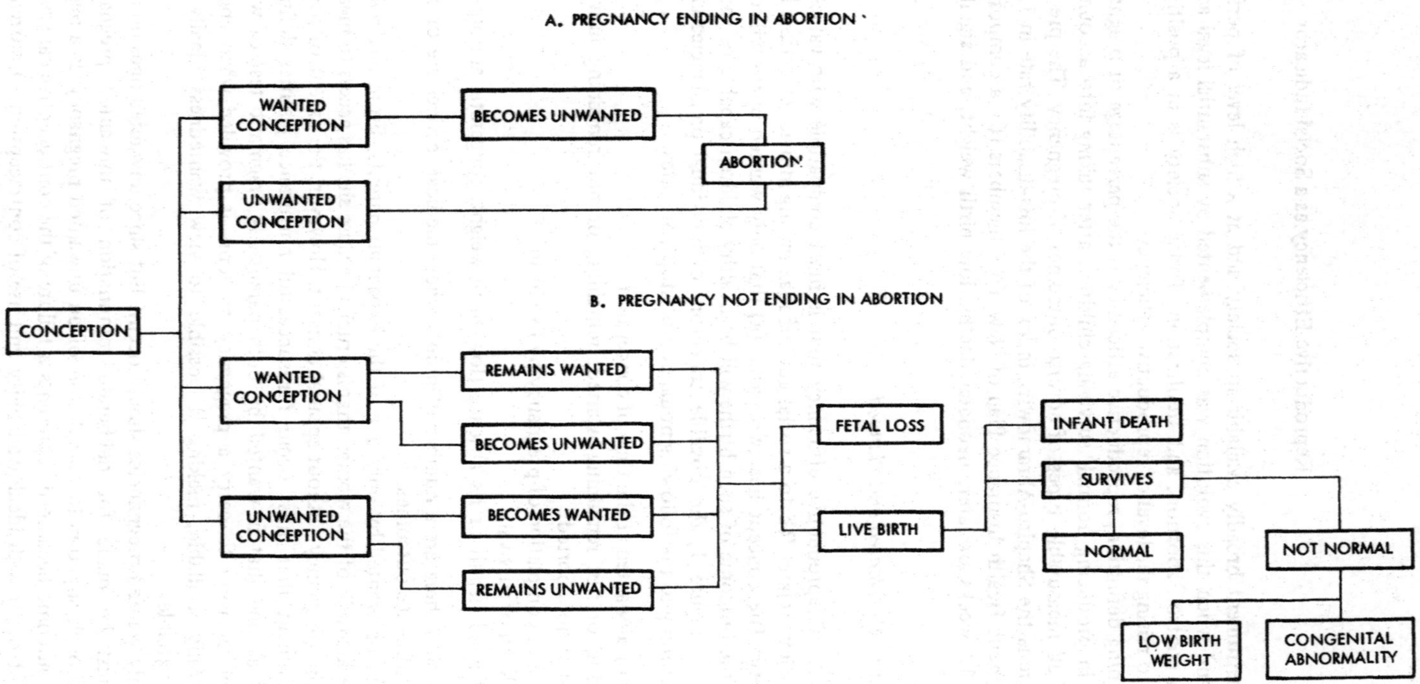

Figure 1. Trajectory of a single pregnancy.

obtainable, owing to its legalization by the Supreme Court decision of 1973 and the entry of abortion into ordinary medical care processes and records. In previous years the level of pregnancy loss, as measured in hospitals, vital statistics and other records, was substantially distorted by the occurrence of illegal abortions. That fact obstructed a clear view of the task of reducing the risks associated with pregnancy. For one thing, the fact that many abortions were recorded as miscarriages set up false trails in the study and prevention of pregnancy wastage. Capacity to articulate a concept of reproductive efficiency and to measure its present level has been greatly improved.

Some pregnancies are wanted at conception but become unwanted as a result of death of the father, disability of either parent, illness of a child, or economic reverses. The occurrence of these events appears random for individuals but is related to social conditions. Unwantedness cannot be simply inferred from the number of previous births and pregnancies or extremes of maternal age, although the probability is enhanced by these factors.

A pregnancy that is unwanted (unplanned) can become an accepted and wanted pregnancy, given a satisfactory marital status for rearing the child and other favorable factors. For already started families, an unplanned pregnancy may be more acceptable if desired family size has not yet been achieved. A revision of desired family size probably calls for more adjustment than accepting a change in schedule. However, for some couples one unplanned pregnancy in a given year may be harder to take than two in later years when family economic circumstances have been stabilized at a desired level.. Permanent socioeconomic status is also relevant: high status could mean confidence of being able to support the child, but could correlate with competing plans for maternal time use. Health status of other children would influence attitudes toward an unplanned pregnancy. Large health bills could impair the asset position and otherwise disposable income of the family.

For unwanted pregnancies not terminating in abortion, there is justification for evaluating pregnancy outcomes because survival of a child with health impairments incurs both financial and nonfinancial sacrifice or cost. If society offers, and people use, adequate contraception and sterilization services as a way of minimizing unwanted conceptions, thus minimizing use of abortion services as a way of insuring against failures in doing so, "gross" RE for all pregnancies, wanted or not, and RE of wanted pregnancies will converge.

Subfecundity adds another consideration to individual reproductive success. Subfecundity, including total infertility, is present in individuals who decide not to marry or are not successful in finding marriage partners, but it is usually revealed and is able to be measured only as couples attempt conception. To account for it properly one would have to start not with desired conceptions as a subset of actual conceptions, but with all conceptions desired among a cohort of women. For wanted pregnancies, maximizing individual welfare requires regular supervision of all pregnancies,[3] and extra measures to protect high-risk wanted pregnancies, such as those in couples not likely to have additional conceptions because of age, health, or known subfecundity.

[3] The month of first prenatal visit correlates with the percentage of infants of 2500 grams or less birth weight in white and black mothers.

End Point for Reproduction

Another major aspect of defining reproductive efficiency is the selection of an end point for evaluation of survival, that is, of "reproduction" as such. Each birth represents success in avoiding early or late fetal death, but the heavy risks of the neonatal period imply that a success cannot be counted merely from the fact of a live birth. The neonatal death is believed to be related to genetic factors and the events of the pregnancy; the postneonatal death to the risks of living and the influence of environment. Although the latter type of death is less likely than the former, the high death rate in the entire first year compared to later years of childhood gives good reason to consider all infant deaths as adverse outcomes of pregnancy.

After one year of age, the end point is debatable. The fall in the child death rate is one factor. As the age of the child increases, the probability that the parents would be able to replace this child with another birth in the event of his death is progressively reduced–i.e. RE could not affect fertility decisions.

The idea of survival to adulthood has some appeal, but it is not unambiguous because the notion of adulthood is socially conditioned by laws relating to marriage, voting, employment and army service, by the economic position of the family, and by educational customs. Also, these factors may relate more to a social view of generational replacement than to determination of individual family size. Parents may wish to see their children survive them, which would greatly postpone the end point for evaluating reproductive success, but parents have no scope for decisions about replacement as children mature and as they themselves pass out of the fertile ages. For simplification, and to use a reproductive success measure to improve decisions on health policy, attention is focused on the events that are associated with biological and social preparation for parenthood (birth timing), pregnancy-related medical care and early infant care, occurrences in the period when risks are relatively high, when replacement pregnancies or alternative choices of timing are possible, and when the utilization and delivery of appropriate health care can be viewed as a continuum.

These considerations can be taken into account by using the time immediately following birth as the end point for study of reproductive outcomes other than infant death. That is, long-run consequences can be taken into account by including all outcomes that incur medical services and costs at the time of pregnancy and birth and do not result in a healthy surviving child. While certain outcomes may lead to a replacement birth, to include replacement costs as well as the costs of the defective outcome would be double counting. However, a weight could be attached to an outcome based on the impossibility or low probability of a replacement given maternal age and other factors in order to express the resulting loss of welfare.

Retrospective correction is needed for the fact that some congenital conditions are not manifest at birth. By extension of the idea of retrospective correction, infant deaths can be brought into the estimate of negative outcomes. That is, the record will have shown that so many infants failed to survive to the age of one year and hence could not be counted among pregnancies resulting in a healthy surviving child, whether or not a pregnancy-related or genetic cause is definitely implicated.

Events Included in Reproductive Efficiency

The basis for choosing the events to be included in reproductive efficiency has to take into account various criteria of importance. The first of these, namely, the possibility of being affected by social policy, has just been used in the discussion of end points in referring to events associated with factors such as timing of pregnancy. Severity is another criterion and can be framed in terms of effect on life expectancy and optimal health during years of life. Another criterion is the costliness of given pregnancy outcomes, in relation both to health care requirements and to educational and child care costs in the event of handicapping conditions.

Maternal health deserves special discussion. It is statistically unimportant in an advanced country like the United States (where, for example, only 477 women died of maternity-related causes in 1973). Conceptually, however, it is an integral part of reproductive efficiency. Individuals would rarely choose to reproduce if they thought that it would cost them their lives, and that the future of the new infant would be impaired. Hence a low risk is a precondition for choosing a personal fertility goal.

Maternal morbidity, representing a more or less protracted impairment of health and function and implied expenditure on health services, is a possible negative outcome of pregnancy and delivery. However, it is not systematically measured, except for statistics on hospital use for complications of pregnancy, delivery, and the puerperium.

Social and Individual Reproductive Efficiency

The important matter of the divergence or agreement of social and individual RE is our final conceptual problem. The possibility of divergence exists largely because of social concern with population trends. A desired *gross* trend toward population stability is consistent with personal disutility of many individuals in the form of unwanted births as well as uncorrected infertility. Society *is* concerned, however, with optimal development of individuals able to mature into social roles and with the possible damage and costs attributable to deficient socialization processes. The ideal timing and supervision of pregnancy and ideal child nurturance required for satisfactory socialization are made more likely by pregnancy being a wanted state.

It appears logical that personal fertility goals are influenced by the tax structure and by expenditure for schools, recreation, housing, and pediatric care, since all of these affect the burdens of child rearing. Additionally, these goals are affected by the acceptance, legalization, and distribution of fertility control services, by school curriculum materials on parenthood, sexuality, marriage, and related factors, and by attitude-forming materials on such subjects diffused through public information networks and other social channels. While ideally this would tend toward a shaping of individual fertility goals to match social priorities, nevertheless a woman who has several children or who is "overage" for optimal outcome may desire a pregnancy even though, if many made a similar choice, total fertility would exceed a socially desired level or some poor pregnancy outcomes would eventuate. The case for voluntary fertility control as a method of attaining social goals for population size depends on willingness to accept a rough social/individual convergence for the sake of the individual freedom to decide, and the belief that the convergence will actually be very good.

Objections to an Index

In proposing an aggregate measure of reproductive efficiency the authors have encountered objections of several kinds. One points out that the *causes* of failure are heterogeneous, and therefore the appropriate control measures (if any) are quite different.

A second objection is that the *consequences* of different kinds of adversity are heterogeneous, that is, the different components of reproductive efficiency are not of equal importance so far as health or welfare is concerned. A death is qualitatively different from a child health deficit. Some low-weight babies have uneventful maturation after compensating for their poor start (7), whereas others have serious health deficits well into life. Some congenital defects are easily repaired, while others form a major intrusion into normal functioning as child or adult. Such objections have indeed obliged the authors to think further about the meaning and purpose of the index.

As to the first objection, heterogeneous causes are implicated *within* several individual variables, notably infant deaths and low birth weight, and heterogeneity is not avoided by considering adverse outcomes separately. As to consequences, we believe that it is an illusion that not combining outcomes into a single index will prevent disagreement over program emphasis. Although the variables we are considering do not have equal outcomes, they do share the use of health services and the potential for being measured and compared in terms of medical care costs incurred. This is a path that we have followed. Also held in common is the potential for influencing personal fertility and generational replacement. That is, how does past pregnancy experience affect family size plans of individuals and overall fertility rates? Other researchers may wish to explore these connections further.

We are particularly struck by the fact that after the gross improvement in infant mortality achievable in advanced societies, one is left with the need for measures of reproductive success that will reflect the risks that women and their mates encounter in seeking a satisfactory reproductive experience. We wish to show what such an index looks like, to what extent it can be estimated from national data currently available, and in particular how the application of economic weights affects the relative proportions of component adverse outcomes.

MEASUREMENT PROBLEMS

The detailed measurement problems in constructing an index concern data limitations of various kinds. Ideally, study of reproductive efficiency would start with a defined sample of pregnancies and follow the outcomes prospectively through the first year of life of all liveborn infants. Overlapping incidence of adversities (for those outcomes that are not mutually exclusive, like fetal death and low birth weight) would be easily corrected. It would be fairly simple, too, to observe the influence of a specific condition on total health in infancy. Weights could be based on empirical data on utilization and costs of medical care when given types of adverse outcomes occurred. Direct determination of the time position of a given pregnancy in relation to family formation as viewed *ex ante* and *ex post* would be feasible.

Hence one of the principal data limitations is related to dependence on retrospective studies. Use of these means understatement of subfecundity, attrition within a cohort of young persons before reproduction occurs, and ill-recalled past fetal losses. Additionally, past abortions may be concealed for reasons related to their illegality, social attitudes, and the effect of disclosure on a present marriage. Or else past abortions may be reported by respondents as miscarriages. Thus population losses implicit in sample design, and data losses due to memory losses and concealment pose difficulties.

Dependence on medical care processes and records also introduces difficulties. *Fetal loss* that occurs within the first few weeks after conception will not be noticed by the woman if she is not aware that she is pregnant. Other miscarriages, although noted by an individual, are not reported to the medical care system as no service is received. *Congenital abnormalities* are very poorly reported on birth certificates. Iowa data for 1963 showed only 39 percent of major malformations in hospital records appearing on birth certificates, and even greater omission of minor malformations. In all, only 18.2 percent of anomalies in the hospital record appeared on birth certificates (8, 9). *Apgar scores* are not recorded in one-third of hospitals, and are less likely to be recorded in nonteaching hospitals; there is also variation in the time at which the score is taken (10). Recording of *birth injuries* is also likely to be variable. While there appear to be variations between hospitals as to whether a case is reported as a fetal death or a stillbirth (11), the possibility of using a combined category and the definiteness of *death* as a measurable event nevertheless make it a useful component of a measure of reproductive outcomes.

Duplications constitute another problem of practical measurement. Babies with congenital defects who die should be counted only once (see figures for 1962-1965 below). Overlap between low birth weight and birth defects is suggested by data on children who were 6 to 11 years old in 1963-1965. Of those who weighed less than 5 pounds at birth, 24.0 percent had a birth defect, which is more than three times the rate (7.3 percent) of defects for those who weighed 5 to 10 pounds at birth (12). As the category of birth defects does not exclude birth injuries, the 24.0 percent figure overstates incidence of conditions due to prenatal factors.

A third important measurement problem arises when comparison of actual reproductive experience with some realistic standard of desired performance is attempted. In an ideal standard, all conceptions would be wanted, and the probability of a successful outcome for them would be 1.0; in a complete ideal, involuntary infertility would be reduced to zero.

A more pragmatic comparison attempts to show what the RE measure would look like if the actual rate of a given adverse outcome was reduced to the minimum observed rate for some population group. What is the "right" minimum to use? The maternal age at which infant mortality is lowest is not necessarily an optimal age, in a given social environment, for child-raising. Rates based on legitimate births have some merit because legitimacy confers several advantages on a pregnancy (13). Married women obtain better medical care during pregnancy, are more likely to be at optimal age, and have better socioeconomic conditions as well as social support. For the most part, health insurance plans do not cover unmarried women for maternity. Furthermore, the unmarried teenager who becomes pregnant is often reluctant to seek medical care because of the attitudes she expects to encounter (14).

Measurement problems are less refractory than they at first appear if one realizes that effects of alternative assumptions can be compared rather than forcing a consensus, and that, once initial gross estimates throw salient problems of pregnancy into relief, refinements can follow and efforts can be made to improve the data base. We have found, too, that a shift in assumptions on some doubtful point has little overall impact on the index.

Miller (15) suggests administratively oriented criteria for evaluating health status indexes. The criteria are designed to evaluate input data requirements and utility. Availability of data is placed on a four-level scale, ranging from total unavailability of reliable data to routine availability through traditional channels. The RE index contains elements at several different levels. Low birth weight and infant deaths are highly reliable and widely collected; congenital abnormalities are clearly incomplete; and early fetal loss is less reliable than stillbirths involving use of medical care. In the future, recording of Apgar scores or related measures that may evolve could be improved with some resource investment. Abortion data should be vastly improved in a context of legality, but further development of a national reporting system may be required. Special national surveys will add to the stock of reliable information and suggest items and classifications that should be added to the regular data collection of the National Center for Health Statistics (NCHS).

Two other input criteria, scaling characteristics and common denominality, are to a large degree satisfied by the unifying concept of pregnancy wastage, the fact that zero wastage is included in the scale, and the fact that numerical reckoning is possible. The question of heterogeneity does enter into utility (an output criterion), but we believe we have suggested ways of dealing with it by applying economic weights.

In regard to output criteria, an index, according to Miller, should cover a broad range of significant health conditions while lending itself to disease (condition)-specific analysis. We believe that this joint canon on comprehensiveness *and* specificity is satisfied by the RE index, since comparisons within an important totality are feasible, as shown by our examples. The utility of an index is based on its sensitivity to changes in the health of a population over time and its relevance to allocation of resources and determination of program priorities. Given some pragmatic consensus as to major items to be included, reproductive efficiency should be very serviceable for these purposes.

REPRODUCTIVE EFFICIENCY IN THE NATIONAL NATALITY SURVEYS

Data from the National Natality Surveys (NNS) conducted by the National Center for Health Statistics provided the opportunity to attempt estimates of reproductive efficiency for the entire United States in the 1960s. Despite the numerous limitations involved in using this particular source for an unintended purpose, and indeed in all retrospective measurements, this trial did give an overview of various components of reproductive loss in a large population of women.

The National Natality Surveys were conceived as a continuing series of surveys designed to extend the amount of information available on the certificate of live birth (16). The file of certificates sent by the states to the NCHS was used as a sampling frame and questionnaires were mailed to the mothers of all births either recorded or inferred to be legitimate. In 1963 and 1972 questionnaires were also sent to physicians and hospitals for all live births to obtain more detailed information on medical care. Descriptions of the samples, response rates, and the survey methodology can be found in the NCHS publications (16-23).

In the successive questionnaires, changes occurred in the subjects of inquiry and the amount of detail. Information recorded on the birth certificate, such as place of and attendant at birth and birth weight, is available for all the surveys, but other information, such as insurance coverage, was collected only at intervals. The first trial computation was based entirely on NNS, but the second one adopted a number of corrections. Most of these were to eliminate known conservative bias in the rates of pregnancy loss, but there was also a correction to avoid double counting of low-birth-weight babies who did not survive.

We believe our final results to be an understatement of pregnancy wastage. One reason is that the data source was limited to legitimate births. A second limitation is that the NNS omitted females with a recent pregnancy not terminating in a live birth during the sample period. Although we dealt with this by ascribing a fetal loss rate to 1962-1966 pregnancies based on reported past experience of mothers of live births in that period, the effect is to understate pregnancy wastage further. Finally, omission of abortions results in underestimation of adverse outcomes if each abortion is taken to represent an unwanted pregnancy. However, the method of aggregating adverse outcomes in an index permits one to measure the proportions of adverse outcomes accounted for by different types of events, and then to study how these proportions were affected by applying economic weights based on medical care costs for each type of event.

In our first trial computation, 10,395 mothers of legitimate live births in 1964-1966 made up the sample. Adverse outcomes included:

- Low birth weight of 6.8 percent (2,500 grams or less) in current pregnancies (707), the rate then being applied to 22,757 previous pregnancies of NNS mothers (2,015).
- Infant deaths of current and past pregnancies totaling 761–the former (198), reported by mothers; the latter (653), from the infant mortality study coordinated with the live birth sample.[4]

[4] The NCHS used the 1964-1966 NNS as its source for the legitimate live births but took infant death figures from the National Infant Mortality Survey of 1964-1966. The surveys collected identical data on reproductive history and socioeconomic variables, which made it possible to compute rates.

- Fetal deaths in a total of 33,152 pregnancies reported by NNS mothers (3,515), including stillbirths plus miscarriages; no length of gestation specified.
- The reported congenital abnormality rate of 0.6 percent, although known to be greatly underreported, was applied in the first trial, yielding 61 cases in current and an additional 117 in past pregnancies.

No data on abortions were sought in the NNS, which was conducted in a period when abortions were illegal except for very narrow indications. The gross result was RE of 80.5 percent or 124.2 pregnancies per 100 "normal" births.

To refine the first estimates of actual reproductive efficiency, a second computation applied incidence rates for certain pregnancy outcomes to the 33,152 pregnancies reported by mothers of the sample births. These rates were derived from NCHS and Health Insurance Plan of New York (HIP) (6) data. In addition, several other changes were made.

The second computation, along with sources of the various rates used, is shown in Table 1. In order to correct for known conservative biases in the original estimates, the rate of congenital abnormalities found in the HIP sample by medical follow-up to age 2, approximately 7 percent of pregnancies, was applied to the NNS group of pregnancies. Another step corrects for the omission of fetal deaths terminating a pregnancy in 1964-1966 that would not be represented in a sample of mothers of current live births at that time. From the fetal death rate in past pregnancies of sample mothers, an estimate of the omitted fetal deaths is derived. However, no correction is made to include a fetal death rate for women who had never had a live birth.

Since we were interested in counting pregnancies and not the total number of conditions, it was necessary to make a correction to avoid double counting of babies in the low-birth-weight category who do not survive and therefore appear again among the infant deaths. Although low-birth-weight babies made up 56 percent of infant deaths in this period, this figure is greatly affected by the out-of-wedlock babies (24). On the assumption that legitimate, low-birth-weight babies would be more favorably situated for survival, the infant death rate applicable to legitimate births in general was used in the absence of more precise information. The percentage of pregnancies with successful outcomes computed this way is 74.5 percent, a decrease of 6.0 percent over the result according to the first trial. The estimate is crude because it largely ignores a pregnancy history for women who had a fetal death in 1964-1966 and past adverse outcomes among women who had completed childbearing earlier. These would reduce the level of reproductive efficiency, possibly by a considerable amount. Within reproductive wastage of about 25 percent, fetal deaths were the leading type of wastage, followed by congenital abnormalities and low birth weight in second and third place, with infant deaths having relatively little impact. Yet infant mortality rates, which rank fourth, are a major indicator in use today, primarily because of ease of measurement.[5]

In order to assess the effect of economic weights on the proportions of the

[5] The continued decline in infant mortality in recent years lends added emphasis to this. The rate for January-December 1974 was 16.6 per 1000 live births, as compared with the 23 per 1000 for legitimate live births at the time of the NNS of the mid-sixties (25).

Table 1

Second computation of reproductive efficiency

A. Estimates for Components

Type of Adverse Outcome	*Rate*	*Method of Deriving Estimate*	*Number*	*Percent of Adverse Outcomes*
Fetal deaths (FD)	11.9% of pregnancies			
Previous pregnancies		Reported – NNS tape	3,515	36.1
Current pregnancies		Computed – NNS tape[a]	1,180	12.1
Congenital abnormalities	7% of pregnancies	Rate from HIP study applied to all pregnancies of NNS mothers	2,403	24.7
Low birth weight	6.8% of live births	Rate from NNS tape applied to current and previous pregnancies	2,016	20.7
Infant deaths	2.3% of live births[b]	NNS (live births) and National Infant Mortality Survey (deaths)	624	6.4
Total			9,738	100.0

B. Reproductive Efficiency as Aggregate Measure

Total pregnancies, NNS mothers (*P*)	34,332
Less adverse outcomes	– 9,738
Net "good" births (*GB*)	24,594
Reproductive efficiency (*GB*/*P*)	74.5%

[a] Total pregnancies of NNS mothers = 29,637 ever live born + 3,515 fetal deaths, or 33,152, making the FD rate 11.9% (i.e. 3,515/33,152). This rate is applied to current pregnancies: FD = 11.9% (10,395 live births + FD). From this, there are 1,180 FD for 11,575 current pregnancies.

[b] Correction for overlap with low birth weight reduces this to 2.1%.

individual adverse outcomes included in our computations, figures from a study of fertility care costs conducted by two of the authors (C.M. and F.S.J.) in Jacksonville, Florida, were applied (26). These were based on prevailing charges in the private sector in 1972.

A pregnancy was priced at $850 on the basis of total medical and hospital costs of a delivery (including office care) with a probability allowance for complications. This was used to construct the weight for an infant death. It omits medical care for an infant preceding death, but about 90 percent of deaths occur very soon after birth, and some who survive longer may be medically unattended. To correct for any omission, however, NCHS data for 1962-1965 infant deaths were used to derive costs of hospital care of infants who die. As the average hospital stay for decedents under 1 year of age is 5 days, or about 2 days longer than the newborn length of stay, an average of $150 is added for the additional days and accompanying medical care. This estimate includes a consideration of infants with congenital abnormalities who die. Of 100,000 infants who died per year in 1962-1965, 13,908 had congenital abnormalities; they used 41.9 percent of the days of care for all infant deaths. For infants with congenital abnormalities who survive the neonatal period, the figure of $1,050 for total costs of a typical corrective surgical procedure, plus a very conservative round-number estimate of $10,000 for extra costs incurred in childhood in 10 percent of cases (prorated to become $1,000 per case) was used. Based on actual hospital utilization in prematurity, the figure of $850 was applied as the cost of caring for a low-birth-weight baby in the first days of life. The figure of $254 for a fetal death combines an average of $200 for medical or surgical treatment of early fetal loss and $850 (same as a delivery) for stillbirths. These events were given probabilities of occurrence of 88 and 12 percent, derived from Shapiro and Abramowicz's HIP sample (6), within all fetal deaths as a group.

These weights, applied to the component outcomes with frequencies assigned based on Table 1, yield the calculations shown in Table 2. The result is expressed as cost per 100 adverse outcomes, and the components' individual shares of total costs are shown. Because a number of assumptions are involved, the results should be understood as indicative of orders of magnitude rather than refined estimates.

The application of weights based on medical care costs has little effect on the relative importance of low birth weight and infant deaths, reducing their share of adverse outcomes slightly. But there is a great shrinkage in the importance of fetal deaths (down from 48.2 to 13.6 percent of the total), frequency being offset by the limited care required in each case. And there is a more than doubling (127.9 percent increase) in the importance of congenital abnormality, implying expensive corrective medical care.

If we take the incidence of successful and adverse outcomes in relation to "good" births, 139.5 per 100 live births in our second computation, then the economic weights can be used in one further step. The total cost of the adverse outcomes would be 39.5 percent of the figure for 100 adverse outcomes in Table 2, or $35,541. The total cost of the 100 successful pregnancies would be $85,000, based on $850 per birth as above. The reproductive wastage would amount to 29.5 percent of the total expenditure resulting in 100 "good" births.

Table 2

Adverse outcomes weighted by health care costs

Type of Adverse Outcome	Percent of Adverse Outcomes	Health Care Cost per Case	Aggregate Cost in 100 Adverse Outcomes	Percent of Aggregate Cost
Fetal death	48.2	$ 254	$12,243	13.6
Congenital abnormality	24.7	2,050	50,635	56.3
Low birth weight	20.7	1,000	20,700	23.0
Infant death	6.4	1,000	6,400	7.1
Total	100.0		$89,978	100.0

Although we have not attempted to include abortion in our calculation, with a weighted average cost (based on 85 percent suction curettage at $150 and 15 percent saline extraction at $500) of roughly $200, abortions occur at the rate of 400 per 1000 live births and involve a considerable increase in the cost of reproductive loss. Forty abortions at $200 per 100 live births would amount to $8,000, adding about 22 percent to the cost of adverse outcomes per 100 live births.

FUTURE DEVELOPMENT AND USE OF REPRODUCTIVE EFFICIENCY

Some of the limitations of our computations can be remedied by availability of similar data on past reproductive history of a sample of women who are not currently having a birth, better reporting of fetal losses and congenital abnormalities, and a continuous national data base for a number of variables. An opportunity is presented by the National Survey of Family Growth and the National Ambulatory Medical Care Survey to relate availability and use of fertility control services to maternal and infant health and health care.

The Survey of Family Growth provides a measure of total gravidity for currently and previously married women, including premarital conceptions followed by a birth within formal or informal marital unions. The Survey does not capture pregnancies terminating before marriage. Not only is abortion history implicitly included in questions about all previous pregnancies terminating without a live birth, but current incidence is specifically asked in a form designed to protect individual privacy (in the 1973 Survey). Certain questions are included on health care for pregnancy.

Fetal loss, infant deaths, low birth weight (under 5.5 pounds), and children living in long-term care institutions are recorded. Infertility, the concordance of actual pregnancies with desired family formation, and methods of fertility control are studied. Hospitalization of infants in the first year of life and of women during a pregnancy are recorded. Some questions on diabetes, hypertension, and anemia make it possible to study maternal morbidity to a limited extent and associate it with the reproductive record.

More information is needed on medical care received in connection with out-of-wedlock births, abortion, and vasectomy outside the hospital setting, the adequacy of insurance, and the influence of pregnancy on employment status and thus on insurance coverage obtained through employment. Furthermore, it is important to disaggregate reproductive efficiency by such variables as age, parity, color, and social class to have a better perception of target populations.

The discrepancy between actual reproductive efficiency and any "optimal" standard has several sources. Teen-age pregnancy, illegitimacy, and poverty are social-demographic variables often noted in association with adverse pregnancy outcomes. They contribute, each in its own way, to the probabilities of inadequate physical development, deficient prenatal care, failure to prevent high-risk pregnancy, and other classic variables (14). High parity births and births to mothers over 35, also found in frequent association with poverty, are responsible for another portion of the problem. Changing opportunities for birth timing and prenatal care, as well as control of overall family size and infant care, are social means of reducing these causes of adverse outcomes of pregnancy, and their effectiveness can be measured by repeated estimation of achieved reproductive efficiency for a given population as interventive programs are applied. As obstetrical and neonatal management still is subject to class and regional discrepancies, similar monitoring seems appropriate.

Successive increments in reproductive efficiency may be progressively more expensive to achieve. As social investment occurs, it will be necessary to compare the amount of expected improvement from a given program with the expected marginal cost. In this connection, it is pertinent that deficient planning and distribution of fertility-related services also entail resource cost. The total care required for infants who eventually die, for management of premature or malformed infants who eventually survive, and for avoidable high-risk pregnancies, represents economic resources that could be put to other health and welfare uses if programs that avert these eventualities were fully available.

It will also be necessary to make a policy choice about objectives. Social funds can be used to try to raise the national average of reproductive efficiency, or to reduce the variance—the contrast in performance between variously advantaged and disadvantaged groups. These objectives may call for different strategies.

REFERENCES

1. Muller, C., and Jaffe, F. S. Financing fertility-related health services in the United States, 1972-78: A preliminary projection. *Family Planning Perspectives* 4(1): 6-19, 1972.
2. Baird, D. Variations in fertility associated with changes in health status. In *Public Health and Population Change,* edited by M. C. Sheps and J. C. Ridley, pp. 353-376. University of Pittsburgh Press, Pittsburgh, 1965.
3. Langer, W. Infanticide: A historical survey. *Journal of Psychohistory* 1: 353-365, Winter 1974.
4. Kellum, B. A. Infanticide in England in the Later Middle Ages. *Journal of Psychohistory* 1: 367-388, Winter 1974.
5. Trexler, R. C. Infanticide in Florence: New sources and first results. *Journal of Psychohistory* 1: 98-116, Summer 1973.
6. Shapiro, S., and Abramowicz, M. Pregnancy outcome correlates identified through medical record-based information. *Am. J. Public Health* 59(9): 1629-1650, 1969.
7. van den Berg, B. J. Morbidity of low birth weight and/or preterm children compared to that of the "mature." *Pediatrics* 42(4): 590-597, 1968.
8. Mackeprang, M., Hay, S., and Lunde, A. S. Completeness and accuracy of reporting of malformations on birth certificates. *HSMHA Health Reports* 87(1): 43-49, 1972.

9. Hay, S., Lunde, A. S., and Mackeprang, M. Background and methodology of a study of congenital malformations. *Public Health Rep.* 85(10): 913-917, 1970.
10. *National Study of Maternity Care. Survey of Obstetric Practice and Associated Services in Hospitals in the United States, A Report of the Committee on Maternal Health.* American College of Obstetricians and Gynecologists, Chicago, 1970.
11. Tokuhata, G. K., Colflesh, V. G., Ramaswamy, K., Mann, L. A., and Digon, E. Hospital and Related Characteristics Associated with Perinatal Mortality. Paper presented at the American Public Health Association, Minneapolis, October 12, 1971.
12. *Prenatal-Postnatal Health Needs and Medical Care of Children, United States.* Series 11, No. 125, p. 22. National Center for Health Statistics, United States Department of Health, Education and Welfare, April 1973.
13. Perkin, G. W. Assessment of reproductive risk in nonpregnant women. *J. Obstet. Gynaecol.* 101(5): 709-717, 1968.
14. *Maternal Nutrition and the Course of Pregnancy,* p. 148. National Academy of Sciences, Washington, D. C., 1970.
15. Miller, J. E. Guidelines for selecting a health status index: Suggested criteria. In *Health Status Indexes,* edited by R. L. Berg. Hospital Research and Educational Trust, Chicago, 1973.
16. *Medical X-Ray Visits and Examinations During Pregnancy, United States, 1963.* Series 22, No. 5. National Center for Health Statistics, United States Department of Health, Education, and Welfare, June 1968.
17. *Educational Attainment of Mother and Family Income: White Legitimate Births, United States, 1963.* Series 22, No. 6. National Center for Health Statistics, United States Department of Health, Education, and Welfare, August 1968.
18. *Employment During Pregnancy, Legitimate Live Births, United States, 1963.* Series 22, No. 7. National Center for Health Statistics, United States Department of Health, Education, and Welfare, September 1968.
19. *Variations in Birth Weight, Legitimate Live Births, United States, 1963.* Series 22, No. 8. National Center for Health Statistics, United States Department of Health, Education, and Welfare, November 1968.
20. *Health Insurance Coverage for Maternity Care: Legitimate Live Births, United States, 1964-66.* Series 22, No. 12. National Center for Health Statistics, United States Department of Health, Education, and Welfare, October 1971.
21. *Differentials in Expectation of Additional Children Among Mothers of Legitimate Live Births, United States, 1964-66.* Series 22, No. 13. National Center for Health Statistics, United States Department of Health, Education, and Welfare, February 1972.
22. *Infant Mortality Rates: Socioeconomic Factors, United States.* Series 22, No. 14. National Center for Health Statistics, United States Department of Health, Education, and Welfare, March 1972.
23. *Infant Mortality Rates: Relationships with Mother's Reproductive History, United States.* Series 22, No. 15. National Center for Health Statistics, United States Department of Health, Education, and Welfare, April 1973.
24. Monthly Vital Statistics Report. *Infant Mortality Rates by Legitimacy Status: United States 1964-66.* Series 20, No. 5, supplement. National Center for Health Statistics, United States Department of Health, Education, and Welfare, August 2, 1971.
25. Monthly Vital Statistics Report. Series 23, No. 11, supplement. National Center for Health Statistics, United States Department of Health, Education, and Welfare, January 30, 1975.
26. Muller, C., Jaffe, F. S., Krasner, M., Carson, D. N., and Whalen, J. *Financing Fertility-Related Health Services in Jacksonville, Florida, 1973-78.* Center for Family Planning Program Development, New York, January 1973.

CHAPTER 7

Indicators of Health Status in Adolescence

Ann F. Brunswick

LOGIC AND STRATEGY FOR AN ANALYSIS OF ADOLESCENT HEALTH INDICATORS

Adolescence is increasingly recognized as a separate life stage where the health risks, in mortality and in morbidity, merit and indeed require distinct attention. An upturn in mortality among teen-aged males has been reported by the National Center for Health Statistics (1-3). A recent survey, which included both personal home interviews and medical examinations of a community cross section of urban black adolescents in the United States, documented the extent of morbidity among that population (4). Better than three-quarters of the young people 12-17 years of age in that study reported at least one health problem; the average number of self-reported health problems was three. Physicians reported a medical problem for two out of three young people they examined; one in three young people, by physician report, had two or more notable health problems.

But to date, much of public and professional concern about adolescent health has been directed at socially deviant behavior—early fertility (5), drinking (6), and use of other drugs (7-10). Little attention has been paid to relating these behaviors to general health status or to developing overall indicators of health status in adolescence. Furthermore, at adolescence, as at other stages, more traditional types of morbidity are more prevalent than the behaviors specified above. For these reasons, when interest turns to measuring the progress and outcomes of health care and of other social change in the adolescent population, indicators which are broadly sensitive in that population will be needed. It is within this context that the approach to developing age-appropriate health indicators for adolescents demonstrated here has been developed.

This attempt at isolating and defining health problems that properly characterize health status among adolescents called into play methodological issues of wider interest. One concerns the domain of subjective, self-reported health status indicators in general. Certainly, the advantages of the household interview for obtaining information about a population's health (self-reported) are well recognized. Beyond economy and efficiency, in no other way can measurements be taken which cover those outside of care as well as those in treatment.

Yet a recognized difficulty of many household surveys lies in assessing severity or seriousness of self-reported morbidity. Functional measures of health in disability days are useful as one way around this major measurement difficulty (11-13). But subjective feelings and attitudes about one's own health cannot and have not been ruled out of consideration either (14). They can, for example, be an important influence on variations in the experienced severity of health problems.

Thus, the paper that follows describes an attempt to come to grips with two *methodological* problems as applied to data obtained from a population of adolescents: (a) to develop a more inclusive measure, i.e. a multiple indicator of health status that incorporates attitudinal as well as functional components; and (b) using this measure, to develop a means of distinguishing seriousness in self-reported health problems through deriving population-appropriate weights that can be applied to those problems.

Because each investigation is based on a particular conception of "health status," the term's meaning as used here will be explained at the outset. Attention has been directed in this study at personal or subjectively experienced wellness or illness, hereafter referred to as "ontological health." The adjective "ontological" is intended to remind us that subjectively experienced health is not the same as that which is more commonly associated with the medical profession. The latter is defined by observable symptoms, signs, and diagnostic categories of disease. The domain to which these refer is identified in this paper as "medical" health. A basic premise of the present investigation is that both health domains—subjectively experienced and professionally observed—need to be recognized. Each contributes to the knowledge of health status something that is missing in the other. "Ontological" health is emphasized here because that is the domain which has been relatively unattended until now.

Such an investigation fits in with emerging interest in the field of health indicators, as part of the broader field of social indicators, whereby quality of life may be periodically assessed and monitored for upward and downward (improvement or deterioration) changes. Specifically, the study reported here fits in with interest in subjective social indicators. In line with this, the target of this inquiry might well be considered "the human meaning of health" (15). The particular importance of subjective factors–perceptions, expectations, attitudes–has been noted to lie "in explicating behavioral correlations that otherwise are often perplexing or ambiguous" (15, p. 9). Specifying this for our own field of interest, subjective factors of "ontological health" are expected to influence or to help explain differences in health behavior, utilization of services, and the like.

CONCEPTS OF HEALTH AND HEALTH STATUS

In approaching these matters, a more basic conceptual problem has been acknowledged: What are we measuring when we say we are measuring health status? And what do we measure when we use various of the available indicators of health status? As posed elsewhere: "What is meant by health status? There are a variety of partial indexes including disability days, hospital days, physician visits and the incidence and prevalence of key diseases" (16, p. 13). The present investigation follows upon Moriyama's exhortation: "More study should be devoted to conceptual problems, especially those relating to the definition of health" (12, p. 597).

Even within the subjective or ontological domain, health was recognized to be a multidimensional experience. As ascribed to attitudinal constructs generally, health was hypothesized to have cognitive, affective, and conative components (17). Accordingly, in the present study, a relatively broad-ranged approach was taken to measuring health, and a variety of health status indicators were incorporated, including: self-ratings; subjective reports of disability and activity limitation; self-reported morbidity; and physician-observed morbidity. Both for conceptual reasons (already described) and empirical criteria (to be discussed shortly) analysis has been focused on a combination of *self-reported,* subjective health measures. Physician observations have been brought into this analysis chiefly to provide perspective on the subjective findings. This is consistent with the view that domains of self-perceived health are not the same as what the professional observes; while there are areas of overlap, there are also areas of distinction specific to each approach.

More particularly, the four self-reported indicators of health status which form the keystone for this analysis of adolescent health indicators are:

- Morbidity–number of self-reported health problems in response to a checklist of current symptoms (within the past year) and illnesses, plus more detailed questions about vision, weight, accidents, menstrual problems, smoking, and eating behavior–57 conditions and behaviors in all.
- Attitude–self-rating of general health obtained in reply to the question: "Most of the time is your health very good, is it pretty good, is it fair or is it poor most of the time?"
- Functional limitation–respondent's response that his health had limited activities in and/or out of school.
- Disability–number of days respondent reported he was absent from school for reasons of health.

These four, when applied to reports of particular health problems obtained in personal interviews with a cross-section sample of 671 black, nonhispanic adolescents[1] permitted examination of certain questions regarding the occurrence and reporting of health problems:

- Are certain health problems more likely to occur in combination with other health problems, while others occur more nearly alone?
- Are some conditions more likely to be associated with a generally lowered sense of physical well-being, while other health problems seemingly make little difference in subjective feelings of healthiness?
- Are some health conditions associated more than others with reduction in activity among adolescents?
- Are there some health problems associated with more absence from school while others seemingly take no special toll on school attendance?

WHAT DIFFERENT HEALTH STATUS INDICATORS MEASURE

These four questions were analyzed by cross-tabulating reports of particular health problems against each of the four separate indicators. The findings presented in Appendix Table 1 point to differences in the association between particular health problems and different health indicators. Eliminating from this discussion conditions reported by very few young people,[2] we see, for example, that hernia, painful or frequent urination, shortness of breath, dizziness-fainting, frequent diarrhea, shaking-trembling, and indigestion in five cases out of six were reported by young people who also reported many other health problems (part A of table). A third or more of young people reporting hernia, blood in bowel movement, and shortness of breath rated their health poorly, while only about one in eight in the entire group evidenced as poor an opinion as this of their own health (part B of table). Those reporting painful or frequent urination or hernia were twice as likely as the sample as a whole to report activity limitation (part C of table). Frequent constipation, frequent earaches, and hernia were conditions most strongly associated with reported disability as denoted by days lost from school.

[1] The sample was comprised of all age-eligible youngsters in a 4 percent systematic probability sample of dwelling units in Central Harlem in the late 1960s. Appreciation for providing this sample is extended to Professor Jack Elinson and to Patricia Collette, then with the Harlem Hospital Department of Patient Care and Program Evaluation, for whose Harlem Health Survey the community sample was drawn. Adolescents 12-15 years old were studied over two years (1968-1969 and 1969-1970); 16- to 17-year-olds were studied only in the second year of study. Before the two age segments were combined, data for 12- to 15-year olds in both years were examined to see if observed differences fell within the limits of normal sampling variation. Since year-to-year fluctuations were minor, the assumption was warranted that youngsters in both study years were drawn from the same universe; the two years' samples were then combined and 16- to 17-year-olds weighted by two to make them proportional to their occurrence in the population. All appendix tables, however, present the raw unweighted "*N*" in parentheses.

[2] If this procedure were applied on a broader scale with findings similar for a proportion, these conditions would be important to consider. Illness, of course, does not follow the "normal" distribution; often (but not always) significant health problems occur with extremely low frequency. However, the reliability of findings is questionable when as few cases as were noted here are involved. For this reason, infrequently occurring conditions (defined here as affecting less than 1 percent of the sample) have been excluded from discussion.

Space does not permit a more detailed review than this of the differential association of particular health problems with the various indicators. The findings in Appendix Table 1 suggest, however, that what are identified as leading types of adolescent morbidity will reflect to a considerable degree what indicator is employed. At the least, these differences reveal a problem in using a measure of morbidity alone, or perhaps in applying any other single indicator of health status, as a representative measure of health.[3]

DERIVATION OF THE COMPOSITE HEALTH SCORE

On empirical grounds (reported above) there was basis for concluding that different health status indicators measure different facets of health. On logical and conceptual grounds, too, different results were expected with different indicators. Health by any criterion and, specifically, self-perceived and self-reported health studied here, is conceived as a multidimensional domain. From this it follows that any single indicator cannot represent all of its dimensions adequately (18).

Furthermore, multiple-item indicators generally are recognized as having greater reliability than single items. While ultimately, the nature and purpose of an inquiry will determine if one or the other indicator is the method of choice, in the present study it was not known ahead of time which would be the most sensitive measure for describing the population's overall health status. We were after a single measure of maximum comprehensiveness and reliability to classify the adolescent sample into different health strata. With these groupings, the relationship between health and other attitudes and behavior would then be analyzed.

Different combinations of the self-reported indicators discussed above (with and without a fifth indicator–number of health problems reported by physician on examination) were tested by means of principal component analysis, run with unity in the diagonals.[4] A composite of the four self-reported indicators *without* physician-observed morbidity was selected. This health status composite accounted for 43 percent of the variance among the four indicators, with a factor reliability of 0.56. For logical as well as methodological reasons, physician-observed data were not included in the composite.

Logically, the analysis would have wider applicability if restricted to one source of data–that self-reported in personal interview. Operating from the premise that self-perceived health has a validity of its own and one that is different from that clinically observed, self-reported data could later be compared to physician-observed data to provide perspective on what each is measuring. Methodologically, the principal component analysis including the clinical measure actually reduced predictiveness

[3] Furthermore, cultural factors are known to influence reporting of morbidity. For example, when boys and girls in the present study were compared on the four health status indicators, they differed only with regard to number of reported problems.

[4] The investigator is indebted to Professor Elmer Struening (Epidemiology) and Professor Joseph Fleiss (Chairman, Biostatistics) at the Columbia University School of Public Health for advice on procedures followed here.

with less variance accounted for and lower reliability than when using the self-perceived measures alone.

Having selected the composite of four self-reported measures equally weighted,[5] a single score was then derived for each individual in the sample by summing his deviation or standard scores on each of the four items, dividing that sum by the number of scores present, and adding a constant of 10 to eliminate negative signs. Composite scores ranged between 8.76-13.06. To facilitate comparisons in the cross-tabulational analyses with particular self-reported conditions, the sample was trichotomized (Appendix Table 2).

WHAT THE COMPOSITE HEALTH STATUS MEASURE MEASURED

Like the component indicators, the composite score also was analyzed for its relationship to particular health problems. This analysis can be seen to address the question: Are some health conditions more likely to occur among sicker adolescents than among healthier? These findings are presented in Appendix Table 2, where conditions are listed in order of their association with poorer health.

Certain conditions with infrequent occurrence showed a stronger likelihood of occurring among sicker young people (e.g. rheumatic fever, jaundice-hepatitis, blood in urine). As before, discussion will be restricted here to those conditions with more than 1 percent self-reported prevalence. Conditions reported by double or more the average proportion of youngsters in poorest health, when health was measured by the composite index, were: *hernia*; painful or frequent *urination; something wrong with heart* (other than thumping hard); frequent *constipation; shortness of breath; chest pains; anemia; heart thumping hard;* a present or prior *pregnancy; dizziness or fainting; vomiting or nausea;* frequent *diarrhea; blood in bowel movement; shaking or trembling.* These were the conditions which, by the criteria used here, posed the greatest overall risk of poor health for adolescents.

What are some of the conditions that did not appear to be associated with poor general health among adolescents? Here, reading up from the bottom of the list in Appendix Table 2, youngsters who reported bed wetting; wore eyeglasses; had hay fever or some other allergy; had weight problems (under or over); and/or who smoked seemed not particularly at risk of poor general health when using this composite of self-perceived and self-reported indicators of health.

USING THE COMPOSITE HEALTH SCORE FOR JUDGING SERIOUSNESS OF SELF-REPORTED HEALTH PROBLEMS

Difficulties in systematic appraisal of seriousness or severity of conditions reported in household surveys were mentioned earlier. The present study lacked such a uniform measure of seriousness in its interview schedule; therefore, all conditions adolescents reported were counted equally when developing the component indicator of number

[5] Factor loadings and coefficients of intercorrelation were comparable among the four components.

of health problems. This raised the question, however, of whether the classification of youngsters according to the composite health status score might be used to distinguish differences in the seriousness of health problems they reported. That is, can we define as more serious those problems reported by sicker youngsters? This bypassed the issue of whether the condition itself or its frequent association with another problem accounts for the observed relationship. A problem's seriousness, or risk to health, would be measured by the average sickness or wellness of the young people who reported having that problem.

Thus, although developed as a means of classifying individuals according to their health status, the composite score was applied in this way to analyze health problems according to their likelihood of association with poor health. In this analysis, the distribution of scores on the composite health status index was divided into *four* segments to increase precision in scoring (as compared to three groups in the prior analysis).

Two methods of scoring conditions for seriousness were tested and their results are compared in Appendix Table 3. The first method involved weighting the proportion of those having the condition who were in the poorest health (25 percent of the sample) by *four,* the group with next poorest health (24 percent of the sample) by *three,* in the second best health segment (31 percent of the sample) by *two,* and in the group with best health (20 percent of the sample) by *one.* The potential range in scores by this method (dropping decimal points) was from 400 (if all who had that problem were in the poorest health quartile) to 100 (if all having a problem were in the best health group). As the table shows, condition scores were actually distributed from 400 (most serious) to 200 (least serious).[6]

The second method of scoring seriousness considered simply the proportion of the sample having that problem who were in the poorest health category. The rank orders in Appendix Table 3 show overall agreement between the two methods, with the increased precision of the former making it the preferred and subsequently used method. The data in the table permit examination of the question: "Do more serious problems occur less frequently?" The answer is "yes," often—but not always. The inverse association between prevalence and seriousness was not perfect. The most prevalent problems *were* more likely to be found at the bottom (the less serious end) of the list in the table (although venereal disease and bed wetting have low prevalence and also appear there). The least prevalent conditions more often were in the upper portion of that table. But, chest pains, shaking-trembling, dizziness-fainting, shortness of breath, vomiting-nausea, and repeated headaches—all identified here to be among more serious adolescent health risks—each had a prevalence of roughly 10 percent or greater.

Such findings may qualify, but do not contradict results from other investigations

[6] That no condition scored lower than 200 was influenced by the fact that the number of health problems was one of the components in the composite score. Any condition was more likely to occur with other conditions than alone (only 10 percent of the sample reported but one health problem); the sample average was three self-reported health problems. Appendix Table 1 (part A) also shows that those reporting *any* condition were less likely to be in "good" health compared to the proportion of the total sample who were so classified in "good" health.

where serious problems were less prevalent (19). The latter conclusions are based on the observation that people who report more serious health problems also tend to report a greater number of health problems. That was true in this study also, but the composite measure by which seriousness was estimated included other indicators as well.

SUMMARY

The accelerating rate of mortality in teen-age and young adult years, the growing awareness of serious social and health problems which overlap considerably in this age group (drugs, early pregnancy, and the like), as well as the significance of the adolescent period for subsequent adult health and health behavior—all of these are reason for interest in identifying indicators of health status for this age group.

Based on data obtained from a representative cross-section sample of urban black youths 12-17 years old, inclusive, this research has been addressed to certain conceptual and methodological issues in measuring health status:

- Many and perhaps most of the current approaches to measuring health status and needs for health care are based on medical definitions and assessments. Subjective experiential factors have received considerably less attention. In line with redressing this imbalance, this research has focussed on the latter, emphasizing the domain of health that is measured by self-reported and subjective indicators and here identified as "ontological health."
- Even restricting concern to the domain of subjective or ontological health, variations in what different health status indicators measure were reported here. Findings from the variety of analyses brought to bear on these indicators were taken as evidence of the multidimensional nature of self-perceived and self-evaluated health. Based on such findings, a multiple-indicator approach to health status was considered better than any single indicator in providing a more representative and more reliable measure. The derivation of one such multiple indicator—a composite of four different health status indicators—was described here.
- Health interview surveys often have lacked a uniform measure for seriousness of self-reported health problems. Yet seriousness or severity is of interest because of its likely association with utilization of health services and other illness behavior. In the present study, the problem of distinguishing seriousness was approached empirically, using the composite measure of four self-reported health status indicators to identify those problems most often reported by the sickest adolescents. Following the logic of the multiple-indicator approach to ontological health, problems identified in this way were suggested to represent the conditions for which adolescent health services are needed most.

Generally speaking, the approach that has been offered for consideration and for critique in this paper is part of an effort at refining conceptualization and modeling tools for age- and race-specific population indicators of health status. Those who study medical care behavior and utilization of services recognize the importance of the individual's perceptions and motivations in health and illness behavior. It is not enough, in planning medical services, to count unmet need in units that the medical profession alone defines. Conceptions of ontological health, as have been emphasized in this research, also are important for determining who selects himself into the medical care system and avails himself of services once they are offered. Obviously, too, health care will never be comprehensive until needs as perceived by the individual himself are also weighed. It is for reasons such as these that the legitimacy of both realms of health–the medical and the ontological–needs to be recognized and has been stressed here. Attention has been focussed on indicators of ontological health in particular because, in health research, *that* has been the relatively neglected realm.

REFERENCES

1. National Center for Health Statistics. *Monthly Vital Statistics Report* Vol. 18, No. 13. Department of Health, Education and Welfare, October 21, 1970.
2. Leading components of upturn in mortality for men. National Center for Health Statistics, Department of Health, Education, and Welfare, September 1971.
3. National Center for Health Statistics. *Monthly Vital Statistics Report* Vol. 22, No. 13, Department of Health, Education, and Welfare, June 1974.
4. Brunswick, A. F., and Josephson, E. Adolescent health in Harlem. *Am. J. Public Health,* 62(10, part 2) supplement, October 1972.
5. Brunswick, A. F. Adolescent health, sex and fertility. *Am. J. Public Health* 61(4): 711-729, 1971.
6. Brunswick, A. F., and Tarica, C. Drinking and health: The relationship among urban black adolescents. *Journal of Addictive Diseases* 1(10): 21-42, 1974.
7. Brunswick, A. F. Health and drug behavior. *Journal of Addictive Diseases,* in press.
8. Jessor, R., Jessor, S. L., and Finney, J. A social psychology of marihuana use: Longitudinal studies of high school and college youth. *J. Pers. Soc. Psychol.* 26(1): 1-15, 1973.
9. Josephson, E., Haberman, P., Zanes, A., and Elinson, J. Adolescent marihuana use: Report on a national survey. In *Student Drug Surveys,* edited by S. Einstein and S. Allen. Baywood Publishing Company, Farmingdale, N.Y., 1972.
10. Kandel, D. Adolescent marihuana use: Role of parents and peers. *Science* 181: 1067-1070, September 14, 1973.
11. Haber, L. Identifying the disabled: Concepts and methods in the measurement of disability. *Social Security Bulletin* No. 30(12): 17-34, 1967.
12. Moriyama, I. M. Problems in the measurement of health status. In *Indicators of Social Change: Concepts and Measurements,* edited by E. B. Sheldon and W. E. Moore. Russell Sage Foundation, New York, 1968.
13. Sullivan, D. F. Conceptual problems in developing an index of health. *Vital and Health Statistics.* Series 2, No. 17. National Center for Health Statistics, Department of Health, Education, and Welfare, 1968.
14. Elinson, J. Toward sociomedical health indicators. *Social Indicators Research* 1: 59-71, 1974.
15. Campbell, A., and Converse, P. E. *The Human Meaning of Social Change.* Russell Sage Foundation, New York, 1972.
16. National Center for Health Statistics. *Health Statistics Today and Tomorrow.* Vital and Health Statistics, Series 4, No. 5 (HRA), DHEW Publication No. 74-1452. Department of Health, Education, and Welfare, September 1973.
17. Rosenberg, M. J., and Hovland, C. I. Cognitive, affective and behavioral components of attitudes. In *Attitude Organization and Change,* edited by M. J. Rosenberg et al., pp. 1-14. Yale University Press, New Haven, 1960.
18. Fishbein, M., and Ajzen, I. Attitudes towards objectives as predictors of single and multiple behavioral criteria. *Psychol. Rev.* 81(1): 59-74, 1974.
19. Mechanic, D. Discussion of research programs on relations between stressful life events and episodes of physical illness. In *Stressful Life Events,* edited by B. S. Dohrenwend and B. P. Dohrenwend, pp. 87-97. John Wiley and Sons, New York, 1974.

Appendix Table 1

Association between individual health conditions and various indicators of health status (self-perceived) ($N = 671^a$)

	A			B			C		D		
	No. of Health Problems			Self-Rating			Activity Limited		No. School Days Absent		
Condition	Low 0-2 (28%)	Med. 3-5 (41%)	High 6+ (31%)	Very Good (33%)	Pretty Good (54%)	Fair/ Poor (13%)	No (68%)	Yes (32%)	Low 0 (32%)	Med. 1-5 (33%)	High 6+ (35%)
Hernia (8 = 100%)	–[b]	–	100	18	18	64	27	73	27	9	64
Jaundice, hepatitis (4 = 100%)	–	(43)[c]	(57)	–	(43)	(57)	(29)	(71)	(20)	–	(80)
Rheumatic fever (2 = 100%)	–	–	(100)	–	(100)	–	–	(100)	(50)	–	(50)
Painful, frequent urination (14 = 100%)	–	17	83	17	61	22	11	89	50	7	43
Heart (other than thumping) (24 = 100%)	3	3	94	27	50	23	50	50	29	21	50
Frequent constipation (28 = 100%)	–	22	78	17	64	19	53	47	19	19	62
Shortness of breath (54 = 100%)	–	16	84	15	53	32	50	50	24	30	46
Chest pains (80 = 100%)	2	20	78	16	57	27	41	59	21	30	49
Blood in urine (3 = 100%)	–	(25)	(75)	(25)	(75)	–	(25)	(75)	(75)	–	(25)
Anemia (23 = 100%)	3	22	75	–	81	19	56	44	18	36	46
Heart thumping hard or racing (33 = 100%)	–	21	79	21	60	19	46	54	24	29	47
Ever pregnant (18 = 100%)	26	32	42	23	58	19	48	52	41	6	53
Dizziness, fainting (52 = 100%)	–	14	86	15	65	20	49	51	17	27	56
Vomiting, sick to stomach (71 = 100%)	1	23	76	19	59	22	44	56	17	29	54
Frequent diarrhea (13 = 100%)	–	12	88	12	69	19	56	44	–	44	56

Blood in bowel movement (13 = 100%)	–	10	90	5	63	32	58	42	13	40	47
Shaking, trembling (55 = 100%)	3	12	85	12	65	23	52	48	27	27	46
Chronic bronchitis (11 = 100%)	–	33	67	17	66	17	42	58	8	33	59
Indigestion (28 = 100%)	–	16	84	11	63	26	47	53	18	32	50
Repeated sinus trouble (55 = 100%)	–	28	72	27	51	22	49	51	25	25	40
Asthma, wheezing (63 = 100%)	4	34	62	12	57	21	53	47	19	31	50
Difficulty hearing (45 = 100%)	2	24	74	15	64	21	55	45	24	36	40
Repeated headaches (123 = 100%)	3	32	65	19	58	23	48	52	18	34	48
Constant cough (68 = 100%)	–	28	72	27	52	21	49	51	16	27	57
Repeated back trouble (55 = 100%)	1	23	76	16	63	21	53	47	24	30	46
Frequent sore throats (87 = 100%)	1	24	75	22	58	20	56	44	19	33	48
Stomach pains (111 = 100%)	3	25	72	21	59	20	53	47	20	30	50
Worms, parasites (5 = 100%)	–	–	(100)	(20)	(80)	–	(60)	(40)	(60)	(20)	(20)
Tuberculosis (3 = 100%)	–	–	(100)	–	(80)	(20)	(40)	(60)	(40)	(20)	(40)
Frequent colds (140 = 100%)	2	31	67	23	58	21	51	49	18	33	49
Frequent earaches, discharge (39 = 100%)	2	27	71	18	55	27	63	37	21	18	61
Limbs: Stiffness, pain, deformity (38 = 100%)	9	22	69	35	47	18	47	53	27	38	35
Nervous-emotional problem (118 = 100%)	8	24	68	26	56	18	54	46	25	39	36
Repeated nosebleeds (59 = 100%)	6	37	57	19	56	25	56	44	33	31	36
Speech problem (91 = 100%)	7	30	63	25	59	16	54	46	31	32	37
Trouble going to sleep (192 = 100%)	13	38	49	23	55	22	60	40	20	35	45
Fair/poor appetite (119 = 100%)	19	37	44	21	55	24	61	39	31	30	39

Appendix Table 1 (Continued)

Condition	A No. of Health Problems Low 0-2 (28%)	Med. 3-5 (41%)	High 6+ (31%)	B Self-Rating Very Good (33%)	Pretty Good (54%)	Fair/ Poor (13%)	C Activity Limited No (68%)	Yes (32%)	D No. School Days Absent Low 0 (32%)	Med. 1-5 (33%)	High 6+ (35%)
Trouble seeing blackboard (117 = 100%)	12	36	52	28	56	16	60	40	30	37	33
Trouble staying asleep (94 = 100%)	24	28	48	26	52	22	61	39	33	35	32
Serious accidents, injuries (61 = 100%)	9	41	50	36	47	17	61	39	28	28	44
Polio (2 = 100%)	–	–	(100)	(50)	(50)	–	(50)	(50)	–	(50)	(50)
Eye problem (other than acuity) (83 = 100%)	16	38	46	26	57	17	57	43	25	30	45
Diabetes (2 = 100%)	–	(50)	(50)	–	(100)	–	(50)	(50)	–	(100)	–
Skin problem (111 = 100%)	8	39	53	31	56	13	59	41	28	33	39
Bad dreams (119 = 100%)	20	35	45	30	59	11	59	41	29	39	32
Teeth, gum problem (217 = 100%)	19	34	47	29	53	18	62	38	26	35	39
Menstrual problem (143 = 100%)	4	40	56	33	53	14	65	35	24	38	38
Gonorrhea (4 = 100%)	(58)	–	(42)	(29)	(43)	(28)	(86)	(14)	–	(67)	(33)
Drink alcohol (136 = 100%)	22	36	42	38	44	18	65	35	39	24	37

Teeth need straightening (138 = 100%)	21	36	43	32	51	17	58	42	29	33	38
Smoke cigarettes (167 = 100%)	30	32	38	40	43	17	68	32	32	24	44
Hay fever, allergy (61 = 100%)	7	43	50	35	53	12	71	29	23	34	43
Obese (180 = 100%)	25	39	36	29	56	15	61	39	26	39	35
Underweight (190 = 100%)	21	42	37	25	57	18	68	32	34	28	38
Wear glasses (248 = 100%)	16	47	37	34	54	12	70	30	32	32	36
Bed wetting (14 = 100%)	29	21	50	36	57	7	93	7	15	46	39
Syphilis (1 = 100%)	—	—	(100)	(100)	—	—	(100)	—	—	—	(100)

[a] Numbers in this and all other tables represent raw unweighted frequencies. Percentages are based on a weighted total of 793 where 16- to 17-year olds were counted twice.

[b] Dash signifies absence of cases in that category.

[c] Parentheses are used to distinguish percentage distributions of conditions reported by less than 1 percent of the young people.

Appendix Table 2

Association between individual health conditions and the composite index of health status (self-perceived)

	Composite[a]		
Condition	Good (31%)	Ave. (35%)	Poor (34%)
Hernia (8 = 100%)	–	–	100
Jaundice, hepatitis (4 = 100%)	–	–	(100)[b]
Rheumatic fever (2 = 100%)	–	–	(100)
Painful, frequent urination (14 = 100%)	5	6	89
Heart (other than thumping) (24 = 100%)	3	13	84
Frequent constipation (28 = 100%)	8	14	78
Shortness of breath (54 = 100%)	6	18	76
Chest pains (80 = 100%)	5	19	76
Blood in urine (3 = 100%)	(25)	–	(75)
Anemia (23 = 100%)	–	28	72
Heart thumping hard or racing (33 = 100%)	9	19	72
Ever pregnant (18 = 100%)	16	13	71
Dizziness, fainting (52 = 100%)	4	26	70
Vomiting, sick to stomach (71 = 100%)	9	21	70
Frequent diarrhea (13 = 100%)	–	31	69
Blood in bowel movement (13 = 100%)	5	26	69
Shaking, trembling (55 = 100%)	10	22	68
Chronic bronchitis (11 = 100%)	–	33	67
Indigestion (28 = 100%)	5	29	66
Repeated sinus trouble (55 = 100%)	15	19	66
Asthma, wheezing (63 = 100%)	9	26	65
Difficulty hearing (45 = 100%)	6	30	64
Repeated headaches (123 = 100%)	8	28	64
Constant cough (68 = 100%)	10	28	62
Repeated back trouble (55 = 100%)	8	29	63
Frequent sore throats (87 = 100%)	11	29	60
Stomach pains (111 = 100%)	7	33	60
Worms, parasites (5 = 100%)	(20)	(20)	(60)
Tuberculosis (3 = 100%)	–	(40)	(60)
Frequent colds (140 = 100%)	9	31	60
Frequent earaches, discharge (39 = 100%)	6	35	59
Limbs: Stiffness, pain, deformity (38 = 100%)	18	24	58
Nervous-emotional problem (118 = 100%)	13	30	57
Repeated nosebleeds (59 = 100%)	13	30	57
Speech problem (91 = 100%)	12	33	55
Trouble going to sleep (192 = 100%)	18	29	53
Fair/poor appetite (119 = 100%)	19	30	51
Trouble seeing blackboard (117 = 100%)	21	29	50
Trouble staying asleep (94 = 100%)	23	27	50
Serious accidents, injuries (61 = 100%)	17	33	50

Appendix Table 2 (Continued)

Condition	Composite[a]		
	Good (31%)	Ave. (35%)	Poor (34%)
Polio (2 = 100%)	–	(50)	(50)
Eye problem (other than acuity) (83 = 100%)	21	29	50
Diabetes (2 = 100%)	–	(50)	(50)
Skin problem (111 = 100%)	23	28	49
Bad dreams (119 = 100%)	24	30	46
Teeth, gum problem (217 = 100%)	22	33	45
Menstrual problem (143 = 100%)	24	33	43
Gonorrhea (4 = 100%)	(29)	(29)	(42)
Drink alcohol (136 = 100%)	29	28	43
Teeth need straightening (138 = 100%)	25	33	42
Smoke cigarettes (167 = 100%)	32	28	40
Hay fever, allergy (61 = 100%)	17	44	39
Obese (180 = 100%)	30	31	39
Underweight (190 = 100%)	22	40	38
Wear glasses (248 = 100%)	26	38	36
Bed wetting (14 = 100%)	29	57	14
Syphilis (1 = 100%)	–	(100)	–

[a] One component of the composite index is the number of self-reported health problems; most of these conditions entered into that sum.

[b] Parentheses are used to distinguish percentage distribution of conditions reported by less than 1 percent of the young people.

Appendix Table 3

Seriousness score for health problems

Condition	Percent Prevalence ($N = 659$)	1 Weighted Composite		2 Proportion in Poorest Health	
		Rank	Seriousness Score	Rank	Percent in Poorest Health Quartile
Rheumatic fever	[a]	1	400	1	100
Jaundice, hepatitis	1	2	386	2	86
Hernia	1	3	382	3	82
Painful, frequent urination	2	4	368	4	78
Frequent diarrhea	2	5	357	9	63
Heart (other than thumping)	4	6	353	15	60
Chest pains	12	7	352	7.5	64
Blood in urine	1	8	350	5	75
Shaking, trembling	9	9	349	7.5	64
Blood in bowel movement	2	10	348	18.5	58
Dizziness, fainting	9	12	346	11	62
Frequent constipation	4	12	346	6	69
Shortness of breath	9	12	346	11	62
Vomiting, sick to stomach	11	14	344	11	62
Heart thumping hard or racing	5	15	343	18.5	58
Repeated headaches	19	16	342	23	54
Indigestion	5	17	340	18.5	58
Anemia	5	18	339	13	61
Difficulty hearing	7	19	333	18.5	58
Stomach pains	17	20	327	30	50
Repeated backaches, back trouble	10	21.5	324	24	53
Frequent earaches, discharge	6	22	322	21.5	55
Frequent sore throats	13	24	321	26	51
Asthma, wheezing	9	24	321	30	50
Frequent colds	21	24	321	34	49

Worms, parasites	1	27	320	15	60
Tuberculosis	1	27	320	15	60
Constant cough	10	27	320	34	49
Repeated sinus trouble	8	29	318	21.5	55
Limbs: Stiffness, pain, deformity	6	30	313	26	51
Repeated nosebleeds	8	31.5	312	26	51
Nervous-emotional problem	18	31.5	312	34	49
Speech problem	14	33	307	36	46
Chronic bronchitis	2	35.5	300	30	50
Diabetes	1	35.5	300	30	50
Polio	1	35.5	300	30	50
Ever pregnant [b]	12	35.5	300	37	45
Trouble going to sleep	29	38	294	39	43
Eye problem (other than acuity)	13	39	293	39	43
Skin problem	18	40	292	41	42
Trouble staying asleep	14	41	289	43	39
Fair/poor appetite	19	42	287	44.5	37
Serious accidents, injuries	9	43	285	42	40
Teeth, gum problems	33	44.5	284	44.5	37
Trouble seeing blackboard	17	44.5	284	46.5	36
Menstrual problems	54	46	280	49	34
Bad dreams	17	47	277	46.5	36
Teeth need straightening	22	48	274	50	33
Obese	27	49	272	51	32
Drink alcohol	24	50	268	48	35
Underweight	29	51	267	52	30
Wear glasses	38	52	261	54	26
Smoke cigarettes	30	53	258	53	29
Gonorrhea	1	54	256	39	43
Hay fever, allergy	9	55	251	55	24
Bed wetting	2	56	242	56	14
Syphilis	[a]	57	200	57	0

[a] Less than half of 1 percent. [b] Percentages are based on females only.

CHAPTER 8

A Measure of Primary Sociobiological Functions

Sidney Katz
C. Amechi Akpom

The increase in frequency of chronic diseases as observed in recent years is, to a large extent, generally attributed to the greater number of individuals who survive into old age, where chronic manifestations of noninfectious diseases are more common. These diseases and their associated dependencies lead to increasing social concern and responsibility for long-term care, broadly defined as activities and interventions by which we ameliorate and manage such dependencies. For those who share the concern and responsibility for long-term care, the ability to evaluate health and illness status is essential. Service providers must assess health and illness status in order to set goals for service and to develop plans for service activities. They also use information about improvement in status, or lack of improvement, to modify service activities as they seek beneficial outcomes. Consumers and service program managers require such information in relation to their concerns for the effectiveness, efficiency, and quality of the services which are provided. Policy makers and planners use information about health and illness status of populations to arrive at rational decisions about priorities and directions for the allocation of health services resources. Not the least, investigators must be able to assess health and illness status to produce needed quantitative information about the direction and degree of efforts required to benefit patients optimally (1, 2).

Functional status of the individual is an important behavioral dimension of health and illness status which reflects both the needs for service assistance and the outcomes resulting from service. When measured in socially relevant terms, information about functional status reflects needs and outcomes in a manner which is broadly useful to the individual and society. Adding such information to existing biological expressions of health and illness status increases the potential for decision making which is socially, as well as biologically, helpful to those with chronic conditions. In addition, at a time when knowledge about etiology and pathogenesis of chronic conditions is not advanced enough to permit measurement in these terms, functional status can be an objectively measured milestone which indicates the existence, stage, severity, and impact of such conditions (3). For purposes which require the classification of populations with a mixture of disease conditions and health problems, classification according to function offers a conceptually defined basis for homogeneous groupings. Terms of function also serve as language bridges for better communication among disciplines and among those who plan, develop, facilitate, serve, and are served (when other disciplinary languages are often jargonized barriers).

In this paper, we focus on the measurement of activities of daily living (ADL), a set of primary sociobiological functions. In particular, we present our experiences in developing and applying the Index of Independence in Activities of Daily Living (Index of ADL) (4). We shall describe its development, the index itself, theoretical observations about the index, and the results of selected applications of the index.

DEVELOPMENT OF THE INDEX OF ADL

Our interest in the measurement of health and illness status in functional terms began about twenty years ago, stemming from attempts to evaluate hypotheses about improved comprehensive care for chronically ill people (5). In these attempts, we were hampered by the lack of outcome measures which could be used to make comparative descriptions of both changes in patient status over time and changes in the course of illness among patients or groups of patients. We saw the need for both socially and biologically relevant measures, and we were aware of the origins and history of efforts such as those of the Commission on Chronic Illness, which, during the early 1950s, had used a classification of function to estimate the potential for improvement in patients with chronic illness (6). The Commission had also expressed the need for a classification of overall function to describe disability in activities of daily living.

As a result, we embarked on a series of studies concerning activities of daily living, mobility, and socioeconomic functioning among severely disabled people. We subsequently extended our efforts to areas of mental function, to role dysfunction such as restricted activities, to other social functions, to physical function, and to the issue of function as a dimension of severity of illness. With regard to activities of daily living, we looked for and identified a set of graded primary functions which were hierarchically related to each other (5, 7, 8). The hierarchical relationships, thus, enabled us to rank individuals on a graded scale, wherein the scale's grades represented standardized functional profiles which could be compared with each other. By also requiring that individual functions in the profile should be sensitive to change over time, the overall scale was sensitive to change. The resulting scale, the Index of ADL, made it possible to rank people in an ordered manner, to make comparisons among them as individuals or groups, and to detect and compare changes over time. The scale also permitted us to describe the profile of the individual as a single grade which, by virtue of the hierarchical nature of the scale, reflected an understandable level of behavior in terms of the component variables (functions) included in the scale.

To derive a scale of the sort specified above, we used a Guttman-type approach to analyze detailed observations of a large set of activities of daily living in patients with fracture of the hip (5, 7). Standardized observations were made systematically and repeated at comparable points during the course of illness. (Importantly, observations of function were defined on the basis of the status of patients rather than on the basis of impressions of ability in order to minimize the effects of subjective interpretation and, thus, increase objectivity and reliability.) Grades of "better" (less dependent) and "worse" (more dependent) were defined for each function, and the resulting patient profiles were compared in search of hierarchical relationships among the variables. As a result, a set of definitions of "better" and "worse" were identified, whereby six daily living variables were strongly related to each other in a hierarchical manner and were, at the same time, sensitive to change. The variables were bathing, dressing, toileting, transfer, continence, and feeding (5, 7, 8).

Developmental studies of the Index of ADL were subsequently extended to other chronically ill people, including those with cerebral infarction, multiple sclerosis, paraplegia, quadriplegia, rheumatoid arthritis, and a large number of unselected types of chronic conditions among institutionalized and noninstitutionalized people (9-14). Methodological studies encompassed children as well as adults, the mentally retarded as well as physically disabled, and ambulatory and noninstitutionalized as well as institutionalized people (4, 7, 8, 15). Early confirmation of the appropriateness of the Index definitions and its use appeared in a report of observations in more than 1000 patients (8), while this and the other studies cited in this paper produced necessary information about its generalizability, reproducibility, and meaning.

THE INDEX OF ADL

The Index of ADL summarizes an individual's overall performance in six functions, namely, bathing, dressing, toileting, transfer, continence, and feeding, organized as a scale of ordered profiles of levels of dependence in carrying out these functions (4). According to the Index, performance is summarized as grades *A, B, C, D, E, F, G,* or "*Other,*" where *A* is the most independent grade relative to the scale and *G* the most dependent grade. These grades are defined in Figure 1 (4).

The category of "*Other*" on the scale usually includes less than 5 percent of patients. In applying the scale to comparative evaluations, instances of occurrence of the category "*Other*" do not have to be excluded from most analyses for the following reasons. By definition, a patient classed as "*Other*" is more dependent than one classed as *A* or *B,* and more independent than one classed as *G.* Therefore, individuals classed as "*Other*" can always be compared relative to those classed as *A, B,* or *G.* Experience

The Index of Independence in Activities of Daily Living is based on an evaluation of the functional independence or dependence of patients in bathing, dressing, going to toilet, transferring, continence, and feeding. Specific definitions of functional independence and dependence appear below the index.

A—Independent in feeding, continence, transferring, going to toilet, dressing, and bathing.
B—Independent in all but one of these functions.
C—Independent in all but bathing and one additional function.
D—Independent in all but bathing, dressing, and one additional function.
E—Independent in all but bathing, dressing, going to toilet, and one additional function.
F—Independent in all but bathing, dressing, going to toilet, transferring, and one additional function.
G—Dependent in all six functions.

Other—Dependent in at least two functions, but not classifiable as C, D, E, or F.

Independence means without supervision, direction, or active personal assistance, except as specifically noted below. This is based on actual status and not on ability. A patient who refuses to perform a function is considered as not performing the function, even though he is deemed able.

Bathing (Sponge, Shower, or Tub)

Independent: assistance only in bathing a single part (as back or disabled extremity) or bathes self completely

Dependent: assistance in bathing more than one part of body; assistance in getting in or out of tub or does not bathe self

Dressing

Independent: gets clothes from closets and drawers; puts on clothes, outer garments, braces; manages fasteners; act of tying shoes is excluded

Dependent: does not dress self or remains partly undressed

Going to Toilet

Independent: gets to toilet; gets on and off toilet; arranges clothes; cleans organs of excretion (may manage own bedpan used at night only and may or may not be using mechanical supports)

Dependent: uses bedpan or commode or receives assistance in getting to and using toilet

Transfer

Independent: moves in and out of bed independently and moves in and out of chair independently (may or may not be using mechanical supports)

Dependent: assistance in moving in or out of bed and/or chair; does not perform one or more transfers

Continence

Independent: urination and defecation entirely self-controlled

Dependent: partial or total incontinence in urination or defecation; partial or total control by enemas, catheters, or regulated use of urinals and/or bedpans

Feeding

Independent: gets food from plate or its equivalent into mouth (precutting of meat and preparation of food, as buttering bread, are excluded from evaluation)

Dependent: assistance in act of feeding (see above): does not eat all or parenteral feeding

Figure 1. Index of Independence in Activities of Daily Living.

also indicates that the unique profile of the occasional person classed as "*Other*" tends to remain unique and thus permits a precise determination of improvement or deterioration when changes occur in that person. For example, a patient who is incontinent and dependent in dressing (grade "*Other*") clearly deteriorates when he/she develops bathing dependence in addition to incontinence and dependence in dressing (grade of *D*).

A modified form of grading the Index of ADL, which has been useful in classifying patients with chronic illness, eliminates the need for the category "*Other*" (16). In this version, grades of the Index of ADL represent the number of activities in which the individual is dependent (see Figure 2). Grades expressed as *0, 1, 2, 3, 4, 5,* or *6* thus reflect the number of areas of dependence as a single summary term. This type of scaling, which correlates highly with the original scale, is made possible by virtue of the inherent consistency of the hierarchically ordered profiles, as will be described later.

As derived in the development of the Index, the observer uses the following definitions to complete the form reproduced in Figure 3 and records, for each function, the most dependent degree of performance occurring during a two-week period (or another defined period as required for any particular study) (4). The observer determines whether another person assisted the patient or whether the patient functioned alone, defining assistance as active personal assistance, directive assistance, or supervision. The actual existence of assistance is considered in the evaluation, not the potential or ability of the patient. Thus, for example, overprotective assistance is defined as assistance though the observer considers the patient as able, and refusal to perform a function is defined as nonfunctioning though the patient is deemed able.

Bathing is the overall complex behavior of getting water and cleansing the whole body. A patient receives "no assistance" (first of the three classes of bathing in Figure 3) if no other person is involved in any part of the process of taking a sponge, shower, or tub bath to wash the whole body. Such a patient goes to the sink by himself if he sponge-bathes at the sink, gets in and out of a tub by himself if he tub-bathes, and is not supervised in the shower if showering is the means of bathing. A patient receives

0 = Independent in all six functions (bathing, dressing, feeding, continence, transfer, toileting)

1 = Independent in five functions and dependent in one function

2 = Independent in four functions and dependent in two functions

3 = Independent in three functions and dependent in three functions

4 = Independent in two functions and dependent in four functions

5 = Independent in one function and dependent in five functions

6 = Dependent in all six functions

Figure 2. Index of ADL (modified Katz Index).

Name ______________________ **Day of evaluation** ______________________

For each area of functioning listed below, check description that applies. (The word "assistance" means supervision, direction, or personal assistance.).

Bathing—either sponge bath; tub bath, or shower.

☐	☐	☐
Receives no assistance (gets in and out of tub by self if tub is usual means of bathing)	Receives assistance in bathing only one part of the body (such as back or a leg)	Receives assistance in bathing more than one part of the body (or not bathed)

Dressing—gets clothes from closets and drawers—including underclothes, outer garments and using fasteners [including braces if worn]

☐	☐	☐
Gets clothes and gets completely dressed without assistance	Gets clothes and gets dressed without assistance except for assistance in tying shoes	Receives assistance in getting clothes or in getting dressed, or stays partly or completely undressed

Toileting—Going to the "Toilet room" for bowel and urine elimination; cleaning self after elimination, and arranging clothes

☐	☐	☐
Goes to "toilet room," cleans self, and arranges clothes without assistance (may use object for support such as cane, walker, or wheelchair and may manage night bedpan or commode, emptying same in morning)	Receives assistance in going to "toilet room" or in cleansing self or in arranging clothes after elimination or in use of night bedpan or commode	Doesn't go to room termed "toilet" for the elimination process

Transfer—

☐	☐	☐
Moves in and out of bed as well as in and out of chair without assistance (May be using object for support such as cane or walker)	Moves in and out of bed or chair with assistance	Doesn't get out of bed

Continence—

☐	☐	☐
Controls urination and bowel movement completely by self	Has occasional "accidents"	Supervision helps keep urine or bowel control; catheter is used, or is incontinent

Feeding—

☐	☐	☐
Feeds self without assistance	Feeds self except for getting assistance in cutting meat or buttering bread	Receives assistance in feeding or is fed partly or completely by using tubes or intravenous fluids

Figure 3. Evaluation form for Index of ADL.

"assistance in bathing only one part of the body" if he functions by himself as defined above, except that he is assisted in washing only one part of the body, as his back alone or one leg alone. The class "assistance in bathing more than one part of the body" includes the individual who is assisted in washing more than one part of the body or who does not bathe. This last, most dependent category, includes also the following: the patient to whom water is brought even though he washes himself; the patient who is taken to the place of bathing though he washes himself; the person who is helped in or out of a tub as regularly as once a week; the patient who is regularly supervised for reasons of safety although he washes himself; and the patient who cannot reach his feet to wash them.

Dressing is the overall complex behavior of getting clothes from closets and drawers and then getting dressed. A patient gets "completely dressed without assistance" (first of the three classes of dressing in Figure 3) if no other person is involved in getting clothes from closets and drawers nor in putting on the clothes, including brace, if worn, and including outer garments and footwear. Fasteners must also be managed without assistance. Footwear includes such items as socks and slippers or shoes. The intermediate category of dressing includes those who get their own clothes and dress independently as defined above "except for assistance in tying shoes." A patient is placed in the third and most dependent category if he "receives assistance in getting clothes or in getting dressed" or remains "partly or completely undressed."

Going to toilet is the act of going to the room termed the "toilet room" for bowel and bladder function, transferring on and off the toilet, cleaning after elimination, and arranging clothes. The patient who functions wholly by himself, including getting to the room, is classed as functioning "without assistance" (first of the three classes in Figure 3). It should be noted that an individual in this class may or may not be using an object for support such as a cane, walker, or wheelchair; and he may be using a bedpan or commode at night, in which case he must empty it himself in order to be considered in the "without assistance" category. If another person assists in any part of the function, the toileting status is recorded as "receives assistance" (intermediate toileting category in Figure 3). Toileting status is also recorded as "receives assistance" for an individual who uses the toilet room at certain times, and at other times uses a daytime bedpan or commode. The third category, namely, "doesn't go to room termed toilet," is self-explanatory. Note that toileting is not concerned with continence. If a patient is occasionally incontinent, but manages himself completely independently insofar as toileting is concerned, toileting function is recorded as "without assistance."

Transfer is the process of moving in and out of bed and in and out of a chair. If no other person is involved in the transfer, the patient is considered to function "without assistance" (first of three classes of transfer in Figure 3). Such a patient may be using an object for support, e.g. cane, walker, or bedpost. The intermediate category, namely, "with assistance," applies if another person is involved in the process. Patients in the third category are bedridden and do not leave the bed at all. In evaluating transfer status, the observer may be told that the patient is not allowed to transfer unless supervised for reasons of safety. The observer then determines whether such supervision is a reality. The observer may occasionally find, for example, that a daughter claims she supervises her mother whenever her mother moves from one place to another, while observation reveals that the mother moves about entirely on her own and the daughter means that she is always within hearing distance.

Continence refers to the physiological process of elimination from bladder and bowel, where incontinence is the involuntary loss of urine and/or feces. The function is thought of as the primitive function of control and does not include any consideration of hygiene, toileting, or constipation. The patient is classed as "controls urination and bowel movement completely by self" (first of three continence categories in Figure 3) if no other person assists. Such a patient can exert some degree of control on the process himself by medication or by self-administered enema (or, in the case of a patient with a colostomy, may manage this by himself). The case in which a slight amount of wetness or slight soiling of underclothes is occasionally noted by others and not perceived as incontinence by the patient is recorded as "controls urination and bowel movement." The patient who does not get to the bathroom or commode on time or who is incontinent at least once during the period of the evaluation is considered as "has occasional accidents," the intermediate category. Patients in the third category are incontinent or controlled by the supervision, direction, or intervention of another person. Presence of a catheter or planned, supervised scheduling for bowel control are included in the incontinent category.

Feeding concerns the process of getting food from a plate or its equivalent into the mouth. It is considered in a primitive sense and without concern for social niceties. A patient feeds himself "without assistance" (first of three classes of feeding in Figure 3) when this primitive process of ingestion is accomplished without the aid of another person. The intermediate category applies to the individual who feeds himself, but receives assistance in cutting meat or buttering bread. The third category, "receives assistance," applies to the individual who is assisted in this feeding process or who is fed partly or completely parenterally.

Data recorded on the assessment form (Figure 3) are converted into an Index of ADL grade (or modified Index grade) with the aid of the definitions presented in Figure 1. Note from Figure 1 that two descriptions would permit one to distinguish between "Independent" and "Dependent" levels for grading purposes; yet three descriptions are presented for the observer to assess on the recording form. Introduction of an intermediate description increases observer awareness of subtle distinctions and, thereby, increases reliability and sensitivity. The intermediate description is classified as dependent for certain functions and independent for others. For grading purposes, the intermediate description of bathing and dressing, for example, is classed as independent.

Environmental artifacts that tend to influence ADL levels are occasionally encountered. For safety reasons, some hospitals require nurses or aides to supervise patients who shower or get into tubs. During the first few days in the hospital, patients are sometimes kept in bed until the staff can assess their behavior and the degree of dependence that is advisable. In some nursing homes, patients are kept in bed and not permitted to dress. For safety and convenience, water for bathing and clothes for dressing are sometimes brought to patients. All these special conditions can result in ADL ratings that are lower than they might be in the absence of such restrictions. A test of actual functional level is possible and is indicated for certain studies.

Reliable reproduction of Index grades depends on adherence to its component definitions. However, widespread use of the Index has shown that these definitions are easily understood and readily applied by those who have experience with people who have chronic conditions. Simple training with regard to the definitions and process of observation leads to a degree of reliability such that differences between observers will occur once in twenty evaluations or less frequently (8).

THEORETICAL OBSERVATIONS ABOUT THE INDEX OF ADL

As described before, the Index of ADL is not an invention. It, rather, represents a description of observed phenomena in a social and biological context. Its grades reflect profiles of levels of human behavior in terms of six basic functions, namely, bathing, dressing, toileting, transfer, continence, and feeding. Based on empirical observations, the method of deriving the scale led to the identification of these six functions as being hierarchically related. Other items of function, such as mobility, walking, and stair-climbing did not fit into the hierarchical system.

The theoretical basis for the hierarchical relationship which permitted orderly scaling of the six functions was not clear at first. The relatively large amount of success we experienced in its application to many purposes and situations, though gratifying, made us increasingly conscious of the possibility of a theoretical explanation. When understanding finally emerged, we felt both stimulated and chagrined, stimulated by the experience of having an insight and chagrined by our slowness in understanding.

Insight began when we noted that the functions which comprise the Index of ADL, and their characteristic order, brought to mind the recognized patterns of child growth and development as well as the behavior of members of primitive societies (17-20).

> Pediatric texts, for example, describe the development of children largely in terms of bathing, dressing, going to toilet, locomotion, elimination, and feeding. Terms used in the Index, which was developed independently, are strikingly similar. Pediatric descriptions distinguish between vegetative and culturally learned behaviors, and an analogous distinction can be recognized in the activities of the Index. The definitions in the Index of feeding, continence, and transfer are, thus, recognized to reflect the organized locomotor and neurologic aspects of simple vegetative functions, exclusive of their more complex cultural and learned characteristics. As defined in the Index, bathing, dressing, and going to toilet also require organized locomotor and neurologic functioning, but these activities are prominently influenced by cultural forces and learning (8).

In early studies of the Index of ADL, we also observed that certain recovering disabled patients passed through three successive stages: (a) return of independence in feeding and continence; (b) recovery in transfer and toileting; and (c) recovery of dressing and bathing functions (8). This pattern is similar to the progression of development of these basic functions in children, since we note that by two years, the child holds a glass securely and takes food into his mouth on a spoon (17, 19). He is not yet completely continent and requires a great deal of assistance and supervision in bathing and dressing. By three years, he feeds himself and can even pour from a pitcher. Nights of wetness occur, and supervision of going to toilet is required in managing clothes and in self-cleansing. The three-and-a-half-year-old child is generally dry at night. By four years, he uses the toilet independently, though he may still require occasional supervision. Between four and five years, he requires only general supervision in bathing and dressing (8). The above parallelism and the observed hierarchical order of function in the Index suggest that common mechanisms underlie the two kinds of progression. It also seems to be consistent with the hypothesis that, just as there is an orderly pattern of development, there is an ordered regression as part of the natural process of aging, since it appears reasonable that loss of function would begin with those activities which are most complex and least basic, while those functions which are most basic and least complex could be retained longer. Observations in the course of our many studies of the aged support this thesis.

Anthropology provides independent confirmation of the biological primacy of the functions which comprise the Index. Here again, a distinction is evident between vegetative and culturally learned functions (21-23). All peoples, primitive and advanced, develop self-regulation of feeding and elimination as requirements for survival. They also develop independent locomotion, moving from one place to another to adapt themselves and their environments to their needs. Bathing and dressing, however, are not necessities of day-to-day physiological functioning, as evidenced by the habits of children of primitive people and adults of the most primitive groups. Modified forms of bathing and dressing are, nevertheless, performed regularly and universally even by primitive peoples, as in the ritual bath and the use of loincloth, headdress, body string, arm band, necklace, mask, and fur. The cultural significance of bathing and dressing is emphasized by the symbolic and ceremonial use of dress to express strength, rank, courage, and sexual maturity, and by the practice of bathing to clean away evil (8).

Studies of the predictive capacity of the Index provide additional theoretical insight. In one such study, the Index of ADL predicted long-term adaptation (in terms of two-year mobility and two-year house-confinement) as well as or better than did selected measures of either mental or physical function (4). In that study, mobility and house-confinement were selected as criteria of long-term outcome which reflect important concepts of adjustment and adaptation of the organism as these are discussed in the writing of such behavioral theoreticians as Freud, Havighurst, and Kuhlen. In Freud's concept, the ego is a system of forces which includes, among others, the cognitive processes, and is responsible for mobility of the organism, and its movement through time and space (24). This movement, biologically and psychologically, is modified by physical, psychological, and social assets and limitations. "Directed by cognitive processes, purposive adjustment or adaptative actions depend, thus, on such factors as the intactness of a coordinated neurological and locomotor system, as well as the adequacy of organized psychological and social behavior patterns. In the presence of strong adjustment or adaptive forces (e.g. neurological, locomotor, and behavioral functions), the injured organism will better recover its mobility, even to the point of making use of substitute devices or new-learned behavior" (4). Adaptation was considered important to the conceptual understanding of the aging process by Havighurst (25), who stated that, to a large degree, the process of growing old is "an adaptation to: (a) changes in the structure and functions of the human body, (b) changes in the social environment." Relatedly, Kuhlen (26) stated that the "achievement and maintenance of good adjustment require the potential of mobility, a certain freedom on the part of the individual to move out of a threatening or frustrating situation into one more satisfying or at least less threatening."

In the light of the foregoing types of information about child growth and development, behavior of members of primitive societies, and definitions of adaptation and adjustment, we gained understanding about the mechanisms which contribute to the hierarchical relationship inherent in the Index of ADL. Observations about the order of recovery of Index functions among disabled people and the ability of the Index to predict long-term adaptation were interpreted as supportive evidence. Supportive also were many reported longitudinal and experimental studies which are not detailed here and which regularly demonstrated the capacity of the Index to discriminate and predict (9-11, 13, 14, 16). Such studies added understanding about its meaning and validity. As a result, we consider that the Index of ADL appears to be based on functions of sociobiological primacy and that it reflects the adequacy of organized neurological and locomotor response.

APPLICATIONS OF THE INDEX OF ADL

Evaluation of independence in activities of daily living among people with chronic conditions has wide application (12). The Index of ADL has, thus, been used to develop information for patient care, planning, policy, teaching, and research purposes. It has been applied to increase knowledge about the outcomes of specific chronic diseases, thereby producing predictive information about the course of illness. It has also been used to add knowledge about benefits that can be attributed to long-term care of chronic conditions. Information has been provided about the aged and about mentally retarded children, about noninstitutionalized as well as institutionalized patients, and about population health status. The following are selected examples of its applications.

The Index of ADL has been used to develop predictive information about the courses of specific illnesses, in its capacity both as a measure of the patient's health status at the onset of illness and as a measure of the sociobiological outcome of the illness. In a study of patients with fracture of the hip, for example, most full and partial recoveries occurred within one year after fracture, and there was little likelihood of recovery after two years (see Figure 4) (14). In that study, recovery in ADL tended to precede recovery in walking, and recovery was generally sustained for two years or longer. Advanced age and prefracture disability (as determined by the Index) were predictors of poor outcome. Such predictive information is useful since it makes possible the avoidance of excessive therapeutic efforts in situations where the chances for successful outcomes are small. It also directs attention to possible limits in therapeutic skills, where the development of new skills and knowledge might be needed.

Similarly, in a group of patients with stroke, a majority of recoveries occurred within six months after stroke, and there was little likelihood of recovery after two years (see Figure 5) (9). In that study, recovery was generally sustained for a year or longer, when such recovery occurred. At the end of two years, six of every ten survivors walked without personal assistance and received minimal or no assistance with activities of daily living, four of the six returning fully to their prestroke functional levels. Advanced age, the absence of early neuromuscular improvement, the

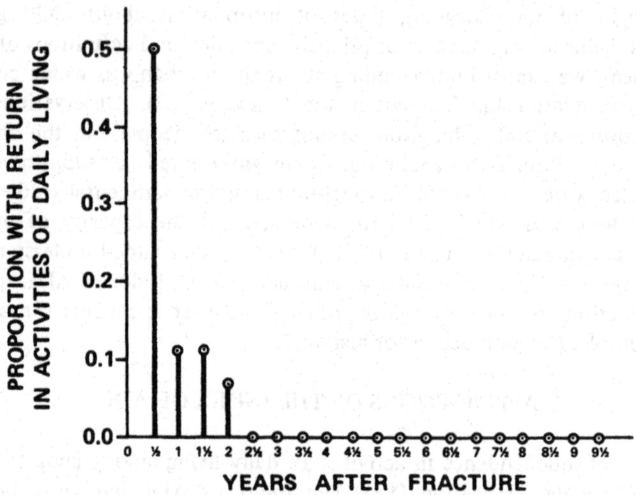

Figure 4. Recovery of Activities of Daily Living in a group of rehabilitated patients with fracture of the hip. (Figure reproduced by permission of *Surgery, Gynecology, and Obstetrics.*)

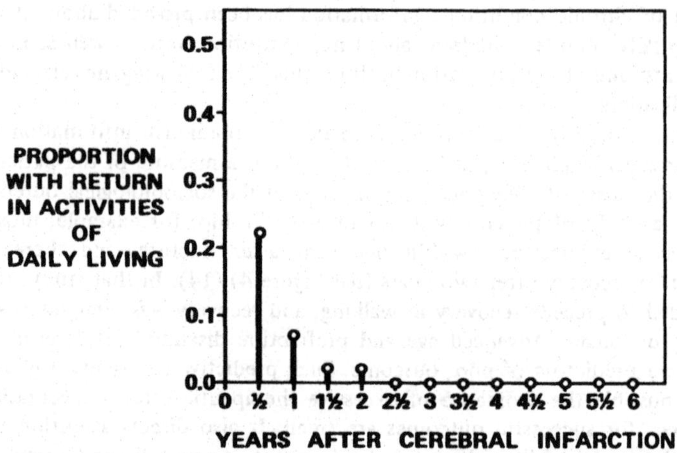

Figure 5. Recovery of Activities of Daily Living in a group of rehabilitated patients with stroke.

presence of more than one stroke, and the presence of coexisting major chronic disease were predictors of poor outcome.

In comparison studies and in experiments dealing with the efficacy of care, the Index of ADL has been used as a control variable to control for health status and as an outcome variable to measure sociobiological function. In a comparison study of the effectiveness of rehabilitation for patients with fracture of the hip, for example, severe deterioration in activities of daily living was significantly more frequent among non-rehabilitated patients than among matched rehabilitated patients (27).

The results of a controlled experiment concerning the effects of coordinated visiting nurses' services for patients with given types of rheumatoid arthritis revealed significantly fewer deteriorations in activities of daily living among those in the treatment group, as well as fewer deteriorations in clinical manifestations of disease activity (10). As yet another example of an application in a controlled study of home nursing care, beneficial effects in physical and mental functions were demonstrated among treated patients who were not severely disabled as measured by the Index of ADL when compared with similar control patients (13). In the latter two studies, the care variable involved more than the activities of a single doctor or nurse. It consisted of comprehensive treatment programs organized and coordinated through joint efforts of community organizations and of professional disciplines with specific skills and goals.

An important contribution of the Index of ADL has been its use as a component of a multidimensional profile which measures severity of chronic conditions. The idea for this grew out of a concept set forth by the Commission of Chronic Illness in its studies of chronic illness in the United States (28). In that study, a classification system was described that combined criteria of disease and dysfunction into three groups of differing degrees of severity. The most severe group included those with maximum disability regardless of diagnosis. The second and third degrees of severity included those having less than maximum disability, the second group having some disease and the third having minor or no disease. A conceptual basis for homogeneous groupings in a large population was, thus, made explicit. Based on this concept, we developed a method of applying the Index of ADL as the disability component in such a classification system (3, 29). We used this classification in the previously cited experimental study of continuing nursing care in the home (13).

As one of several measures, the Index of ADL has been used in multidisciplinary screening designed to detect chronic conditions and disability among ambulatory young and middle-aged outpatients (4). In that study, dysfunction was highly correlated with major chronic diseases, and most of the disabled patients were identified as disabled by more than one disability measure. In larger population studies, the Index has been incorporated into interviews in a survey of the Health Care Needs of the Elderly and Chronically Disabled in Massachusetts (30), and in a national study of cerebral palsy in adolescence and adulthood in Israel (31). Such studies have contributed information which is useful for planning and policy making with regard to long-term care.

Contributing also to usefulness in planning and policy making is the observation that Index levels reflect service needs in terms of the type and amount of personal assistance. For example, all patients graded as *A* according to the Index in a study of hemiplegic patients had no nonfamily attendants and, by definition, received no assistance (4). Of these, 98 percent lived in nonprotective residences. With increasing dependence according to the Index, increasing proportions were found in nursing homes, hospitals, or custodial institutions. Of those in the most dependent level (*E, F,* or *G*), 95 percent received nonfamily attendant care and more were correspondingly in nursing homes or other protective institutions. Relatedly, among hemiplegic patients discharged from a rehabilitation hospital, 79 percent of those graded as *D* or more dependent at discharge were receiving nonfamily attendant care one year after stroke, while 45 percent of those graded as *B* or *C* at discharge were receiving such care after one year (8).

The hierarchical nature of the scale was reflected in the observation that the presence or absence of dependence in a single function, namely, toileting, predicted significantly different amounts of nonfamily assistance and entry into long-term care institutions. Comparative follow-up studies of ADL function among patients accepted and not accepted into a home care program contributed to a decision by the administrators of that program to test the value of its services experimentally and, on the basis of subsequent results, to modify its service program (4). A similar course of events stemmed from comparative follow-up studies of ADL function among patients discharged from a rehabilitation hospital (13).

The Index offers a measure of objectivity which has appealed to practitioners of medicine, nursing, and rehabilitation because of its relevance to patient problems. It focuses on functional deficits of major importance which could be improved by interdisciplinary team care. The Index can establish the status of the patient at the point of instituting therapy, can serve as a guide to progress during therapy, and can identify the point of maximum service benefit. It can serve as a basis for allocating service resources within service programs and can be incorporated into quality assurance information systems, both as an element in the classification of patient problems and as an element of broadly relevant sociobiological outcome. In addition to its use in service program planning and management, the Index of ADL can be used to obtain information which reflects needs and outcomes in populations, thereby serving planning and policy-making purposes. Its use in research has been well-documented; and the fact that the Index is objective and based on physical, psychological, and social principles has made it a useful device in teaching. Its broad foundation in methodological and applied experiences has led to its inclusion in contemporary systems for the profiled classification of long-term care patients (32).

REFERENCES

1. Commission on Chronic Illness. *Chronic Illness in United States.* Vol. II, *Care of the Long-Term Patient*, pp. 325-361. Harvard University Press, Cambridge, Mass., 1956.
2. Reed, L. J. The changing role of chronic disease. *J. Chronic Dis.* 1(1): 86-87, 1955.
3. Katz, S., Ford, A. B., Downs, T. D., and Adams, M. Chronic-disease classification in evaluation of medical care programs. *Med. Care* 7: 139-143, March-April, 1969.
4. Katz, S., Downs, T. D., Cash, H. R., and Grotz, R. C. Progress in development of the Index of ADL. *Gerontologist* 10: 20-30, 1970.
5. Staff of the Benjamin Rose Hospital. Multidisciplinary study of illness in aged persons: I. Methods and preliminary results. *J. Chronic Dis.* 7: 332-345, 1958.
6. Commission on Chronic Illness. *Chronic Illness in the United States.* Vol. IV, *Chronic Illness in a Large City*, pp. 66-67. Harvard University Press, Cambridge, Mass., 1957.
7. Staff of the Benjamin Rose Hospital. Multidisciplinary studies of illness in aged persons: II. A new classification of functional status in activities of daily living. *J. Chronic Dis.* 9: 55-62, 1959.
8. Katz, S., Ford, A. B., Moskowitz, R. W., Jackson, B. A., and Jaffe, M. W. Studies of illness in the aged. The Index of ADL: A standardized measure of biological and psycho-social function. *JAMA* 185: 914-919, 1963.

9. Katz, S., Ford, A. B., Chinn, A. B., and Newill, V. A. Prognosis after strokes: II. Long-term course of 159 patients with stroke. *Medicine* 45: 236-246, 1966.
10. Katz, S., Vignos, P. J., Moskowitz, R. W., Thompson, H. M., and Svec, K. H. Comprehensive outpatient care in rheumatoid arthritis: A controlled study. *JAMA* 206: 1249-1254, 1968.
11. Steinberg, F. U., and Frost, M. Rehabilitation of geriatric patients in a general hospital: A follow-up study of 43 cases. *Geriatrics* 18: 158-164, 1963.
12. Kark, S. L. Disease and disability. In *Epidemiology and Community Medicine*, Ch. 3, p. 35. Appleton-Century-Crofts, New York, 1974.
13. Katz, S., Ford, A. B., Downs, T. D., Adams, M., and Rusby, D. I. *Effects of Continued Care: A Study of Chronic Illness in the Home.* DHEW Publication No. (HSM) 73-3010. U.S. Government Printing Office, Washington, D.C., 1972.
14. Katz, S., Heiple, K. G., Downs, T. D., Ford, A. B., and Scott, C. P. Long-term course of 147 patients with fracture of the hip. *Surg., Gynecol., Obstet.* 124: 1219-1230, 1967.
15. Grotz, R. T., Henderson, N. D., and Katz, S. A comparison of the functional and intellectual performance of phenylketonuric, anoxic, and Down's Syndrome individuals. *Am. J. Ment. Defic.* 76: 710-717, 1972.
16. Stroud, M. Highland View Hospital W-120 Study. Cleveland, Ohio (unpublished manuscript).
17. Gesell, A., and Ilg, F. L. *Infant and Child in Culture of Today*, pp. 98-233. Harper and Brothers, New York, 1943.
18. Mussen, P. H., and Conger, J. J. *Child Development and Personality*, pp. 81-104, 110-111. Harper and Brothers, New York, 1956.
19. Gesell, A. *First Five Years of Life*, pp. 13-51, 242-248. Harper and Brothers, New York, 1940.
20. Almy, M. *Child Development*, p. 157. Henry Holt, New York, 1955.
21. Murdock, G. P. *Our Primitive Contemporaries*, pp. 56, 170-172, 270, 342. Macmillan Company, New York, 1934.
22. Miller, N. *Child in Primitive Society*, pp. 110-128, 196. Brentano's, New York, 1928.
23. Warner, W. L. *Black Civilization*, pp. 325-338, 475-483. Harper and Brothers, New York, 1937.
24. Krech, D., and Crutchfield, R. S. *Elements of Psychology.* Alfred A. Knopf, New York, 1958.
25. Havighurst, R. J. A social-psychological perspective on aging. *Gerontologist* 8: 67-71, 1968.
26. Kuhlen, R. G. Aging and life-adjustment. In *Handbook of Aging and the Individual*, edited by J. E. Birren. University of Chicago Press, Chicago, 1959.
27. Katz, S., Jackson, B. A., Jaffe, M. W., Littell, A. S., and Turk, C. E. Multidisciplinary studies of illness in the aged persons: VI. Comparison study of rehabilitated and nonrehabilitated patients with fracture of the hip. *J. Chronic Dis.* 15: 979-984, 1962.
28. Commission on Chronic Illness. *Chronic Illness in the United States.* Vol. IV, *Chronic Illness in a Large City*, pp. 375-377. Harvard University Press, Cambridge, Mass., 1957.
29. Akpom, C. A., Katz, S., and Densen, P. M. Methods of classifying disability and severity of illness in ambulatory care patients. *Med. Care* 2(suppl.): 125-131, 1973.
30. Branch, L. G., and Fowler, F. J. *The Health Care Needs of the Elderly and the Chronically Disabled in Massachusetts*, pp. 46-56. Monograph from Massachusetts Institute of Technology and Harvard University, Cambridge, Mass., 1975.
31. Margulec, I., editor. *Cerebral Palsy in Adolescence and Adulthood.* Project No. OVR-6-61, sponsored by the Vocational Rehabilitation Administration–U.S. Department of Health, Education, and Welfare, and the American Joint Distribution Committee Services in Israel ("Malben"), Academic Press, Jerusalem, 1966.
32. Jones, E. W., McNitt, B. J., and McKnight, E. M. *Patient Classification for Long-Term Care: User's Manual.* DHEW Publication No. (HRA) 74-3017. U.S. Government Printing Office, Washington, D.C., 1973.

PART 3

Some Applications of Sociomedical Health Indicators

CHAPTER 9

Health Indexes Sensitive to Medical Care Variation

Carlos J. M. Martini,
G. J. Boris Allan,
Jan Davison,
E. Maurice Backett

THE PROBLEM

A feature of much planning of medical services is our ignorance about the extent to which many indexes which are assumed to reflect the effects of medical care actually do so rather than reflecting other circumstances affecting the lives of the populations concerned.

This paper presents the results of a study which attempted to extend the limited area of current knowledge concerning the relative importance of medical care in the determination of outcome indexes. Only by identifying many more outcomes which are specifically sensitive to one or other aspect of medical care, and eliminating others, which respond most readily to changes in extraneous variables, can more effective decisions be made in health services planning. This is not to deny that indexes which are more sensitive to variation in socioenvironmental conditions are not valid measures

This work was supported by a grant from the United States National Center for Health Statistics, Department of Health, Education, and Welfare, to the Department of Community Health of Nottingham University.

of health status, but that for the evaluation of medical care, which is the main concern of the authors, interest must be focused on outcome measurements.

The general hypothesis underlying this project was that some indexes of health are more sensitive than others to variations in the pattern of provision and the resources invested. The essential points are:

1. Health can be measured in terms of outcomes which for most planning purposes are still expressed as mortality, morbidity, and disability indexes.

2. Health outcomes are affected by three main types of circumstances: health services, environmental conditions, and socioeconomic patterns.

3. The contributions of each type of circumstances can be distinguished and hence a weighting obtained.

4. Not all measurable health outcome indexes are equally influenced by all three kinds of external circumstances.

5. It is therefore possible to detect some which are particularly (though not necessarily exclusively) sensitive to different levels of provision of health services.

6. These indexes can also be combined into more comprehensive measurements, which would be less subject to random fluctuations and more able to evaluate the effectiveness of the care provided.

THE RATIONALE

The degree to which health outcome indexes are influenced by health services, environmental conditions, and socioeconomic patterns will be reflected in varying degrees of correlation between indexes and the three circumstances. Our rationale assumed that there is a meaningful real entity which can be seen in several normally distributed constituents, with health indexes as their proxy measures.

These constituents can be seen as the results of (1) random circumstances, (2) the differential provision of medical care, and (3) social, economic, and environmental factors. Average levels of the various constituents of health are chosen in order to minimize the effects of random fluctuations. The problem then arises of measuring "differential provision of medical care" and which are the most relevant "social, economic, and environmental factors." In a manner similar to that used to approximate "health," approximations to the medical, social, economic, and environmental constituents of the factors affecting health can be derived by the use of selected indexes. These approximations may then be analyzed to determine the sensitivity of outcome indexes to the provision of medical care and the extent to which there is incomplete separation of the main factors (i.e. the "overlap" or the collinearity effect).

RESULTS

A large number of variables measuring various aspects of outcome (dependent variables), facets of the medical care process, and sociodemographic and environmental characteristics (independent variables) have been extracted from the routinely published statistical sources for the years 1970 to 1972 in the United Kingdom. Many of these independent variables and all the dependent variables, relating to outcome of care, were standardized by age, sex, and diagnosis.

Since it was clearly not feasible to include indicators for all possible diagnoses and operations in the study, a number of criteria were applied to their initial selection and in the selection of age and sex groups. These were that the diagnoses should be firm, well established, and simple; the number of cases should be sufficient to enable rates to be calculated (this was the basis for the selection of age and sex groups); several types of health professionals should usually be involved in the management of the patient; the diseases should be important in economic and human terms and, preferably, costly in terms of hospital time and skills; and information should be available for the diagnostic groupings from the major sources of data. Seventeen diagnoses for both immediate admissions and all admissions[1] and four operations were selected. These are listed in Table 1. Only two of these diagnoses, Cerebrovascular disease and Pneumonia, were used in the last stages of the analysis, to represent the whole group.

On examination of the available data, it was concluded that the fifteen Regional Hospital Boards of England and Wales would be the most suitable units of analysis. The selection of these units of analysis necessitated aggregation or splitting of data, in some instances, as comparable areas of the country are not always used by the major government agencies collecting health and health-related information. The actual numerical values obtained by such manipulation of the data can only be approximations to the exact values and, for this reason, it was decided to convert the calculated values to ranks and use these ranks in subsequent analyses. Ranking was also used because in many cases it was uncertain which measure of central tendency should be used, and the values of the mode, median, or mean appeared to maintain the same rank order throughout the fifteen Hospital Regions.

The variables were grouped on the basis of a priori theoretical and substantive considerations. Among the 321 independent variables, one group represented Sociodemographic characteristics, a second group, Environmental pollution, and five groups various aspects of the medical care system, namely Community expenditure, Traditional general practice, Hospital resources and performance, Met demand,[2] and Efficiency of care.[3]

The 409 variables measuring final outcome were represented by five groups: Deaths under one year, Total mortality, Deaths in hospital, Multiple diagnoses (measures of care complication), and Certified incapacity (the latter comprised the only variables available as measures of morbidity in the total population).

[1] In the United Kingdom a large proportion of patients referred to hospitals with less severe diagnoses are not admitted immediately, but through a waiting list, which, in some cases, is of many weeks' duration.

[2] This group consists of hospital utilization variables which are population based such as outpatient attendance and discharge rates.

[3] This group comprises those variables relating to hospital activity such as time on waiting list and duration of stay.

Table 1

Diagnoses and operations selected for inclusion in the study

ICD Code[a]	Diagnosis
140-99	All malignant neoplasms
151	Malignant neoplasm of stomach
162	Malignant neoplasm of trachea, bronchus, and lung
174	Malignant neoplasm of breast
185	Malignant neoplasm of prostate
204-7	Leukemia
250	Diabetes mellitus
410	Acute myocardial infarction
411-4	Other ischemic heart disease
430-8	Cerebrovascular disease
454	Varicose veins of lower extremities
480-6	Pneumonia
531-3	Peptic ulcer (excluding gastrojejunal ulcer)
540-3	Appendicitis
550-3	Hernia (with or without mention of obstruction)
574-5	Cholelithiasis and cholecystitis
N820	Fracture of neck of femur
GRO Code[b]	**Operation**
410-1	Inguinal hernia repair
520-9	Gall bladder operations
441-4	Appendicectomies
893-4	Varicose veins operations

[a] International Classification of Diseases code.
[b] General Register Office's Classification of Surgical Operations code.

The initial stage of the analysis was concerned with determining the most "relevant" variables from among the large number selected in the first instance. In a preliminary analysis the outcome (dependent) variables were cross-correlated (using Spearman's rho) with each of the sociodemographic/medical care (independent) variables. Following the correlation analysis, it was possible to rank the variables in terms of their number of "large" correlations ($R \geqslant 0.7$). This enabled the most consistently relevant variables to be identified. However, it was recognized that the importance of a particular variable may be masked in a strict count of large correlations. Therefore, further criteria were also used to select variables based on their possible relevance in epidemiological and medical care terms.

The rank values for each of the fifteen Hospital Regions of 66 independent variables and 38 final outcomes so selected from the larger number introduced into the preliminary cross-correlation analysis were converted to standard scores and the correlation coefficients recalculated. On factor analyzing the two groups of variables separately, certain variables were found to be of low communality and were dropped from subsequent runs.

The environmental pollution variables were eliminated at this time as a separate entity. The manipulation required to generate pollution data for the Hospital Regions was considerable, and the reliability of the more recent data thus obtained varied from region to region. Even though the Environmental pollution variables frequently had a high predictive value for many of the outcome variables, the beta coefficient was often greater than unity, indicating some essential defect in the data. This view was reinforced by the finding of a correlation of 0.95 between these variables and others representing socioeconomic status. It was therefore assumed that socioeconomic status could be considered to include environmental influences.

After this further selection process, 44 independent variables and 32 final outcomes were retained. From factor analysis it was possible to identify clusters of variables within the three groups. The distinctive clusters conformed closely to the a priori groupings that had been used in the first stage of the analysis. Within the sociodemographic set, two subsets could be distinguished: "status" and "urbanization." The clusters and their constituent variables are shown in Table 2.

A principal factor analysis was then performed for each cluster; each variable was weighted by its factor score;[4] and the weighted variables were aggregated in an additive manner to form combined indexes representing as far as possible the theoretical dimension associated with each cluster of variables.

Table 2

Clusters and their constituent variables identified by factor analysis within the theoretical groupings of sociodemographic characteristics, characteristics of the medical care system, and measures of final outcome

Cluster and Variable	Factor Score	No. of Large Correlations ($R \geqslant 0.7$)
SOCIODEMOGRAPHIC CHARACTERISTICS		
1. Socioeconomic status		
Demographic:		
Lower quartile age of total population	0.8	53
Upper quartile age of male population	0.6	34
Socioeconomic:		
Households per car	-0.5	101
Socioeconomic group:		
Foreman and supervisors, skilled manual workers, own account workers	-0.9	91
Employers and managers	0.9	89

[4] The factor score for each variable is shown in Table 2. The number of large correlations associated with each variable is also shown in this table.

Table 2 (Continued)

Cluster and Variable	Factor Score	No. of Large Correlations ($R \geqslant 0.7$)
Percent of households having rateable values £100 or less	-0.9	85
Percent of students remaining in school after statutory school-leaving age	0.7	44
2. Urbanization		
Population per hectare	1.0	50
Percent of females economically active	1.0	50
CHARACTERISTICS OF THE MEDICAL CARE SYSTEM		
1. Community expenditure		
Executive Council expenditures on general medical services	0.7	73
Local Authority expenditures on social services	0.7	55
Total expenditures on health and social services	0.9	44
2. Traditional general practice		
Percent of general practitioners in solo practice	1.0	84
Median age of general practitioners	1.0	48
3. Hospital resources and performance		
Hospital manpower:		
Nurses and midwives per 10,000 population	0.9	52
Total hospital manpower per 100,000 population	0.9	49
General Medical Senior Hospital Medical Officer and Consultants per 100,000 population	0.8	54
Hospital inpatients:		
Average daily occupied beds per 1000 population	0.9	92
Obstetrics: ante- and postnatal beds per 1000 females aged 14-44	0.7	68
Teaching hospitals:		
Deaths and discharge as a percent of all deaths and discharges	0.3	57
Beds per million for:		
Malignant neoplasm	0.9	76
Hernia	0.8	74
Acute myocardial infarction	0.9	73
Peptic ulcer	0.7	72
Cholelithiasis	0.5	60

Table 2 (Continued)

Cluster and Variable	Factor Score	No. of Large Correlations ($R \geqslant 0.7$)
Malignant neoplasm of trachea, bronchus, and lung	0.9	53
4. Met demand		
Outpatient attendances per 1000 population	0.8	50
Discharge rate from hospital per 10,000 population for:		
Peptic ulcer	0.7	19
Hernia	0.5	16
All diagnoses	0.9	13
5. Efficiency of care		
Time on waiting list before admission to hospital for:		
Peptic ulcer	−0.6	10
Hernia	−0.8	31
All diagnoses	−0.7	21
Median duration of stay in hospital for:		
Peptic ulcer	0.8	42
Hernia	0.8	30
All diagnoses	0.8	34
Median duration of stay (immediate admissions) for:		
Acute myocardial infarction	0.7	17
Peptic ulcer	0.6	29
Cholelithiasis	0.6	11
Median time on waiting list (operations) for:		
Gall bladder	−0.8	33
Varicose veins	−0.8	28
Waiting time in hospital before operation for:		
Gall bladder	0.5	12
Duration of stay in hospital (operations) for:		
Varicose veins in males	0.8	17
Gall bladder in females	0.6	17
MEASURES OF FINAL OUTCOME		
1. Deaths under one year		
Infant mortality per 1000 live births	1.0	8
Perinatal mortality per 1000 live births	1.0	8
Neonatal mortality per 1000 live births	1.0	7
Environmental deaths per 1000 total births	1.0	6
Infant death rate for pneumonia	1.0	10
2. Total mortality		
Death rates (adjusted) per 1000 home population	0.9	8

Table 2 (Continued)

Cluster and Variable	Factor Score	No. of Large Correlations ($R \geq 0.7$)
Standardized mortality ratios for:		
Malignant neoplasm of trachea, bronchus, and lung in males	0.5	13
Cerebrovascular disease in males	0.9	19
Age-sex specific death rates:		
Malignant neoplasm of trachea, bronchus, and lung in males 65-74	0.3	20
Cerebrovascular disease in males 65-74	0.9	17
Pneumonia in males 65-74	0.8	9
3. Deaths in hospital		
Case fatality rate per 100 discharges within 48 hours of admission (all admissions):		
Cerebrovascular disease	0.3	1
Pneumonia	0.8	3
All diagnoses	0.4	3
Case fatality rate net per 100 discharges (all admissions):		
Cerebrovascular disease	0.8	3
Pneumonia	0.8	3
All diagnoses	0.8	2
Case fatality rate per 100 discharges within 48 hours of admission (immediate admissions):		
Cerebrovascular disease	0.3	1
Pneumonia	0.7	8
All diagnoses	0.4	3
Case fatality rate net per 100 discharges (immediate admissions):		
Cerebrovascular disease	0.9	3
Pneumonia	0.9	3
All diagnoses	0.8	3
4. Multiple diagnoses (complicated cases)		
Maternity complications: Abortions, therapeutic and other	0.3	6
Multiple diagnoses rate per 100 discharges for:		
Cerebrovascular disease	0.6	0
Pneumonia	0.8	9
All diagnoses	0.7	10
Multiple diagnoses rate per 100 discharges (immediate admissions) for:		
Cerebrovascular disease	0.7	3
Pneumonia	0.9	5
All diagnoses	0.9	4

Table 2 (Continued)

Cluster and Variable	Factor Score	No. of Large Correlations ($R \geqslant 0.7$)
5. Certified incapacity		
Inception rate per 1000 males	1.0	12
Days certified incapacity per 1000 males	1.0	13

The combined indexes were factor analyzed, and three factors extracted using the principal factor solution. (The total variance extracted by the three factors was 87.6 percent, being 39.1 percent, 35.4 percent, and 13.1 percent for Factors 1, 2, and 3, respectively.) An oblique transformation of these three factors still resulted in the correlations between them remaining almost zero so that they may be considered as being effectively orthogonal. This is important as no assumption was made of nonrelatedness among the theoretical dimensions.

Examination of the factor pattern matrix (Table 3) shows that Factor 1 appears to represent an urbanization/medical care dimension, Factor 2 a socioeconomic status/community mortality and morbidity dimension, and Factor 3 an urbanization/hospital mortality dimension. A number of the combined indexes are loaded on more than one factor. Thus urbanization appears to contribute equally to Factor 1 and Factor 3. Although socioeconomic status appears to be mainly loaded on Factor 2, it does also make some contribution to Factor 1. Of the outcome indexes, Deaths in hospital appears to be measuring a different dimension of outcome because, although

Table 3

Oblique factor pattern matrix of the combined indexes after rotation

Combined Index	Factor 1	Factor 2	Factor 3	Communality
Sociodemographic Indexes				
Socioeconomic status	0.42	0.82	−0.13	0.86
Urbanization	0.61	0.06	0.70	0.92
Medical Care Indexes				
Community expenditure	0.67	0.40	0.34	0.78
Traditional general practice	0.90	−0.02	0.20	0.87
Hospital resources	0.97	−0.11	−0.08	0.95
Met demand	0.91	−0.20	−0.26	0.91
Efficiency of care	0.91	−0.12	−0.06	0.83
Final Outcome Indexes				
Deaths under one year	0.20	−0.90	0.17	0.84
Total mortality	0.07	−0.94	0.25	0.92
Deaths in hospital	−0.19	−0.41	0.90	0.93
Certified incapacity	0.03	−0.93	0.03	0.84
Multiple diagnoses	−0.32	0.84	0.19	0.85

loaded on Factor 2, which is the main factor representing outcome, its largest contribution is to Factor 3.

A multi-stage regression technique developed by one of the authors (1) from a method of Mood (2) was used to partition the variance in each combined outcome index between the sociodemographic and medical care components.[5] The indexes constituting these two components are those shown in Table 3.

The bar diagrams in Figure 1 show the proportion of variance in each of the five combined outcome indexes explained by the medical care and sociodemographic components, respectively, and the joint contribution (collinearity) of these two components. The collinearity is a measure of the degree of overlap or lack of independence of the two components.

Each combined outcome index consists of a weighted combination of a number of individual indicators in which the weightings are the appropriate factor scores. If, within each combination of variables, there are considerable differences among the individual indicators in sensitivity to variation in medical care, which are not reflected in the weightings, the effect of those indicators more sensitive to medical care variation may be masked by those in which the relative contribution from the sociodemographic component is large. A number of individual outcome indicators were therefore selected for a similar analysis from within each of the five groups of variables which constitute the combined outcome indexes. The bar diagrams showing the partitioning of variance in each individual indicator between the medical care and sociodemographic components can also be seen in Figure 1 grouped with the representation for the combined index to which they contribute.

Deaths Under One Year

The proportion of variance explained in this combined index is 0.70. The contribution to the variance explained from the sociodemographic component is 0.36 compared to 0.25 from that measuring medical care. Thus sociodemographic influences appear to make a slightly greater contribution to this index of Deaths under one year.

The five individual indicators contributing to this index have equal weightings (see Table 2). Two indicators, Infant mortality per 1000 live births and Perinatal mortality per 1000 live births, were selected for further analysis. The contribution of the sociodemographic component to the variance explained in Infant mortality is more than twice that from the medical care component, while for Perinatal mortality the contribution from the two components is almost equal. As Perinatal mortality comprises stillbirths and deaths during the first week of life, this finding confirms what is currently known about the effects of medical care on infant mortality shortly before, during, and shortly after childbirth when socioeconomic and environmental factors appear to be of lesser importance.

[5] The term "component" is defined as a group of indexes and is not to be confused with the terminology used in principal component analysis.

Dependent Variable	Proportion of Variation Explained by: Medical Care	Proportion of Variation Explained by: Sociodemographic	Collinearity	Proportion of Total Variance Explained
Deaths under one year	0.25	0.36	0.09	0.70
Infant mortality per 1000 live births	0.18	0.39	0.06	0.63
Perinatal mortality per 1000 live births	0.26	0.29	0.06	0.61
Total mortality	0.14	0.56	0.05	0.75
Death rates (adjusted) per 1000 home population	0.29	0.24	0.01	0.54
Standardized mortality ratio : cerebrovascular disease in males	0.08	0.29	0.25	0.62
Age-sex specific death rate : pneumonia in males 65-74	0.07	0.78	-0.03	0.82
Deaths in hospital	0.37	0.65	-0.14	0.88
Case fatality rate : all admissions				
All diagnoses	0.56	0.30	-0.11	0.75
Case fatality rate within 48 hours : immediate admissions				
Cerebrovascular disease	0.11	0.03	0.09	0.23
Pneumonia	0.09	0.47	0.08	0.64
All diagnoses	0.17	0.08	0.00	0.25
Case fatality rate : immediate admissions				
Cerebrovascular disease	0.31	0.64	-0.12	0.83
Pneumonia	0.27	0.59	-0.10	0.73
All diagnoses	0.57	0.43	-0.07	0.93
Multiple diagnoses	0.50	0.13	0.16	0.79
Multiple diagnoses rate : all admissions				
All diagnoses	0.21	0.39	0.22	0.82
Multiple diagnoses rate : immediate admissions				
Cerebrovascular disease	0.37	0.01	-0.01	0.37
Pneumonia	0.63	0.03	0.06	0.73
All diagnoses	0.41	0.21	0.22	0.84
Certified incapacity	0.22	0.50	0.05	0.77
Days certified incapacity per 1000 males	0.29	0.26	-0.01	0.54

Figure 1. The sensitivity of combined outcome indexes and individual health indicators to medical care.

Total Mortality

The proportion of variance in this index of mortality explained by the medical and sociodemographic components is 0.75, which is slightly higher than that for Deaths under one year. Further examination of the partitioning of the variance between these two components shows that the sociodemographic component explains four times as much of the variance in this outcome index as the medical care component, indicating that the sociodemographic variables account for most of the variation in this index.

Three individual indicators were selected from within this group for further analysis, Death rates (adjusted) per 1000 home population, Standardized mortality rate for cerebrovascular disease in males, and Age-sex specific death rate for pneumonia in males aged 65-74. The proportion of variance in these individual indicators explained by the medical care and sociodemographic components varies from 0.54 for Death rates (adjusted) to 0.82 for Age-sex specific death rate. The partitioning of variance between the two components also differs markedly for these three indicators. The indicator, Death rates (adjusted), appears to be equally sensitive to medical care and environmental influences. The other two indicators in this group do not show a similar sensitivity to medical care. In Age-sex specific death rate for pneumonia in males 65-74, the contribution from the sociodemographic component is very large (0.78), which is probably reflecting deficiencies in the environment of the patients. The joint contribution of the sociodemographic and medical care components to the variance explained in the indicator, Standardized mortality ratio for cerebrovascular disease, is of the same order of magnitude as the individual contribution from the sociodemographic component, implying an incomplete separation of medical care and environmental influences for this indicator.

Deaths in Hospital

The proportion of variance explained in this combined index is high (0.88), but the contribution of the medical care component is just over half that of the socio-demographic. The collinearity is negative, indicating the existence of suppressor effects.

Examination of the partitioning of variance in the seven individual indicators selected from this group, shown in Figure 1, reveals first the existence of two distinct groups, namely deaths within 48 hours and all deaths (the latter group is divided into immediate admissions and all admissions). The former group, which describes the mortality experience of patients admitted as emergencies and dying in the first two days following admission, is characterized by a relatively low proportion of variance explained, a small contribution from the medical care component, and either a small positive collinearity or no joint contribution from the sociodemographic and medical care components. The relatively low proportion of variance explained, particularly in the case of Cerebrovascular disease and All diagnoses, implies that certain variables of significance in emergency admissions and very severe cases have not been included. These missing variables are probably related to the seriousness of the patient's condition, and not to the medical care system, as the distinct contribution of the medical care component to the variance explained is similar for the two individual diagnoses and for all diagnoses. The proportion of variance explained for these three individual indicators parallels the factor score weightings, shown in Table 2, which were used in the construction of the combined index, Deaths in hospital.

The remaining four variables selected from those contributing to this combined index are measures of Case fatality rates for all deaths (both before and after 48 hours of admission). The proportion of variance explained in these individual indicators is relatively high, ranging from 0.73 for Immediate admissions for pneumonia to 0.93 for Immediate admissions for all diagnoses. For the two specific diagnoses selected, Cerebrovascular disease and Pneumonia, the distinct contribution from the medical care component is less than half that from the sociodemographic component. The proportion of the variance in Case fatality rate for all diagnoses explained by the medical care component alone is the same for all admissions and immediate admissions. However, the contribution from the sociodemographic component is higher for immediate admissions and this also accounts for the higher proportion of total variance explained in this indicator.

Multiple Diagnoses

The combined index, Multiple diagnoses, is currently used as a proxy measure of case complication rate, albeit a crude one, as the additional diagnoses may be concurrent conditions and not necessarily complications affecting the principal diagnosis. This index appears to be most sensitive of the five outcome indexes to variation in medical care. The contribution from the medical care component is almost four times as large as the contribution from the sociodemographic component. However, it is perhaps questionable whether this indeed can be considered as a true measure of outcome. It appears to be more strictly a measure of process—a function of the available technology, the sophistication of the system of medical care, and the attitudes of health professionals. This is borne out by the pattern of the factors extracted on factor analyzing the correlations between the combined indexes, shown in Table 3. It can be seen that Multiple diagnoses is the combined outcome index that loads most highly on Factor 1, which is the factor representing characteristics of the medical care system.

Four individual indicators were selected for further analysis from the group of variables comprising this index. With the exception of Multiple diagnoses rate (immediate admissions) for cerebrovascular disease, the proportion of variance explained by the sociodemographic and medical components is higher, varying from 0.73 to 0.84. For the two individual diagnoses, Cerebrovascular disease and Pneumonia, there is essentially no contribution from the sociodemographic component to the variance explained. The contribution from the medical component is high for Pneumonia, being almost twice that for the other single diagnosis, Cerebrovascular disease. The partitioning of variance between the medical care and sociodemographic components shows a different pattern for immediate admissions and all admissions when calculated over all diagnoses. In the former case the contribution from the medical care component is almost twice that from the sociodemographic component, but, for all admissions, the reverse situation applies (probably, in the case of immediate admissions, for more severe cases, more intensive and dedicated care is common, which may mean that additional problems are more likely to be diagnosed). The collinearity is relatively high for Multiple diagnoses rate for all diagnoses for both immediate and all admissions, implying an incomplete separation into medical care and sociodemographic components.

Certified Incapacity

The only measures of morbidity that could be obtained from the routinely published statistics related only to the working populations and their days and spells of incapacity for work as certified by general practitioners. For the combined index, Certified incapacity, the contribution of the medical care component is less than half that of the sociodemographic component.

This index comprised two individual indicators. One of these, Days certified incapacity per 1000 males, was selected for further analysis. This indicator showed the same degree of sensitivity to medical care as the combined index, but the contribution from the sociodemographic component was almost halved. This reduction in sensitivity to sociodemographic influences accounted for the decrease in the proportion of variance explained.

DISCUSSION

It would be outside the reasonable length of this paper to discuss extensively all the possible implications of each individual finding. However, the overall results of this study seem to indicate that indexes constructed from the traditional outcome measures are more sensitive to variations in the sociodemographic circumstances of the population than to the amount and type of medical care provided and/or available. This seems to be especially true for those indexes, such as Infant mortality or Certified incapacity, which are community based. By contrast, those indexes such as fatality rates (especially Case fatality rate: immediate admissions for all diagnoses), which apply to care provided in hospitals, appear to be relatively more sensitive to medical care. Possible implications could be, first, that these indexes are not really measuring health outcomes, and, second, that health outcomes are even less affected by medical care than is currently assumed; or a combination of both could be responsible. However, before statements as condemnatory as these can be justified, it is necessary to consider the problems of validity and reliability of the indexes. This is a difficult area due to a lack of criteria external to the indicators themselves. The indexes used in our study are a function of the quality of the data input. The quality of the data used, although the "best" available, was less than perfect, if, for no other reason, than aggregation and splitting of the data were necessary in those cases in which comparable areas were not used by the agencies collecting this information. Deductions made from analyses of existing data, however complete, cannot, in a case like this, be a satisfactory substitute for those based on experimental methods, though they can form the basis of hypotheses. Experimental evidence is required both to sustain the hypotheses and to establish the magnitude of the cause-and-effect relationship between given factors. Causal relationships cannot be proved from the results of such a study; they can only be inferred.

The regression method is sensitive to the strengths or weaknesses of the material used. The more precise and detailed the observations, and the greater the understanding of the structure of the medical care system, the greater the confidence that can be placed in the conclusions. To obtain the best picture, particularly when regression analysis is employed, the numbers of units of analysis and of variables are of crucial importance. In our case, there was a need to obtain enough information (usually produced by different agencies) in as many units of analysis as possible. In our study only fifteen units were used, and possibly these are too few for an ideal use of multivariate analysis techniques. However, as incremental contributions to the variance were estimated rather than regression coefficients, a small number of units of analysis is less critical.

There were a number of theoretically important variables in both the independent and dependent groups which could not be incorporated because no information was available. These included survival rates for certain diseases, patient satisfaction, restoration of physical and social function, and also the amount of residual morbidity outside the hospital (Certified incapacity is not a good indicator of the amount of illness in the community). Indexes of health measuring disability presented a particularly intractable problem. There was very little information available and the local registers were incomplete and thus inadequate for our purposes. Among these missing variables were some that may have provided the most satisfactory measurements of outcome of care, but a population survey would have been necessary to provide this information. If special studies of this type were able to show that these missing indicators were strongly associated with the indicators measuring aspects of medical care, then a good case could be made for keeping augmented records routinely.

A possible fallacy which could be of importance and which has caused difficulty in previous social research is that the patients who provided the information for the outcome indexes may not have the socioeconomic characteristics of the resident population from which some of the independent variables were derived. In general it is assumed that utilization of health services does in fact vary according to social class (even within a health services system in which there is open access to medical care), so probably the patients are not a representative cross-section of the population. Conclusions are, however, drawn about areas and not individuals and it was assumed, in this study, that the extent of the discrepancy does not differ between the units of analysis.

To eliminate this difficulty would require either specific studies on the patients to determine their socioeconomic characteristics, or that such information should be collected routinely about each patient, which is not at present done in the study areas.

Most of the other pitfalls of the methods in this study have been mentioned as the relevant methods were explained. However, there is one further point that needs discussion: the combination of indicators which may have elements in common.

In a weighted combination of two indicators, which have a common element, the size and sign of the weightings must be taken into account in the interpretation of the combination. If both weightings are of the same sign, the importance of the common element is increased; when the weights are of opposite sign, the importance of the common element is reduced. For example, in the combination of Perinatal mortality (stillbirths and deaths within one week of birth) with Infant mortality (deaths within a year of birth), the importance of "deaths within one week of birth" is accentuated.

A different problem arises when studying individual indicators, one of which is included within the other: for example, the partitioning of variance in the case of hospital deaths within 48 hours due to cerebrovascular disease, and total hospital deaths (within and over 48 hours) for the same diagnosis. The variance explained for deaths within 48 hours is low (0.23) with the largest contribution from the medical care component (0.11), while the variance explained for total deaths is high (0.83) with a high sociodemographic component (0.63). Two separate issues are apparent in explaining the difference in the partitioning of the variance in these two indicators. First, the low proportion of variance explained for deaths within 48 hours suggests that the variables included in this study were not appropriate to the consideration of more urgent cases (for instance, no data on availability of intensive care units were included). Secondly, the contribution from the sociodemographic component is high for total deaths in comparison to that for deaths within 48 hours, indicating that, for those cases in which death does not occur within 48 hours, recovery is more dependent on sociodemographic characteristics (probably due to the different case-mix of these patients).

From these findings it would appear that the weakest group of independent variables may be those measuring medical care, while the socioeconomic/urban characteristics of the population are better described by the variables included in the sociodemographic group (this last type of information was mainly census based). This is borne out by the partitioning of variance in some of the other indicators of outcome.

At this point it must also be emphasized that although, in most cases, the "combined indexes" explained a larger proportion of variance, they were not more sensitive to medical care than all their constituent indicators. These combined indexes, however, have other advantages, as outlined previously.

After this necessarily brief review of some of the possible methodological shortcomings in this study, let us assume that these results may be expressing, albeit crudely, a real phenomenon. In other words, the impact of medical care on the indexes measuring outcome is only secondary to the effect of the sociodemographic circumstances of the population. This does not necessarily mean that medical care is not affecting health but that the traditional measures (with the possible exception of case fatality rates) may be inappropriate for use in at least part of the planning of health services.

Two very important stages in this planning process are: initially, the detailed description of the actual situation in terms of health status, and, later, after implementation of policy decisions, a periodic focused evaluation of the achievement of objectives.

The first analysis is based mainly on information on the frequency and distribution of health problems, and it is for this purpose that most of the outcome indexes analyzed in this study could be used. These indexes still remain the most readily available proxy measurement of health status of a community, and it must always be borne in mind that the events which comprise rates have an intrinsic value in themselves (for example, the death of a child) which goes beyond the statistical meaning of the rates. One must consider individuals (even single cases) when formulating social policy.

However, it is in the later stage of evaluation, mentioned previously, that a very important problem arises. To be able to evaluate the effectiveness and quality of our programs, it is necessary to focus on those aspects of the health-sickness process that theoretically can be affected by our efforts. This is where the value of many of the indexes used in our study is very limited. Most of the important advances of medical care in the last 20 or 30 years are related to the quality of life before death for which we do not have, as yet, any precise measurements. An example of this is osteoarthritis of the hip which seriously restricts mobility and produces sufficient pain to very severely disable the patient. In many cases regular analgesics are needed even when the patient is resting. However, since the early 1960s, an entirely successful operation can be performed, the arthroplasty of the hip, which changes those patients affected by this gross disablement into practically normal individuals. It is difficult to imagine a more dramatic improvement in the quality of life due to medical care. Measurements of improvement such as these are not to be found among the traditional indicators of outcome (case fatality rate of arthroplasty of the hip operations is only 1.2 percent).

This lack of appropriate indicators is even more pronounced in the area of primary medical care, only a small part of which is concerned with mortality, and where evaluation based on measures of morbidity does not give credit to the work of those health teams who are concerned also with the patient's social, emotional, and psychological well-being.

To conclude, it is important to emphasize that health is not fully describable in terms only of mortality, morbidity and disability, and it is probably in the search for new indicators of quality of life that the way forward lies.

REFERENCES

1. Allan, G. J. B. Simplicity in path analysis. *Sociology* 8(2): 197-212, 1974.
2. Mood, A. M. Partitioning variance in multiple regression analyses as a tool for developing learning models. *American Educational Research Journal* 8(2): 191-201, 1971.

PART 4
Sociodental Indicators

CHAPTER 10

Toward the Formulation of Sociodental Indicators

Lois K. Cohen
John D. Jago

Sociomedical health indicators for oral health may be discussed in terms of the following referents: (a) status of oral health, and (b) delivery of services related to oral health. One of the chief virtues of assessing oral health is that the teeth and surrounding structures are definite and relatively easy to observe, carrying with them much of their previous disease and/or treatment history. Of course, some oral conditions, such as dental caries, are easier to measure and provide more knowledge of past treatment than other conditions, such as herpes simplex, canker sores, or periodontal disease. But the oral cavity, being a distinct area of the human anatomy, is a relatively closed system which provides the researcher with a unique opportunity to obtain necessary clinical measurements which can act as validators for measures of normative or value-laden self-reports of oral health status or oral health history.

Viewed from this perspective, the most common diseases occurring within the oral cavity, those affecting the teeth, could be considered as paradigmatic of chronic physical disease for they reflect the life-style of the individual, have a multifactorial etiology, are largely or wholly preventable, and are insidious in onset and relatively painless, yet have acute stages. Like many chronic diseases, they incur low mortality, but their very commonness transforms them into an important economic, if not social, problem for the maintenance of a healthy individual.

STATUS OF ORAL HEALTH

The present paper describes existing oral status indexes and their uses. With the possible exception of indexes of occlusal traits, all of the indexes are morbidity indexes or describe conditions which precede morbidity. All represent provider assessments only. All were designed for community assessments by dental epidemiologists. None has been tested against variables measuring disability or dysfunctional behavior. Yet all have elements of usefulness for the researcher of social indicators because they provide a relatively well-defined basis on which to begin correlational research.

The distinct advantage of any index is that it enables summarization of diverse elements into a single meaningful concept expressed as a number. In the field of health, there seems to be no such single comprehensive index akin to, say, the national income or gross national product. Rather, there are profiles of indicators. Similarly in dentistry, there are several indicators, each summarizing a distinct disease or condition, but there is no single comprehensive index of total oral health. One of the problems is that the qualitative range of oral disorders is as incredibly diverse as the incidence and prevalence of such disorders are incredibly universal (1). A single summary indicator might serve little in the way of differentiating types of needs for dental care. Except in the case of malignant neoplasms of the mouth, victims of which have a low survival rate (2), oral diseases have little effect on life expectancy.

Weighting oral conditions other than cancer in terms of severity might have little significance in an aggregated index because each disorder is as severe as the next. Because everyone has some dental disorder, to a certain extent, dental disorders may be described as statistically normative. And because an undue loss of time from work or usual activity is not involved in most cases, Sullivan's disability components for an index of health (3) would not be useful. The definition of "undue" may be at issue since it has been estimated that in the United Kingdom, for example, 19 million hours of work were lost annually in travelling to, waiting for, and getting treatment from the dentist (4). It is intriguing to note that 19 million hours is less than half an hour per person per year in the United Kingdom. Whether this number is of sufficient magnitude to contribute to disability is an unknown since most of the relevant data have not been collected. Similarly, Chiang's model (5) could not work because it measures severity in terms of duration of illness in a year or as termination in death. Time in a year free of dental disorder may be totally inappropriate because the probability of one or another dental disorder existing in an individual, and certainly in a group of individuals, is close to 100 percent.

Three measures have been described which attempt to deal with the general concept of dental health. These are: the *Index of Dental Need* developed in the United States by Lambert and Freeman and coworkers (6); the *Oral Health Grading* used by Bulman and coworkers in the United Kingdom (7); and the *National Dental Health Index* (NDHI) which has been in process of development in Canada since 1958 for the purpose of studying national variations and trends in dental disease (8). The Index of Dental Need and the Oral Health Grading will be discussed later in this paper. The National Dental Health Index provides comparative data in four main areas: (a) relative prevalence of dental caries, (b) relative prevalence of periodontal disease, (c) relative prevalence of malocclusion, and (d) relative degree of treatment level. Definitions of 20 indexes of dental health are provided for the NDHI, but up to the present it has not been possible to calculate a Canadian national dental health index from a dental health survey of Canadian Provinces during 1968-1970 (9). The failure to produce such a dental index raises the question of whether or not a single dental health indicator is feasible or meaningful at the present time.

Dental Caries

Bodecker and Bodecker (10) introduced epidemiological indexes for caries when they formulated the Caries Index and the Caries Susceptibility Index. Perhaps the most widely applied dental index today is the DMF (D = Decayed, M = Missing, F = Filled) (11). This index describes prior treatment as well as needs for treatment and it may be used either for teeth or for the surfaces of the teeth. It is arrived at by examining all the permanent teeth in the mouth and making a count of the number of teeth (or surfaces) that are decayed, are missing (extracted), and have been filled, and then adding the individual frequencies together. DMF = D + M + F is a shorthand expression, not a mathematical one. It describes an additive operation that does not imply equivalence. It measures *two* processes instead of the usual *one*: disease and treatment.

Dental caries is an irreversible condition. Once it occurs in a tooth, decay usually progresses. If the tooth has not been treated, it is counted in the DMF Index as D (decayed). If it has been treated, it is counted as either a restoration (F) or an extraction (M). Technically, (M) is restricted to teeth extracted because of caries and does not refer to tooth loss caused by trauma, impactions, periodontal disease, orthodontics, or other causes. The DMF Index thus reflects the caries life-history or experience of the teeth. However, as noted above, teeth may be missing for reasons other than caries destruction. For example, sound teeth may be extracted to correct or prevent a malocclusion, and most tooth loss after the age of 35 is the result of periodontal disease. Therefore, while the DMF Index is a fairly reliable estimator of caries experience among young subjects, it is less reliable in adults. Indeed, Jackson (12) argued that the DMF Index ceases to be an effective measure of caries experience in patients aged 25 years and older, at least in England. Furthermore, adults tend to forget why or when a tooth was extracted several years after the event.

When the number of carious (D) teeth or surfaces is enumerated, a large component of dental need (i.e. a condition that requires professional treatment) is reflected. Filled (F) teeth reflect treatment; decayed (D) teeth reflect unawareness or neglect; and missing (M) teeth reflect neglect or treatment resulting in extraction. The latter may be expressed by the ratios D/DMF or DM/DMF. It should be stressed that knowledge of the total DMF as such does not enable an estimate of current need for treatment; for this, the D component must be known.

The DMF is the most common index in use today in public health dentistry. Modifications of the basic index, such as those suggested by Knutson (13), Smyth et al. (14), and Viegas (15), have also been used in dental epidemiology. There are other measures of some aspects of caries experience (number of lesions, number multiplied by size of lesions, for example), but they do not contain components of prior treatment along with treatment needs. There are, however, disadvantages in the use of the DMF Index. While it indicates prevalence, it does not indicate severity of caries. In order to overcome this disadvantage, Wagg (16) devised the Extrapolated Carious Surface Increment Index (ECSI) as a means of measuring caries progression. However, the ECSI is an index of caries alone; there are no treatment components in it.

A different approach in the epidemiology of dental caries was suggested by Grainger (17, 18). The method makes no actual count of carious lesions but employs a hierarchical system whereby individuals are assigned to one of five zones of increasing severity, on the basis of occurrence of caries or restorations in specified locations in the mouth. This method has been evaluated by Conchie, Scott, and Philion (19) and Poulsen and Horowitz (20).

Periodontal Disease

To measure disease in the supporting structures of the teeth is far more difficult than to measure caries. Periodontal disease involves three processes which are usually sequentially related although not necessarily so. These are inflammation of the gums (gingivitis), formation of pockets beneath the gingival margin, and loss of alveolar bone surrounding the roots of the teeth. Children rarely exhibit pocket formation or bone loss. Gingivitis is the easiest of the three processes to observe, and is a reversible process if good home care is practiced by the patient or following frequent professional care. Pocket formation, while not observable by surface scanning, is easily discovered by probing. It is usually irreversible and requires professional care.

Alveolar bone loss can be observed in radiographs, may be inferred by recession of the gums, is a component of pocket formation, and is usually not reversible, but may be stopped or slowed following professional care. Bone loss may be an indicator of past disease activity but not always of present disease activity. Since the greatest incidence of bone loss occurs later in life and people may have lost teeth for other reasons, the observed findings tend to be less accurate for the assessment of previous periodontal disease than is the case for the DMF Index in assessment of caries. Furthermore, while it is possible to measure need and previous periodontal disease activity with radiographs and other devices, it is not possible to measure past periodontal treatment accurately. The reversible nature of gingivitis following treatment usually leads to an underestimate of previous treatment. And while a gingivectomy would constitute some tangible evidence of previous periodontal therapy, it is much less observable and therefore less quantifiable than is a filling material in the case of caries treatment.

Within the past 25 years several indexes have been devised to measure the presence and relative severity of periodontal disease. Some of these indexes were developed for epidemiological screening of populations, others to assist the clinician in the ongoing management of the individual patient. All of them indicate current need for treatment, but the existence of several indexes highlights the fact that there is no one comprehensive but simple index available for periodontal disease. Some indexes measure only gingivitis: the PMA (P = Papillary, M = Marginal, A = Attached Gingiva)

Index (21, 22) and the Gingival Index (GI) (23) are in this category. The other periodontal indexes indicate all three disease processes; among these are the Periodontal Index (PI) (24), the Gingival-Bone Count (GB) (25), and the Gingival-Periodontal Index (GPI) (26, 27).

The Periodontal Treatment Need System (PTNS) proposed recently differs from the above indexes in that it expresses periodontal needs according to the type of therapy and the corresponding time necessary for providing the treatment (28). It thus establishes a basis for calculations of human power and costs. The PTNS classifies treatment needs into three procedures: Class A–individual hygiene motivation and instruction, Class B–scaling and elimination of overhangs, and Class C–periodontal surgery. Time averages for performing the different types of treatment have been estimated as: Class A–60 minutes per patient, Class B–30 minutes per mouth quadrant, Class C–60 minutes per quadrant.

The authors of the PTNS found a high association between age and PTNS. They speculated that the need for periodontal treatment in a population might be calculated directly from the age distribution of the population, provided that the endentulous distribution is known. It should be noted that the PTNS does not provide an index of need for treatment expressed numerically. It is an ordinal scale; Classes A, B, and C, respectively, indicate mild, moderate, and severe periodontal disease states. A broadly similar index to the PTNS is the Periodontal Treatment Requirement Index (PTR) (29), which assigns a severity score to six segments within a mouth but makes no estimate of time required for treatment.

An index which does not measure periodontal disease as such, but rather factors exerting a direct mechanical influence on the gingiva (including caries) is the Retention Index (30). This index takes cognizance of the fact that mineralized deposits on teeth surfaces both above and below the gum margin, ill-fitting margins of tooth restorations, and untreated carious lesions constitute a group of retentive elements which may lead to gingivitis. The theoretical interest of this index is that it combines elements of caries and periodontal disease.

Malocclusion

Malocclusion is the most difficult of all oral conditions to measure, not least because there are no clear definitions of what constitutes "malocclusion." From one viewpoint, dental occlusion is a feature of physical anthropology which varies in individuals just as does blood group or eye color. To what extent any particular occlusion may be labeled a malocclusion requires a value judgment; this is made on several grounds, the most important being cultural values such as body image and esthetics, anatomical deviations from morphological norms as defined by clinicians or dental scientists, and functional considerations such as not being able to masticate or enunciate well. Accordingly, the definition of malocclusion is not one to be made by orthodontic clinicians or dental scientists alone. The person with the malocclusion (the "patient") also has a role in its definition, explicitly or implicitly. Several workers have devised descriptive measures classifying various occlusal traits on anatomical dimensions (31, 32), but these do not necessarily differentiate functional interference or perceived treatment needs. Whether anatomical deviations interfere with function may depend on individual adaptability. Indeed, available measures for estimating the severity of malocclusion may be of more assistance to the orthodontist in differentiating "simple" treatment cases from more complex cases than they are for public health administrators who must differentiate among priorities for care. The recently developed Malocclusion Treatment Severity Index (MTSI) is being used for such a purpose of distinguishing between simple and complex therapy cases at the University of Toronto (33).

Thus, need for treatment is not an absolute concept in the area of occlusal relations. While orthodontic services are in many cases provided for esthetic reasons only, it is difficult to estimate the extent to which the arrangement of teeth in a person's mouth constitutes a psychological hazard. Some individuals actively participate in societal activities in spite of gross physical deformity while others are greatly concerned because they have minor tooth crowding. Which conditions are dysfunctional for the individual to operate in his or her environment becomes a subjective decision on the part of the patient, the parents, and the dentist. Precisely because this is such a subjective decision, malocclusion has not been deemed a public health problem in the great majority of places in the world (except possibly for New York State, which attempts to define "handicapping" cases) (34).

Because the social dimension has been diffusely defined, the value assessment attached to the customary descriptive clinical classifications may be described as one of low priority, a luxury for the rich, and perhaps even a status symbol for aspiring members of the middle class in the United States. Other societies may attribute other values to various occlusal relations, most or all of which are still unidentified in the literature. A five-year follow-up study of orthodontically rehabilitated cases suggests the possibility that such treatment may make some difference with respect to occupational rank, engagement and marriage, assessment of personal appearance, and anxiety levels. The small statistical differences, however, suggested to the researcher either that malocclusion does not often serve as a basis for social discrimination or that untreated persons compensate for their malocclusion in their role performance (35).

In an attempt at collaborative research between sociology and clinical dental epidemiology, a study was initiated to examine the perceptions of children with respect to occlusal appearance (36). These data were related to actual clinical measurements taken on these same children by standardized dental examiners. The results suggest that the preference patterns of children differ from the classification of severity formed by dental professionals, further suggesting that any specific occlusal condition needs to be studied in relation to the psychological impact on the patient and significant others, for nonclinical judgments by these consumers can and do modify the provision of the professional service itself. Other studies have found similar discrepancies between patient opinion and professional opinion (37, 38).

The indexes of occlusal relations available today still depend upon provider judgments typical, of course, of the indexes for all other oral conditions. Yet in the case of occlusion where esthetic judgment underlies the decision of the patient and the society at large regarding the extent of the associated handicap, there seems to be a salient need for the development of a tool containing appropriate social-psychological as well as clinical criteria (the former giving weight to consumer and other nonprofessional and professional perceptions). Once an issue is defined as a problem for society (as handicapping malocclusion has been in New York State), some effort must be made to measure that problem in the social or behavioral dimensions now appropriate to it. Thus, Draker's work on the Handicapping Labio-Lingual Deviation Index (HLD) (34) begins to define what is handicapping to the individual. It attempts to draw a line for the program administrator which may be adjusted to budgetary changes without abandonment of some degree of objectivity in clinical assessment.

Indexes of Other Oral Conditions

Very few other specific oral indexes have been developed. Methods for measuring the severity of enamel opacities and enamel hypoplasias have been described by Beck (39). Methods of classifying traumatic injuries to teeth have been devised for purposes of treatment planning, but not necessarily to take account of previous treatment. Dean (40) devised a seven-point nominal scale ranging from normal to severe to measure the mottling of tooth enamel which, however, does not have relevance to previous treatment. Subsequently, Dean (41) assigned weights to a revised six-point scale and calculated an index of dental fluorosis for population groups ranging from 0 to 4. There is a relationship between the index of dental fluorosis and the level of fluoride present in the community water supply. Dean's data showed that up to 1.3 parts per million fluoride could be present in drinking water and the fluorosis index would remain below 0.6. Dean (42) regarded an index of dental fluorosis of 0.4 or less as of no concern, but when it exceeds 0.6, it becomes a public health problem warranting attention.

There is one index which does not measure disease, but which was developed as a measure of oral cleanliness. This is the Oral Hygiene Index (OHI) (43) and a subsequent variant, the Simplified Oral Hygiene Index (OHI-S) (44), which can be regarded as the same index for our purposes. The OHI quantifies oral hygiene status by recording degrees of stain and debris on the teeth and the presence of calculus both above and below the gum margin. As an indicator of whole mouth cleanliness, the OHI may be used as a measure of dental neglect or the effectiveness of past personal oral hygiene practices. The component which measures debris reflects oral hygiene experience in the recent past (e.g. days and weeks). It does give some clue to the degree of assiduousness which the individual has applied in order to maintain the cleanliness of his mouth. As such, it is the closest epidemiological measure available with which to compare past and current dental habit patterns.

Another index for the assessment of oral hygiene behavior which is a refinement of the OHI is the PHP (Patient Hygiene Performance) (45). The latter was originally developed for assessing the effectiveness of a patient's education in oral hygiene. Basically, it is the same index though the tooth itself is subdivided into five sections for measurement in the PHP compared to three in the OHI. There are sometimes technical differences in the meaning of results yielded from the indexes but, in general, they both are to some extent measures of behavior.

There are no indexes for oral cancer nor are there reliable simple screening systems for this disease. The only definitive diagnostic procedure for oral neoplasms is the biopsy, i.e. the surgical removal of some suspected tissue for histological examination. Although exfoliative cytology (scraping off the superficial layer of a suspected lesion for cell examination) has proved valuable in stimulating professional responsibility for early detection of oral cancer (46, 47), it is not a foolproof screening method. In fact, it usually produces substantial false negative identifications (48). But biopsies, which are more accurate, are unfortunately impractical for field surveys because they involve surgical procedures.

The Index of Dental Need

In their study of dental care utilization and oral status of teen-agers in Boston, Lambert and Freeman and coworkers (6) developed a comprehensive multidimensional Index of Dental Need (IDN) comprised of the number of carious tooth surfaces, periodontal condition as measured by the Gingivial-Bone Count, and orthodontic conditions divided into those needing treatment and those which do not. The IDN was expressed not as a numerical value but on a nominal scale as low-medium-high.

The authors of this study stated that all of the measures of dental need are correlated with each other at the 0.01 level with the exception of the occlusion rating. They were not disturbed by the latter deviation; the reason they gave for this was that "severe malocclusions are relatively rare and largely hereditary." The IDN is a first attempt to develop a multifactor index of dental conditions. However, it does not take into account either the condition of traumatized teeth or the need for prostheses, both of which occur relatively frequently in teen-agers, nor conditions such as hypoplastic and fluorosed teeth. To be applicable to adults, an index of dental need would also need to provide for the full range of oral diseases and conditions both common and rare.

A further merit of Lambert and Freeman's study was that they were the first to associate the three basic oral conditions simultaneously with social and behavioral patterns. They classified the dental behavior of teen-agers into three categories (preventative, treatment, and neglect) which take into account the recency, frequency, and reasons for having seen a dentist. Preventative behavior describes a person who sees a dentist for check-up at least twice a year and has visited the dental office within the past 12 months. Treatment behavior characterizes three subgroups: (a) those who see a dentist for check-up yearly or less often, and have seen a dentist within the past 12 months; (b) those who see a dentist for check-up but last saw a dentist over a year ago; and (c) those who do not go for check-up but have had dental treatment within the past 12 months. Neglect behavior includes persons who do not go for check-ups and last saw a dentist over a year ago, and those who have never been to a dentist. Although the authors used the term Index of Dental Behavior (IDB), they did not put it in numerical form, or even on a low-medium-high scale, but only in the qualitative levels of preventative, treatment, and neglect.

These two indexes do not appear to have been used by other workers in this field.

Lack of uniform record systems and lack of comparability of dental examiners collecting the component data are obvious barriers to be overcome when trying to apply these indexes to another situation. In *The Clinic Habit* study (6), these problems were minimized by the use of a limited number of well calibrated examiners and a single recording system.

The Oral Health Grading

In their sociodental study of two contrasting urban areas in England, Bulman and coworkers (7) developed a measure which they described as an oral health index. They regarded it as "merely one step towards a satisfactory solution" to the compilation of an index of oral health which will take into account the condition of all oral tissues. In the Oral Health Grading, there are three main divisions: dental, periodontal, and prosthetic; and there are three grades for each of the divisions: good, fair, and poor. These workers asserted that more than three gradings leads to confusion in definition and interpretation, and less than three to lack of adequate information (except in the prosthetic division, where two grades suffice–satisfactory and unsatisfactory). A six-digit code, therefore, gives a measure of the oral health of any subject. The three divisions are referred to by letters, i.e. A (dental), B (peridontal), and C (prosthetic), and the three grades by figures–1, 2, and 3, or in the case of the prosthetic division, 1 and 3. Thus, an entirely healthy mouth would be classified as A1B1C1, while severe dental caries in an otherwise healthy mouth would be classified as A3B1C1. The British workers recognized two problems in the interpretation of the grading. First, that it provides a measure of oral neglect rather than oral needs, and second, that it is not possible to differentiate between denture wearers and others.

Under this classification, all subjects may be placed in one of 17 categories, which may be listed in a descending order of oral health. The British experience was that three-quarters of an adult population tended to fall into six categories, while at the other end of the scale another five categories accounted for only five percent of an average population. Bulman and his associates, therefore, regraded the 17 categories into a seven-point ordinal scale so that any individual could be assigned an oral health score between one and seven.

Bulman believed that such a score should accurately reflect the state of oral health, but pointed out that, with the exception of the extreme scores one and seven, the measure would give little indication of treatment needs. By the use of this seven-point scale, they were able to show that the oral health of the population of Salisbury tended to be better than that of Darlington, and that in both areas the oral health of women was better than that of men.

QUALITY OF SERVICES

Ultimately, the quality of services is judged on the basis of relative change in the status of oral health of a population before, during, and after services have been provided. The relationships between treatment and change of status of oral health are highly complex and much remains to be learned. Crude measures such as the ratio of restorations to extractions (F/M) or the percentage of teeth extracted have been used for several decades as indexes of dental treatment, computed from basic data available from annual reports of health departments. Such indexes do enable an administrator to make a rough evaluation of his service. For instance, the number of patients per day, coupled with frequency counts of the various kinds of services provided, enables an appraisal of the extent of comprehensive care rendered. The rate of completed cases is another measure of accessibility to care as an indicator of quality of service. The higher the fillings/extraction ratio, the more comprehensive the services might be considered to be. Comparison with the same categories of data for previous years may lead to conclusions as to whether the quality of care for the consumer group is improving or otherwise.

At least five treatment indexes have been devised to measure the extent to which dental caries is dealt with or not dealt with. Two of these utilize the complete DMF Index described previously and are accordingly applied to young or relatively young populations. They are the Care Index (49) and the Treatment Index (12). The Care Index is simply F/DMF × 100.

The Treatment Index (TI) is a weighted index based on three grades of successful treatment, namely, a filled tooth (F), which is the most successful form of treatment; a filled carious tooth (FC), which is less successful; and an extracted tooth (M), which is the least successful form of treatment. The weighting is purely arbitrary and Jackson's formula is

$$TI = \frac{3\left(\frac{F}{DMF}\right)\% + 2\left(\frac{FC}{DMF}\right)\% + \frac{M}{DMF}\%}{3}$$

Two other indexes do not use the whole DMF, only the D and F components. The Unmet Restorative Treatment Needs (UTN) is defined D/DF × 100 (50). The Restorative Index (RI) is the obverse of the UTN and is defined by F/DF × 100 (51). These two latter indexes for treatment of caries may be applied in communities of all age groups.

There is, finally, the Dental Services Index (39), which may be applied to individuals or population groups. On the individual basis, it is directly related to the cost of dental services (excluding prosthodontics) required to become dentally fit (assuming a standard schedule of fees). On a population basis, the index is directly related to the dental humanpower and physical resources needed to make the population dentally fit. The Dental Services Index varies directly with the annual caries increment of age-specific populations and indirectly with the amount of dental treatment received before examination.

An important question which has only recently been begun to be investigated is the relationship between long-term restorative care and tooth mortality in a community. Two recent English studies have begun to provide some clues. Holloway (52) analyzed data from surveys conducted by Gray, Todd, Slack, and Bulman (53) and Jackson, Murray, and Fairpo (54), and concluded that regular attendance for restorative dentistry postponed the breakdown of the natural dentition by five years. Lennon, Davies, Downer, and Hull (55) examined the prevalence and pattern of tooth loss from skeletal remains of a nineteenth-century British population and compared the findings with those reported by Gray et al. (53) for a contemporary British population. They found that for persons under 35 years of age, the percentage of teeth missing in the nineteenth-century population was higher than for the twentieth-century population for all teeth except the first molars. However, for persons aged 35 years and above, the differences for most teeth between the two populations were not significant. Comparisons of the data for two populations a century apart would suggest that modern restorative dentistry, at least in England, has not been effective for the older age group.

Technical aspects of quality have been considered which refer to the degree of precision and adequacy of treatment represented on the tooth itself, but these are strictly matters of mechanical perfection to be measured by the profession itself. Nontechnical aspects of quality such as thoroughness of the examination and diagnosis, referral of cases, skill in patient relationships, completeness and accuracy of record-keeping, and the like have been considered for study to a far lesser degree.

Beyond the unit of analysis of dentist and patient, there is the issue of whether the totality of the professional manpower in a given geographical area meets the needs of all people in that constituency. Quality of services can then be viewed as to whether or not there are available services, whether there is adequate access to services, and whether those services are acceptable to the consumers, providers, and administrators involved in service delivery. An example of this approach is shown in the grouping of available statistical measures prepared by a working committee on evaluation of dental health services convened by the Regional European Office of the World Health Organization (56). In that report, data from service records and evaluation surveys could be organized according to four concepts: effectiveness, efficiency, appropriateness, and adequacy. Thus, changes in the DMF Index in two points in time would be one indicator of effectiveness of a dental program. Costs in terms of expenditure per unit of work, per patient visit, and per patients completed could indicate efficiency. Appropriateness might be viewed in terms of cost effectiveness. Adequacy might be reflected in a series of percentages such as population group examined, population group needing treatment, population group treated, or population group with treatment completed.

Abramowitz and Mecklenburg (57) described the approach of the United States Indian Health Service (IHS) to the assurance of quality in its dental program. The IHS standards for acceptable quality are established as the minimum measurable levels which are considered desirable, attainable, and adequate as determined by those persons who must work to achieve the standards. In the IHS system, the standards refer to a level of health expressed as the frequency of acceptability per the total number of services provided, and the criteria refer to the conditions required to attain acceptability per service.

The assessment of the quality of dental care has also been the subject of the work by Friedman (58) on the Dental Care Index (DCI). Friedman based his index on the structure of the DMF, which he asserted could be applied to other dental diseases and could be used as the ultimate measure of the effectiveness of a dental health care program:

> For example, let D stand for any disease rather than just caries, M for failure of treatment, and F for success of treatment. The M or the F factors could be further modified by an R, or replacement factor. There are two main problems, however, with this approach. First, it is very difficult to define success and failure except in the absolutes of the presence or absence of teeth. Second, these factors are essentially end-results and do not adequately measure the process of treatment which is essential for the financing and organization of dental care programs. . . .
>
> The Dental Care Index combines both process and outcome features of dental care. Like other indexes, it is patterned after incidence, prevalence and severity, but of care, not disease. In terms of care, incidence refers to the initiation of care for the newly eligible population (primary utilization), prevalence to the on-going process of care (maintenance utilization), and severity to the extent or depth of care (scope of services and completion).

The DCI is quite complex. Its description contains features which estimate volume of services and costs for on-going and new programs, but are not necessary to the evaluation of the quality of the program. It does not measure the technical quality of care. For this purpose, Friedman developed a *Guide for the Evaluation of Dental Care* (59) as an adjunct to the DCI.

Other methods of assessment of quality of dental care are in use or are being developed. At a workshop on the evaluation of quality of dental care programs held at Asilomar, California, in March 1971, the general consensus was that no one index, particularly a simple index, will provide an absolute or even a relative measure of the quality of a dental care program (60). Schonfeld's comprehensive review of the literature on the evaluation of the quality of oral care systems (61) builds a strong case for mapping out detailed procedures for assessing all possible facets of oral care systems. He includes measures of the quality of education and training of dental manpower, evaluations of qualified active personnel, indications of the provision of oral care services themselves, and, finally, measures of ultimate outcome, health status.

TOWARD SOCIODENTAL INDICATORS

In the dental field, there is a unique research project in progress which attempts both to define quality in global terms and to relate these measures to oral health status indicators. In some instances, services in the dental field can be related to the need for services (see discussion of F/DMF). Using a record linkage technique, data on consumers' oral health status can be related to the services which consumers either remember receiving or for which evidence can be obtained by clinical examination of the oral cavity.

The example alluded to is from the protocol for the "World Health Organization/ Division of Dentistry International Collaborative Study of Dental Manpower Systems in Relation to Oral Health Status (62)" and represents that view of sociodental indicators which assesses not just the level of health of a population but a society's capacity to care for its dentally ill population. The purpose of the study is to examine structural characteristics, e.g. of nationally developed dental care delivery systems, and relate them to an outcome of services and needs. Structural variables are treated as independent variables. Dependent measures are not viewed as oral health status outcomes alone, for any of these could reflect differences not only in system features but in the natural environment as well (natural fluoride in water supply, nutritional patterns, genetic characteristics, etc.). Rather, the dependent measure is a ratio of services provided to need within that population, posing the research question of whether or not, or to what extent, dental services provided in a given society fill the oral health needs of that society. This reduces the risk of faulty international comparisons whereby mortality and morbidity rates may be the sole measures of health or disease without consideration of base line need or differential aspects of services. Treatments and services are not necessarily standard from one country to another. For instance, in some countries periodontal treatment consists of electronic massage and similar kinds of therapy, but in the United States an entirely different set of principles underlies treatment for the same disorders. When the country-specific services are related to the periodontal health needs of the respective populations, one might have a more accurate notion about the delivery subsystem for each society and the relative oral health status associated with that subsystem.

Mediating between the structural features of the systems (independent variables) and the outcome variables of service/need (S/N) are variables having to do with the efficiency with which the system operates. At what social and economic cost is any given ratio of S/N achieved? Thus, the monetary cost to the consumer, the provider and the administrative components, and the social cost to the society (reflected sometimes in out-migration of medical and dental manpower, or dissatisfaction with work or irregular, symptomatic dental visit patterns) are viewed not as outcome measures in themselves but as qualifying data specifying the condition with which the S/N level for that population is associated. The mediating, qualifying, or specifying variables represent *process*, while the independent variables represent *structure* and the dependent variables logically represent *outcome.* Outcome is a ratio of administrative activities (services) over measures of vitality (health status). This approach to measurement of outcome is not unlike an underlying premise of the Northeast Ohio Regional Medical Program, where the action program itself was designed to measure health services in relation to manifest needs of their target populations (63).

A word about the development of the dependent variable seems in order. The International Collaborative Dental Study was initiated for the purpose of supplying information to administrators concerning the type of system components which may be recommended for demonstration in their societies or in subgroups of their societies. The administrators did not say that they were striving for any particular given level of oral health status. Rather, they wanted suggested system components. It was the task of the research team to determine how systems and system components might be evaluated, which led to the formulation of the S/N ratio.

In order to find an appropriate measure, the research team tried to view the problem in terms of a health care system model with the principal actors, goods and services, and media of communication defined as specifically as possible. Given the listing of components for measurement, a hypothetical ordering occurred which facilitated hypothesis formulation. It then emerged clearly that the dependent variable was "oral health status." Some variables, such as services or treatment provided, were logically closer to oral health status than were others, such as cost measures or number of dentists. Thus, services were viewed as an "adjustment" (64) for the outcome measure. Dimensions of psychological or social well-being were eventually viewed not as outcome but as specifying conditions in the total schema. The idea was not to put all possible facts into the dependent variable, but to relate as many factors as appropriate to the dependent variable.

Of course, combining measures is an exercise and the usefulness of the exercise will be in the testing of the results. It is also possible post hoc to analyze the data using an Automatic Interaction Detection (AID) program (65), whereby a new ordering may be obtained explaining variance in S/N. But this protocol allows for sets of statistics to measure model parameters, which in turn may permit a deeper understanding of why our indicators vary from subsystem to subsystem.

INDICATORS OF GENERAL HEALTH AND ORAL HEALTH

Measuring health (or in operational form, the absence of disease) constitutes the raison d'etre of the present work concerning sociomedical health indicators. Such indicators, based on data collected at any given time, provide some measure of the present status of health (or the current disease state) of a population. And that status, wherever it may be pinpointed along a hypothetical continuum from disequilibrium to equilibrium, from total positive to total negative health, may be the end result or final outcome for the researcher, administrator, or policy maker. Status of health is an outcome of several social factors, including personal life-style and cultural and ecological factors, in addition to level of physical well-being. The addition of the social dimension to the indicator expands the concept to include a direct measure of normative interest. The social dimension enables the research data to be transformed and expanded for purposes of policy. Such value judgments about data on health status may be concerned with the degree to which health services provided in a given group or society are functionally optimum for that group or society. Defining dysfunctions and disturbances of usual performance are matters for personal, community, or national concern. For instance, a condition causing bad breath or body odor may upset an individual sufferer, and may be serious enough to spur the deodorant industry, but it still does not warrant national concern. This example illustrates a real cost to society, not an outcome in itself but a cost associated with a given level of morbidity in a society.

A final comment needs to be made with respect to the feasibility at this time of incorporating dental components into any global index of health. The weighting of dental components (which are rarely associated with either mortality or gross disability) with components having definite association with mortality or serious disability would obscure the issue of dentistry's cost to society. It costs a great deal to maintain a level of oral health in the face of these ubiquitous oral conditions. But though dental care has an impact on total health, it is one of low priority for many governments, insurance funds, and members of the human community. Perhaps dentistry's greatest contribution is in the degree to which dental care contributes to the quality of life. Dentistry's impact may be more a statement about the efficiency of a health care delivery system than it is an end result. Dollars which might be spent in lowering fatalities from other conditions are used instead for restoring teeth. This is not to imply that dollars should not be spent on filling teeth, for, if they were not, perhaps as many or more dollars might be spent on making and periodically remaking dentures, thus siphoning even more money away from illness with a life-death impact on society (to say nothing of the human cost involved in the discomfort of prosthetic appliances). Dental diseases constitute a case in which the behaviorally expressed impact on society cost that society more in social disability (i.e. inability to perform a social role optimally) than it does in absolute loss of life. Defining all the dimensions of that social disability is yet an incomplete exercise as evidenced by the Canadian Royal Commission of Health Service's attempt to view the relative magnitude of health problems, including dental health, in terms of their effects and consequences (66).

Despite the difficulty of assessing the actual impact of dental health, within the total scheme of health, dental health is a system in microcosm. Studying this relatively closed system may permit clearer definitions to be made about sociomedical health indicators, because there are a limited number of diseases and conditions with which to deal, to measure and combine into an indicator, and to match to behaviors. Thus, the research worker has a unique opportunity in dental health to polish the methodology for assessing social definitions for goals of well-being (67). Those goals, their measurement, and the eventual guarantee of equal access for all to them, perhaps constitute the essence of what has been called the "new social contract" (68).

REFERENCES

1. *International Classification of Diseases; Manual of the International Statistical Classification of Diseases, Injuries and Causes of Death,* Vol. 1, pp. 201-206. World Health Organization, Geneva, 1967-1969.
2. Adams, R. A. Epidemiology of oral carcinoma in Victoria, Australia. Abstract No. 15, Australia-New Zealand Division of International Association for Dental Research, 12th Annual Meeting, August 9-11, 1972. *J. Dent. Res.* 52: 569, 1973.
3. Sullivan, D. F. Conceptual problems in developing an index of health. National Center for Health Statistics, *Vital Health Stat.,* Series 2, No. 17, May 1966.
4. Moser, C. A., Gales, K., and Morpurgo, P. W. R. *Dental Health and the Dental Services: An Assessment of the Available Data,* pp. 26-27. Oxford University Press, London, 1962.
5. Chiang, C. L. An index of health: Mathematical models. National Center for Health Statistics, *Vital Health Stat.,* Series 2, No. 5, May 1965.
6. Lambert, C., Jr., and Freeman, H. E., with Dunning, J. M., Hughes, H. M., Maloof, E. C., Morris, R., and Taubenhaus, L. J. *The Clinic Habit,* pp. 45-53. College and University Press, New Haven, Conn., 1967.
7. Bulman, J. S., Richards, N. D., Slack, G. L., and Willcocks, A. J. *Demand and Need for Dental Care: A Socio-dental Study,* pp. 97-103. Oxford University Press, London, 1968.
8. *The Evaluation of Canadian Dental Health. A System for Recording and Statistical Analysis at the Community, Provincial, and National Level.* Canadian Dental Association, Public Health Committee and Research Committee, Toronto, July 1959.

9. *Dental Health Survey of Canadian Provinces 1968-1970. Results of a Field Trial of a Survey Method.* Published by Authority of the Honourable Marc Lalonde, Minister of National Health and Welfare, Ottawa, 1973.
10. Bodecker, C. F., and Bodecker, H. W. C. A practical index of the varying susceptibility to dental caries in man. *Dental Cosmos* 73: 707-716, July 1938.
11. Klein, H., Palmer, C. E., and Knutson, J. W. Studies on dental caries. 1. Dental status and dental needs of elementary school children. *Public Health Rep.* 53: 751-765, 1938.
12. Jackson, D. An index for assessing the efficacy of dental treatment in the control of dental caries. *Dental Practitioner* 11: 226-229, March 1961.
13. Knutson, J. W. An index of the prevalence of dental caries in school children. *Public Health Rep.* 59: 253-263, 1944.
14. Smyth, J. F., MacLachlan, J. S., and Pengelly, J. P. B. Simplified investigation into caries incidence. An interim report. *Br. Dent. J.* 116: 185-190, 1964.
15. Viegas, A. F. Simplified indices for estimating the prevalence of dental caries experience in children seven to twelve years of age. *J. Public Health Dent.* 29: 76-91, 1969.
16. Wagg, B. J. ECSI–A new index for evaluating caries progression. *Community Dent. Oral Epidemiol.* 2: 219-224, 1974.
17. Grainger, R. M. In International Dental Epidemiological Methods Series: Dental Health Evaluation, Level A Survey. *Manual No. 3* (first draft). World Health Organization, Geneva, 1967.
18. Grainger, R. M. In *International Statistical Classification of Diseases, Injuries and Causes of Death,* Vol. 1, pp. 201-206. World Health Organization, Geneva, 1967-1969.
19. Conchie, J. M., Scott, K. L., and Philion, J. J. A simplified method of determining a population's needs for dental treatment. *J. Public Health Dent.* 31: 84-95, Spring 1971.
20. Poulsen, S., and Horowtiz, H. S. An evaluation of a hierarchical method of describing the pattern of dental caries attack. *Community Dent. Oral Epidemiol.* 2: 7-11, 1974.
21. Schour, I., and Massler, M. Prevalence of gingivitis in young adults. *J. Dent. Res.* 27: 733-734, 1946.
22. Massler, M. The P-M-A Index for the assessment of gingivitis. *J. Periodontol.* 38: 592-598, 1967.
23. Löe, H., and Silness, J. Periodontal disease in pregnancy. I. Prevalence and severity. *Acta Odontol. Scand.* 21: 533-551, 1963.
24. Russell, A. L. A system of classification and scoring for prevalence surveys of periodontal disease. *J. Dent. Res.* 35: 350-359, 1956.
25. Dunning, J. M., and Leach, L. B. Gingival-bone count: A method for epidemiological study of periodontal disease. *J. Dent. Res.* 39: 506-513, 1960.
26. O'Leary, T. J., Gibson, W. A., Shannon, I. L., Schuessler, C. F., and Nabers, C. L. A screening examination for detection of gingival and periodontal breakdown and local irritants. United States Air Force School of Aerospace Medicine, Technical Documentary Report 63-51, July 1963. *Periodontics* 1: 167, 1963.
27. O'Leary, T. The periodontal screening examination. *J. Periodontol.* 38: 617-624, 1967.
28. Bellini, H. T., and Gjermo, P. Application of the periodontal treatment need system (PTNS) in a group of Norwegian industrial employees. *Community Dent. Oral Epidemiol.* 1: 22-29, 1973.
29. Newcomb, G. M. Periodontal treatment requirements of a group of defense forces' personnel. *Aust. Dent. J.* 20: 183-186, June 1975.
30. Bjorby, A., and Löe, H. The relative significance of different local factors in the initiation and development of periodontal inflammation. Scandinavian Symposium in Periodontology 1966, Abstract No. 20. *J. Periodont. Res.* 2: 76-77, 1967.
31. Jago, J. D. The epidemiology of dental occlusion: A critical appraisal. *J. Public Health Dent.* 34: 80-93, 1974.
32. F. D. I. Commission on Classification and Statistics for Oral Conditions. Working Group 2 on Dentofacial Anomalies, 1969-72. A method for measuring occlusal traits. *Int. Dent. J.* 23: 530-537, 1973.
33. Fisk, R. O., and Wilson, R. E. Selection of patients amenable to simple orthodontic procedure using a malocclusion treatment severity index. *Canadian Dental Association Journal* 39: 468-471, 1973.
34. Draker, H. L. Handicapping labio-lingual deviations: A proposed index for public health purposes. *Am. J. Orthod.* 46: 295-305, 1960.
35. Rutzen, S. R. The social importance of orthodontic rehabilitation: Report of a five year follow-up study. *J. Health Soc. Behav.* 14: 233-240, 1973.

36. Horowitz, H. S., Cohen, L. K., and Doyle, J. Occlusal relations in children in an optimally fluoridated community: IV. Clinical and social-psychological findings. *Angle Orthodontist* 42: 189-201, 1971.
37. Howitt, J. W., Stricker, G., and Henderson, R. Eastman Esthetic Index. *N. Y. State Dent. J.* 33: 215-220, 1967.
38. Kean, M. R., Harkness, E. M., and Koskinen, L. K. Malocclusion in Dunedin schoolchildren. Abstracts No. 11 and 12, New Zealand Section of International Association for Dental Research, 9th Annual Meeting. *J. Dent. Res.* 52: 584-585, 1973.
39. Beck. D. J. *Dental Health Status of the New Zealand Population in Late Adolescence and Young Adulthood.* Department of Health Special Report, Series No. 29, Government Printer, Wellington, N. Z., 1968.
40. Dean, H. T. Classification of mottled enamel diagnosis. *JADA* 21: 1421-1426, 1934.
41. Dean, H. T. Chronic endemic dental fluorosis (mottled enamel). In *Dental Science and Dental Art,* edited by S. M. Gordon, pp. 387-414. Lea and Febiger, Philadelphia, 1938.
42. Dean, H. T. The investigation of physiological effects by the epidemiological method. In *Fluorine and Dental Health,* edited by F. R. Moulton, pp. 23-31. American Association for the Advancement of Science, Washington, D. C., 1942.
43. Greene, J. C., and Vermillion, J. R. The oral hygiene index–A method for classifying oral hygiene status. *J. Am. Dent. Assoc.* 61: 172-179, 1960.
44. Greene, J. C., and Vermillion, J. R. The simplified oral hygiene index. *J. Am. Dent. Assoc.* 68: 7-13, 1964.
45. Podshadley, A. G., and Haley, J. V. A method for evaluating oral hygiene performance. *Public Health Rep.* 83: 259-264, 1968.
46. Cohen, L. K. Dentists and oral cytology. *JADA* 74: 967-970, 1967.
47. Cohen, L. K. Reaching practitioners by mail: An experiment in dissemination of a dental innovation. *Public Health Rep.* 81: 735-741, 1966.
48. Folsom, T. C., White, C. P., Bromer, L., Canby, H. F., and Garrington, G. E. Oral exfoliative study. Review of the literature and report of a three-year study. *Oral Surg.* 33: 61-74, 1972.
49. Walsh, J. International patterns of oral health care–The example of New Zealand. *New Zealand Dental Journal* 66: 143-152, April 1970.
50. Gluck, G. M., Knox, C. D., Glass, R. L., and Wolfman, M. Dental health of Puerto Rican migrant workers. *Health Services and Mental Health Administration Reports* 87: 456-460, May 1972.
51. Jackson, D. Measuring restorative dental care in communities. *Br. Dent. J.* 134: 385-388, May 1, 1973.
52. Holloway, P. J. The success of restorative dentistry? *Int. Dent. J.* 25: 26-30, March 1975.
53. Gray, P. G., Todd, J. E., Slack, G. L., and Bulman, J. S. *Adult Dental Health in England and Wales in 1968.* Her Majesty's Stationery Office, London, 1970.
54. Jackson, D., Murray, J. J., and Fairpo, C. G. Regular dental care in dentate persons: An assessment. *Br. Dent. J.* 135: 59-63, July 17, 1973.
55. Lennon, M. A., Davies, R. M., Downer, M. C., and Hull, P. S. Tooth loss in a 19th century British population. *Arch. Oral Biol.* 19: 511-516, July 1974.
56. *Planning and Evaluating Dental Health Services.* World Health Organization, Regional Office for Europe, Copenhagen, 1972.
57. Abramowitz, J., and Mecklenburg, R. E. Quality of care in dental practice: The approach of the Indian Health Service. *J. Public Health Dent.* 32: 90-99, 1971.
58. Friedman, J. W. Non-clinical assessment of clinical care: The Dental Care Index. In *Report of the 23rd National Dental Health Conference,* Chicago, April 24-26, 1972, pp. 420-438. American Dental Association, Chicago.
59. Friedman, J. R. *A Guide for the Evaluation of Dental Care.* University of California, School of Public Health, Los Angeles, 1972.
60. Schoen, M. H., editor. The Evaluation of the Quality of Dental Care Programs. Summary of Workshop, Asilomar, Calif., March 1971.
61. Schonfield, H. K. Evaluation of the quality of oral care systems. In *Oral Health, Dentistry and the American Public: The Need for an Improved Oral Care Delivery System,* edited by W. E. Brown, University of Oklahoma Press, pp. 229-278, Norman, Oklahoma, 1974.
62. World Health Organization/Division of Dentistry International Collaborative Study of Dental Manpower Systems in Relation to Oral Health Status. Dental Unit, World Health Organization, Geneva, Switzerland, 1972.

63. *Northeast Ohio Regional Medical Program: Part II. Health Related Data. Section IV. Hospital Discharge Study,* p. 25. Northeast Regional Medical Program, Cleveland, Ohio 1968.
64. Bice, T. W. Comments on health indicators: Methodological perspectives. *Int. J. Health Serv.* 6(3): 509-520, 1976.
65. Andersen, R., Smedby, B., and Eklund, G. Automatic Interaction Detector program for analyzing health survey data. *Health Serv. Res.* 6: 165-183, 1971.
66. Kohn, R. *The Health of the Canadian People,* pp, 283-297. Royal Commission on Health Services, Queen's Printer, Ottawa, Canada, 1967.
67. Patrick, D. L., Bush, J. W., and Chen, M. M. *Toward an Aperceptional Definition of Health.* Health Index Project, Department of Community Medicine, University of California, San Diego, July 1972.
68. Social futures relating to health care delivery. *Center Report,* Center for Study of Democratic Institutions, pp. 14-15, February 1973. Fund for the Republic, Santa Barbara, California.

PART 5
Perspectives

CHAPTER 11

Comments On Health Indicators: Methodological Perspectives

Thomas W. Bice

Current interest in developing health indicators is one manifestation of what Sheldon and Freeman have termed the "social indicators movement" (1). Bertram Gross (2, 3) one of its founders and persistent spokesmen, argued in 1965 that social policy in the United States was being informed and guided by a lopsided array of quantitative information. Symptomatic of the "new philistinism" he observed was an imbalance of information due to the ready availability of varieties of economic indicators and the paucity of "transeconomic" indicators, a situation which reinforced the natural tendency of our acquisitive and economically competitive society to equate social policy with economic policy. To remedy this imbalance, a plea was voiced for the collection, reporting, and use of more "transeconomic" information, i.e. social indicators. His recommendations, joined with others inside and outside of government, gave impetus to the movement, whose most visible signs at present are symposia, publications, and suggestions about how to proceed (for a bibliography of these materials, see reference 4).

The vision of the future that motivates participation in the movement is that of a highly rational and compassionate society whose allocations of scarce resources are based on directions indicated by "social accounts." The basic elements of these are to be social indicators, quantitative measures that describe the society's "social health," as economic indicators describe its economic vitality. Just as such measures

This article was prepared for the Seminar on Health Indicators, Columbia University, August 1973. The author holds a Career Development Award [5-K02-HS-337775] from the National Center for Health Services Research, U. S. Department of Health, Education, and Welfare.

as the gross national product, labor force participation, wholesale price indexes, the Dow Jones averages, and others monitor the pulse of the economy, indicators of educational attainment, health, welfare, morale, and others will be employed to describe, evaluate, and project social well-being.

Proponents of social accounts and social indicators envision their application at several levels of policy making, and include among their functions: (a) description of the social state of society, (b) evaluation of the performance of social organizations and institutions, (c) anticipation of future trends, (d) indication of policy directions, and (e) guidance of social research (5). Thus, social indicators are to be the data that inform us about what is, why it is, what it will be, how it might be different, and what else we should know about a variety of things social, ranging from education and health to the arts and leisure. The least exacting in the movement will be satisfied when the requisite data become a part of the ongoing information-gathering and reporting apparatus of society; the visionary foresee the day when social policy will be made somewhere between the input terminals and printers of computers.

To date, the hopes and promises of advocates of social indicators have not resulted in significant changes in our nation's social bookkeeping. Several proposals have been advanced for minor improvements in the collection and reporting of various data, and several "GNP-like" indexes have been constructed which purport to summarize essential elements of various social conditions. Reviewing the stock of such indexes in the health sector, we are inclined to side with Sheldon and Freeman (1) in the observation that the movement is producing vague conceptions of what social indicators are and exaggerated claims of their utility. Furthermore, we concur with their view that much of the current effort in the social indicators movement should be redirected toward solving fundamental conceptual and methodological problems that stand between the present capabilities of social science and the ends to which the more optimistic aspire.

The purpose of this paper is to examine some of the critical conceptual and methodological problems in the construction of one type of social indicator, namely, *health indicators*. Specifically, we contrast views about what social (or health) indicators should indicate, and discuss some of the problems involved in constructing an indicator of health status that will serve the putative purposes of social indicators.

WHAT SHOULD SOCIAL INDICATORS INDICATE?

Although their advocates agree that more and better social data are needed, there is little agreement about what social indicators should measure. Some propose that they should be confined to measures of *outputs* of social subsystems; others contend that social indicators should be devised to measure all significant aspects of various subsystems as determined by theoretical models. The narrower output-oriented conception is illustrated by the definition of social indicators that guided the selection of data in the Department of Health, Education, and Welfare-commissioned *Toward a Social Report* (6):

> A social indicator . . . may be defined to be a statistic of direct normative interest which facilitates concise, comprehensive and balanced judgments about the condition of major aspects of society. It is in all cases a *direct measure of welfare* and is subject

> to the interpretation that, if it changes in the "right" direction, while other things remain equal, things have gotten better, or people are "better off." *Thus statistics on the numbers of doctors or policemen could not be social indicators, whereas figures on health or crime could be* [emphasis added].

Wilbur Cohen, while Secretary of Health, Education, and Welfare, advanced a similar conception of social indicators as "statistics which indicate clearly and precisely present conditions in our society, including, for example, the magnitude of existing social problems and their rate of change" (7). While noting that other types of statistics are also needed by policy makers, he excluded them from the class of social indicators.

The output-oriented conception of indicators is consistent with the tendency among many to equate "health indicators" with "health status indicators." For instance, among Gross and Springer's suggestions for needed data (8), better uses of existing information, and work on various social indicators, entries for health indicators include only measures of health. Specifically, they recommend "more refined surveys of mortality and life expectancy by income groups and by localities–including major slum areas; readjustment of 'Cause of Death' data, with improved interpretation; and more research on the development of positive measures of health and vitality."

It is not surprising to find that proponents of the output definition are likely to have relatively limited aspirations for its use. Gross and Springer (8), for instance, are arguing primarily for greater consideration of social indicators in policy making within a traditional political process, not for the abandonment of the process in favor of complete managerial rationality. It would seem, however, that definitions of social indicators restricted to output measures contain logical contradictions which, strictly interpreted, would greatly diminish their utility in policy making. The definition cited from *Toward a Social Report,* for instance, denies, or at least grossly understates, the possibility that output measures are causally related to other things to which people attach value. According to this definition, changes in health status indicators occurring in the "right" direction signal improvement only when "other things remain equal." Thus, if health status indicators move upward over time, while use of medical services (which is not a health indicator) also increases, we presumably conclude that things have not "gotten better." Similarly, we presumably conclude that a person is "better off" after having spent his last dime to purchase an increment of better health as measured by a health status indicator. Clearly, output-oriented health indicators would permit only absolute decisions by policy makers, when, in principle, allocations of scarce resources are made on the margin (9). Marginal decision making, however, requires more than output information; it also incorporates data about ratios or marginal costs of alternative factors of production. Rational choices among various courses of action to improve health demand not only knowledge of whether health is improving or deteriorating, but also information about why changes are occurring.

Recognizing the limitations of output measures, Land (10) has argued for a broader conceptualization of social indicators. He proposes that

> the term *social indicators* refers to social statistics that 1) are components in a social system model . . . or of some segment or process thereof, 2) can be collected and analyzed at various times and accumulated into a time-series, and 3) can be aggregated or disaggregated to levels appropriate to the specification of the model.

This formulation includes two improvements over the output-oriented conception. First, it admits input as well as output statistics to the set of social indicators; second, it provides a criterion for classifying a statistic as a social indicator, namely, its "*informative value* which derives from its empirically verified nexus in a conceptualization of a social process" (10). Thus, health indicators would, according to this perspective, be neither solely health status indicators nor only disembodied statistics describing health manpower, use of health services, health care expenditures, and the like. Instead, they would comprise sets of statistics that measure the parameters of a health services system model (for an attempt to devise a model of the health sector, see reference 11). These might include input statistics describing the stock personnel and facilities, supply of services, and availability of funds; intermediate production and consumption indicators such as utilization rates, drug consumption and the acquisition of health information; environmental and other hazards to health such as air pollution levels, cigarette consumption, and caloric intake; and, finally, output measures such as mortality rates, prevalence of disabling conditions, illness days per year, emotional stability, and others.

Viewing social indicators from this perspective, it becomes apparent that two sets of criteria are employed in selecting indicators. Choices among output measures are made primarily by political institutions, which transform social values into expressions of social policy (12). Answers to questions such as what levels of infant mortality are "acceptable," how many days of illness per person per year are "tolerable," and the like cannot be determined by purely scientific means. (Strictly speaking, answers that could be provided by empirical research were mortality and morbidity conceptualized as causes of another output, say happiness.) However, the choice of other health indicators–inputs, production and consumption factors, health hazard statistics–is an inherently empirical and thereby scientific matter.[1] Once society's health objectives are formulated by its political process (which hopefully incorporates objective information derived from competing definitions of "health"), the selection of health indicators beyond those that measure outputs must ultimately be guided by a theory of what causes variations in output indicators (for an example, see Blalock's discussion of the causal approach to measurement of discrimination (13)). Seen from this perspective, measurement problems of social indicators lose their mystique and uniqueness: our measurement of a particular indicator will improve and its utility in policy making will be enhanced in proportion to advancements in our theoretical understanding of its causes and effects (14).

Once most of the crucial parameters in a model are specified, even the more advanced uses of social indicators–projection, evaluation, and simulation–become feasible. Unfortunately, the present store of knowledge of why health levels vary among population groups and over time is insufficient to construct models of well-specified state and rate equations. (For a purely hypothetical simulation of this type of modeling, see reference 15.) To hasten the arrival of this type of model, consider-

[1] Sheldon and Freeman's argument that the selection of indicators is an inherently value-laden process and that social indicators do not "make social policy development any more objective" overlooks this point (1).

able effort must be devoted to the conceptualization and measurement of output health indicators on the basis of at least partial theories of the causes of their variations.

THE CURRENT STATUS OF HEALTH INDICATORS

Assuming that a set of health indicators is comprised of politically and socially defined output measures and their scientifically determined causes, it is somewhat fruitless to discuss inputs and outputs separately (except, of course, in regard to formal characteristics such as reliabilities and validities). The state of the art in health indicators development and, therefore, their utility for policy makers, are associated with the degrees of certainty that can be attached to both expressions of values and statements of cause-effect relationships.

These are, in Thompson's words, "the *basic variables* of decision" (16). The most advanced state of decision making is achieved when there is certainty regarding both preferences for desired outcomes (i.e. a value consensus) and knowledge about cause-effect relationships. In such circumstances, decisions are based on a computational strategy, or what Simon (17) terms a "programmed decision." The worst of all worlds for those who deal in indicators is one in which there exist no consensus regarding desired outcomes and only meager knowledge about cause-effect relationships among contending formulations. Lacking these, one cannot be confident that results of his modeling efforts (which will be highly imperfect) are being directed toward socially and politically relevant outcomes. A rational first step in such situations would be to encourage agreement about desired outcomes, after which focused scientific search for causes could be pursued. In the health field, one might begin by determining what society wants and what the relative priorities are. With this knowledge, relevant indicators of health status could be devised and revised as priorities change and as information about causes of variations in health status accumulates.

This sequence has not occurred to any significant degree within the health indicators branch of the social indicators movement. Owing in large part to the lack of national health policy stated in operational language, researchers have fashioned a plethora of outcome indicators of varying relevance to current or potential social policy. This is, of course, not wholly undesirable: data about health status derived from various conceptions of health may focus attention on conditions and aspirations that might go unnoticed were researchers only to slavishly pursue official goals established by policy makers.

Recognizing that the line between this potentially desirable pluralism of intellectual effort and unproductive, piecemeal chaos is not easily drawn, it is our view that much effort is currently misplaced, especially with respect to two trends in this area. One is the effort to devise a *single* concise, quantitative, GNP-like expression of health status; the other is the attempt to move prematurely from indicators of "negative health" to others that signify "positive health." Certainly, conceptual and methodological efforts to devise parsimonious expressions of health status and to prepare for the day when society's major health problems will be due to lack of vitality rather than physical disease are intellectually exciting and may yet prove pragmatically useful in the long run. For the shorter run, however, the confusion of such efforts with the work needed now to construct useful health indicators may deter progress toward accomplishment of objectives more nearly within reach.

POSITIVE VERSUS NEGATIVE HEALTH STATUS INDICATORS

The issue of whether health indicators should measure positive as well as negative health is symptomatic of a fundamental conceptual problem that stems from the lack of a real definition of health.[2] Health, like beauty, goodness, and love, implies good things; namely, the often-cited World Health Organization definition:

> Health is a state of complete physical, mental, and social well-being, and not merely the absence of disease and infirmity.

Although we may agree that health connotes more than mere absence of undesirable states, there is as yet, however, no consensually accepted statement in measurable language of what constitutes well-being. (For a listing of other definitions similar to that of the World Health Organization, see reference 19.) Yet, several serious advocates of health indicators appear to believe that hope for progress rests on solution of this conceptual matter. As noted earlier, Gross and Springer (8) identify the development of positive indicators of health and vitality as the most important task in developing health status measures. Goldsmith (19) offers the tautological opinion that "a clear (or clearer) conceptualization of health is needed before significant progress can be made in measuring health." While agreeing with Goldsmith's statement (but not its intent), we fundamentally disagree with Gross and Springer's choice of priorities. From our admittedly pragmatic perspective, effort directed toward positive indicators is not likely to bear fruit relevant to short-run policy making for some time to come.

Lacking an adequate conceptual basis for measuring positive health, researchers apply indicators that are distributed toward the low end of the presumed continuum of health, with the result that indicators discriminate only among levels of poor health. This would be a serious problem were the preponderance of a nation's population concentrated above the imaginary threshold that distinguishes poor health from good health. Our view is, however, that this is not the case in the United States today, nor probably anywhere else in the world. Epidemiological studies of presumed well populations typically find that majorities of people have at least one health problem that would benefit from medical attention.

Indeed, Zola (20) concluded from a review of literature that, "instead of [illness] being a relatively infrequent or abnormal phenomenon, the empirical reality may be that illness, defined as the presence of clinically serious symptoms, is the statistical *norm*." If this assertion is accurate, a health status index with discriminating power in the positive health region of the health continuum would still, for the most part, be ranking people in terms of negative indicators, such as the presence of disease (as

[2] We use the term "real definition" in its technical sense as an empirical analysis, i.e. a definition "that states characteristics which are, as a matter of empirical fact, both necessary and sufficient for the realization of the phenomenon under analysis" (18).

currently defined by clinicians), disability, or discomfort. Surely, one can accept the intellectual construct of health as a continuum that ranges from a blissful compatibility with a benign nature to absolute death without necessarily subscribing to the opinion that being able to measure bliss is of great and immediate importance in the development of health indicators.

Rather than concern ourselves excessively with the utopian end of the health spectrum, we should concentrate our attention on refining measurements of negative health and, additionally, toward calibrating scales and indexes in terms of socially and politically *useful* units. It is curious indeed that many who list criteria for assessing health indicators fail to state at the outset that the first and foremost criterion of a health indicator is its *usefulness to decision makers,* be they consumers, health professionals, planners, or legislators.[3] Perhaps this oversight accounts for the apparent ascendance of conceptual expansiveness and methodological rigor over practical utility in much of the health status indicators literature.

THE INDEX OF HEALTH STATUS

Until quite recently, mortality rates told all there was to tell about a population's health. While man lived in the fear of dying during infancy or of being struck down by ancient pests and plagues, health and life were nearly synonymous. Accompanying rising standards of living and control over environmental threats to life, however, have come increasing incidences and prevalences of lifetimes spent with chronic ailments and medicated survival. In consequence, mortality rates have become insensitive to relevant regions of the health spectrum, and morbidity takes its place alongside mortality as an important health indicator.

Application of these two types of indicator poses an interesting problem, namely, how to summarize them in a single index number. Several mathematically ingenious, albeit conceptually naive, solutions to the problem have been advanced. A sampling from these provides a flavor of the general approaches advanced as well as their assumptions and limitations.

Chiang's Index of Health (23) is proposed as a quantitative summary of a population's health, in which health is defined as "the fraction of the year in which an individual . . . is living and free from illness." The index, H, for an entire population is

$$H = \frac{1}{P} \sum_x P_x H_x,$$

the weighted average of the mean duration of health per year of the population's age groups. An age group's mean duration of health per year (H_x) is comprised of two components: the effect of illness ($\bar{I}$) and the effect of mortality (m_x), where

[3] A sampling of criteria from Goldsmith's review article illustrates the point (21). It should show changes over time in significant aspects of the health of the living as well as in mortality, and it should be subject to analysis in components which provide useful description of health problems underlying index values. Moriyama (22) lists six criteria, the first being that "it should be meaningful and understandable"; the others are technical considerations. Goldsmith (19) states only that "the purpose of the health status indicator should be clearly stated."

$$\overline{I} = \overline{N}_x \overline{T}_x$$

$\overline{N}_x$ = the observed average number of illnesses per person per year,
$\overline{T}_x$ = the average duration of an illness episode,

and m_x is the age-specific mortality rate. Assuming that, on average, deaths result in the loss of a half-year's time,

$$H_x = 1 - (\overline{I}_x + \tfrac{1}{2} m_x).$$

We need not pursue a lengthy analysis of this index. A hypothetical example suffices to demonstrate its insensitivity to widely different circumstances. Suppose we wish to compare the health of two populations using Chiang's Index. Further suppose that in Population A everyone was ill during an entire year. Then, $I_A = 1$, and $H_A = 0$. In Population B, everyone was also ill during the first six months of the year, after which they all succumbed. Then, $H_B = 0$. Although everyone in Population A survived, albeit in unhealthy conditions, and everyone in Population B died midway through the year, Chiang's Index rates average health as equal in the two populations. Clearly, the failure to distinguish between a day lost to illness and a day lost to death leads to unacceptable results. Likewise, the failure to account for the severity of illnesses jeopardizes the index' claims to validity or even common sense. A day lost to cancer is equated in the index to a day lost to the common cold, a trade no reasonable person would accept.

Sullivan's Index of Life Free of Disability also purports to express mortality and morbidity in a single quantitative summary (24). Defined, computed, and interpreted as an elaboration of the concept of average life expectancy, the Index also produces an uninterpretable blend. Sullivan's Index is, in fact, the average life expectancy minus the average disability experienced during a lifetime. Time lost is for Sullivan the leveler of mortality and morbidity, and, by definition, one person's disability equals another, regardless of their causes or consequences.

Chiang and Sullivan base their indexes on conventional measures of health status. Therefore, although both indexes lack meaningful units for comparison and fail to weight mortality and morbidity differentially, they give the appearance of plausibility. Other investigators, in their eagerness to construct a GNP-like summary index, have dumped other types of indicators in the stew, resulting in incredible combinations of components. Spautz (25), for instance, defines average health, an "area indicator" of the more global Index of Social Health. Computed from national data, the average health index is composed of the total death rate, accidental death rate, infant mortality rate, health expenditures per capita, the ratio of medical care costs to the consumer price index, the number of physicians per 100,000 population, and numbers of draftees disqualified from service for medical reasons. Although Spautz allows that the selection of indicators poses as yet unresolved problems, he offers the practitioner little guidance.

If indexes of health status are ever to become more than interesting solutions to the question "how can we express mortality and morbidity as a single numeral?", they must be scaled in terms of some socially, economically, or clinically relevant criterion. Economists have attempted to do so by estimating the costs to society of death and illness (26); others have tried to scale self-reported illnesses in terms of the types and amounts of health services that would be required to care for them (27). Such approaches to health indicators illustrate how scaling an output measure on the basis of its causes or effects provides a context within which resulting indicators have meaning. Expressing mortality and morbidity due to specific causes by reference to their direct and indirect costs to society–monetary and otherwise–provides more information than health status indexes scaled with units of "time lost." Likewise, morbidity scaled according to implied service need is obviously of more value than GNP-like health status indicators, which, to be informative, must be disaggregated into their component parts.

CONCLUSIONS

Taking seriously claims of advocates of social indicators that such information is intended primarily to assist decision making, we have identified tendencies that we regard as impediments to that end. In our opinion, quests for *the* single, global index of health status and for the ultimate definition of well-being, where the mirage of health congeals, are the principal offenders. Both obscure more than inform, and both raise conceptual and methodological difficulties that predispose unnecessary pessimism. In pursuing these objectives, we risk becoming casualties of our own overambition, and thereby becoming unsatisfied with what is possible because it compares unfavorably with unrealistic aspirations.

There can never be an all-purpose health status index precisely because information about health must serve several purposes. Indicators of functional status are required for evaluation of long-term care programs; measures of chronic diseases are needed to project requirements for specific services; and so on. Were a single, all-encompassing health status index available, we would soon find that, in specific applications, it would have to be disaggregated in various ways. This being so, one might reasonably question the rationale behind aggregating in the first place.

One often-cited reason is that degrees of detail required for highly specific applications are perhaps unnecessary and certainly unfeasible when indicators are applied to more general domains. But, the feasibility argument rests on expedience: it is not responsive to our skepticism of the utility of aggregated, general-purpose indexes. Moreover, the history of measurement runs counter to the claim that loss of detail accompanying aggregation is necessarily offset by greater generality. Progress in measurement is marked by increasing ability to discriminate among quantities and qualities of phenomena, not by devising quantitative summaries that obscure differences. The critical consideration here is relevance to some purpose: if global indexes provide decision makers with useful information, costs of increments of greater (or less) detail must be justified in terms of their added marginal utility. Finding that optimal level of detail is a far more important objective than is construction of a mathematically elegant, global index.

Complicating the search for optimal detail is the notion that a concept of health should embrace various elements of what some label the quality of life. An extension of the view that indicators should measure positive health, it sweeps under the umbrella of health such disparate dimensions as happiness, social effectiveness, moral worth, and physical vitality (28). In consequence, the integrity of any reasonable conception of health is vitiated; the possibility of operationally defining "it" is greatly diminished; and identification of social institutions and technologies to ameliorate it is virtually precluded. Like the search for *the* index, definitional expansiveness is more dysfunctional than helpful. This is not to say, however, that these added dimensions are unimportant, only that their immediate conceptual relevance to health status is dubious.

Proponents of expansive definitions typically proceed from the premise that health status is multidimensional to specify domains of phenomena including traditional notions of health status supplemented by others. From this premise and the resulting augmented definition follows the conclusion that no single index can possibly capture its totality.

This being so, we question the wisdom of stretching the concept of health, like Procrustes bed, to fit any definition. Empirically, "multidimensional" implies that specification of a variable and location of units with respect to it involve combining in some manner information about identifiably different things which may covary in varying degrees. If the various dimensions included under expansive definitions are orthogonal, the conceptual issue about what constitutes health evaporates: that is, some may prefer to retain traditional conceptions and therefore refer only to scores on one of several dimensions; others may prefer to consider the entire conceptual space as containing different *types* of health status, and therefore refer to typologies or profiles. Both routes can lead to the same empirical end. Thus, little is gained, unless, again, the inevitable conceptual complexity introduced by typologies is matched by enhanced utility to decision makers.

The more likely situation is that various proposed dimensions of health status are intercorrelated. For instance, healthy people are happier than the unhealthy (as measured by traditional indicators). Application of statistical techniques, such as factor analysis and path analysis, can clarify (but not prove) whether correlated variables are better considered as indicators of a general concept of health or as causally related but conceptually distinct phenomena. Our guess is that the latter interpretation will prove more plausible in most instances. If so, persons interested in improving happiness, the quality of life, and other such global matters do themselves and others a disservice by confusing these with health status. In effect, health status becomes only one of several potential determinants of general well-being. Treating it accordingly in multivariate models that include other factors will permit estimation of its impact on outcomes of interest. If such analysis demonstrates that its effects, direct and indirect, are trivial, health status can be deleted from further consideration. Where its influences predominate, attention will turn to investigation of other phenomena that influence health status, and to the causal paths that link it to indicators of well-being. We are, at that point, back where we began: searching for the causes and consequences of traditionally defined and measured indicators of negative health.

Acknowledgement—The author wishes to thank Mrs. Renate Wilson for her generously given editorial assistance.

REFERENCES

1. Sheldon, E. B., and Freeman, H. E. Notes on social indicators: Promises and potential. *Policy Sciences* 1: 97-111, 1970.
2. Gross, B. M. Planning: Let's not leave it to the economists. *Challenge* 14(1): 30-33, 1965.
3. Gross, B. M. Social state of the union. *Trans-Action* 3(1): 14-17, 1965.
4. Agocs, C. Social indicators: Selected readings. *Annals of the American Academy of Political and Social Science* 388: 127-132, March 1970.
5. Springer, M. Social indicators, reports, and accounts: Toward the management of society. *Annals of the American Academy of Political and Social Science* 388: 1-13, 1970.
6. Cohen, W. J., editor. *Toward a Social Report,* p. 97. University of Michigan Press, Ann Arbor, 1970.
7. Cohen, W. J. Social indicators: Statistics for public policy. *American Statistician* 22: 14, 1968.
8. Gross, B. M., and Springer, M. New goals for social information. *Annals of the American Academy of Political and Social Science* 373: 211, 1967.
9. Olson, M. An analytic framework for social reporting and policy analysis. *Annals of the American Academy of Political and Social Science* 388: 112-126, 1970.
10. Land, K. C. On the definition of social indicators. *American Sociologist* 6(4): 322-325, 1971.
11. Feldstein, P. J., and Kelman, S. A framework for an econometric model of the medical care sector. In *Empirical Studies in Health Economics,* edited by H. E. Klarman, pp. 171-190. Johns Hopkins University Press, Baltimore, 1970.
12. Henriot, P. T. Political questions about social indicators. *Western Political Quarterly* 23(2): 235-255, 1970.
13. Blalock, H. M., Jr. The measurement problem: A gap between the language of theory and research. In *Methodology in Social Research,* edited by H. M. Blalock and A. B. Blalock, pp. 18-23. McGraw-Hill, New York, 1968.
14. Stinchcombe, A. L. *Constructing Social Theories.* Harcourt Brace Jovanovich, Inc., New York, 1968.
15. Forrester, J. W. *Urban Dynamics.* Massachusetts Institute of Technology Press, Cambridge, Mass., 1969.
16. Thompson, J. D. *Organizations in Action,* p. 134. McGraw-Hill, New York, 1967.
17. Simon, H. A. *The New Science of Management Decision.* Harper and Row, New York, 1960.
18. Hempel, C. G. *Fundamentals of Concept Formation in Empirical Science,* p. 8. University of Chicago Press, Chicago, 1952.
19. Goldsmith, S. B. The status of health status indicators. *Health Services Reports* 87: 213, 1972.
20. Zola, I. K. Culture and symptoms—An analysis of patients' presenting complaints. *American Sociological Review* 31: 616, 1966.
21. Sullivan, D. F. Conceptual Problems in Developing an Index of Health. Public Health Service Publication No. 1000, Series 2, No. 17. National Center for Health Statistics, Washington, D. C., 1966.
22. Moriyama, I. M. Problems in the measurement of health status. In *Indicators of Social Change,* edited by E. B. Sheldon and W. E. Moore, pp. 573-600. Russell Sage Foundation, New York, 1968.
23. Chiang, C. L. An Index of Health Mathematical Models. Public Health Service Publication No. 1000, Series 2, No. 5. National Center for Health Statistics, Washington, D. C., 1965.
24. Sullivan, D. F. A single index of mortality and morbidity. *HSMHA Health Reports* 86(4): 347-354, 1971.
25. Spautz, M. E. The socio-economic gap. *Social Science Research* 1(2): 211-229, 1972.
26. Rice, D. P. Estimating the cost of illness. Health Economics Series, No. 6. U. S. Department of Health, Education, and Welfare, Washington, D. C., 1966.
27. Kalimo, E., and Sievers, K. The need for medical care: Estimation on the basis of interview data. *Med. Care* 6(1): 1-17, 1968.
28. Lerner, M. Conceptualization of health and social well-being. In *Health Status Indexes,* edited by R. L. Berg, pp. 1-11. Hospital Research and Educational Trust, Chicago, 1973.

CHAPTER 12

A Classification of Sociomedical Health Indicators: Perspectives for Health Administrators and Health Planners

Athilia E. Siegmann

The essence of a society should be able to be presented in a quantitative way in order to assess where a society is and where it is going (1, p. 1). In the United States, the similar view of a 1929 Presidential Research Committee on Social Trends was the harbinger of the present social measurement effort (2). It was not until after the Soviet launching of Sputnik in the 1950s that impetus from space-age technology on the redefinition of United States national goals and priorities created a 1960s setting favorable for the development of systematic social measurement (3). With the publication of the study sponsored by the National Aeronautics and Space Administration of the space program's effect on society, the measurement of social trends and change was labeled the "social indicator movement." The measures themselves were called "social indicators" (1, p. 1). The success of Keynesian structural manipulations of the economy by the Council of Economic Advisors in the early 1960s engendered prospects and legislative proposals for a similar Council of Social Advisors with a system of social accounts analogous to the national economic accounts and the global gross national product indicator.

The early expectations were that social indicators would (a) assist in program evaluation, (b) develop a system of social accounts, and (c) help set national goals and priorities. The years 1966-1969 were characterized by an interest in the information base for social policy decisions, as well as an interest in the information base for determining the consequences of these decisions (4, p. 2). These ambitious expectations have since been modified. Experience has demonstrated that "evaluation research" is necessary for the assessment of program outcome (5-7). Indicators that are not part of a causal model cannot demonstrate that general environmental variables or program activities have determined the measured changes. As long as there is no general social system theory from which to extrapolate a system of social accounting, the development of a social accounts system analogous to the economic accounts is not feasible (8). The hope of a direct role for indicators in policy determination has been muted. While indicators are forces that influence the setting of priorities and goals, these latter are more dependent on national values than on assembled data (9, p. 99, 10, p. 139). Currently the social indicator movement concerns itself with identification and specification of crucial societal concerns; the development of descriptive, analytic (4), objective (11), and subjective (12) measures; the estimation of their magnitude and trends over time; as well as use of these measures to serve as input for social policy decisions and resource allocation that relate to the process of national goal setting and priorities.

At present, suggested formulations for indicators include the application of economic account measurement techniques to social measurement (13, 14), replication of past surveys to establish time series (15), and social indicators developed as components of social system models (16). Analysis of current social indicators reveals, however, that none of these efforts are the products of application of causal social modeling; neither do they relate to other societal concerns; nor are they parts of an interrelated system of social accounts (17, pp. 40-56).

When the United States Government published *Social Indicators, 1973* (18), a compendium of statistics and tables that describe United States social conditions and trends, it joined those countries which for many years have issued series of social indicators for the total society. Eight major social areas were developed in *Social Indicators, 1973*: health, public safety, education, employment, income, housing, leisure and recreation, and population. Within these areas broad categories of social interest, or social "concerns," were identified. The area of health identified the social concerns of long life, life free from disability, and access to medical care. The measure, "Life Expectancy at Birth," presented as a time series from 1900 to 1971, was chosen to operationalize the social concern of long life.

In February 1974, shortly after publication of *Social Indicators, 1973,* the Social Science Research Council's Center for Coordination of Research on Social Indicators convened an international review symposium attended by researchers and administrators from universities, private organizations, and government agencies to discuss and evaluate *Social Indicators, 1973.* The aim was to highlight the potential utility of the publication and its data base, as well as to encourage its dissemination and use (19). As a consequence of the symposium, a multidisciplinary Advisory Committee on Social Indicators to the Executive Office of the President, Office of Management and Budget, was created to advise on development, revisions, additions, or deletions from the social indicators to be presented in the 1976 volume. In this edition the health area has been expanded to incorporate nutritional indicators of qualitative and quantitative dietary inadequacy (20).

Health indicator measurement antedates most other social indicator efforts. The era of scientific medicine was already established on the European continent when the 1910 Flexner Report (21) on the United States and Canadian medical education ushered in scientific medical education and its emphasis on precise and unambiguous scientific measurement. The linkage of distinct diagnostic entities to specific prescriptive technologies that were directed at the underlying causes of illnesses ensued. At this juncture mortality and morbidity measures indicated both the receipt of this care as well as its short-run impact upon individuals' health status. Thus, a felicitous dual use of these measures for either descriptive or analytic assessment of the phenomenon being examined was achieved. However, with changes in disease patterns and with population age shifts it has become necessary to develop new measures.

The remainder of this paper will examine the interrelationship of health problem patterns and frames of reference for both defining and measuring health. The paper is divided into three sections. The first section, "Traditional Health Indicators," explains why mortality and morbidity rates, by themselves, no longer serve to assess a population's health status. Their identified deficiencies serve as background to the next section, "A Classification Schema for Sociomedical Health Status Indicators." This second section relates a society's predominant disease patterns and the associated measures necessary to describe and explain the population's health status. In conclusion, the third section, "The Uses of Sociomedical Health Indicators," assesses the role of some selected sociomedical health indicators in the current developmental process of formulation of health status indicators.

TRADITIONAL HEALTH INDICATORS

Prior to the consideration of a classification schema for health status indicators, it is helpful to examine the deficiencies of mortality and morbidity rates as health assessors for the larger portion of the population in developed societies. This examination helps explain the more recent indicator developments.

Dependence of Health Status Measures Upon Disease Patterns

Accompanying each era's and group's predominant patternings of disease or health problems is the appropriate selection or construction of health indicators. Outcome measures are used where the health problems are acute, explicitly diagnosable (22), and are accompanied by a prescriptive technology that has the capacity to alter the course of disease. Under these circumstances, an outcome measure is sufficiently sensitive to relate a change in health status to medical care in the short run, as well as to account for the outcome. This relationship characterizes the earlier stages of modern social development. The developing society's problems are mainly infectious and acute disorders with predictable and unambiguous preventive or cure outcomes that are directly linked in the short run to the provision of sanitarian and medical care technology. Today we still find a similar array of health problems in deprived neighborhoods in the urban areas of developed nations as in developing nations that lack a preventive health care focus. In these settings mortality rates and morbidity rates are the outcome measures that serve to adequately assess the population's health status.

Nowadays, the basic problem with traditional health indicator measures as adequate assessors of a population's health status is the question of continuing relevance of the measures themselves. Moriyama (23), Logan (24), and Sullivan (25) have reviewed changes in health problems and demographic patterns resulting from antibiotic therapies that have made mortality and morbidity measures less relevant. With the decrease in communicable and infectious diseases which primarily affect children and young persons, the population age shifts toward middle-aged and aged persons. Mortality measures, however, are compromised even as assessors of the aged population's health status. In industrialized societies half the women survive to past 75, and half the men to past 70 years of age. When the aged die, death is often no longer ascribable to a single specific cause of death. These deaths are due to multiple causes of a generalized systematic breakdown associated with old age. It should be noted, however, that there is an opposing view that ascribes most of these deaths to coronary heart disease (26). Nevertheless, it is generally conceded that this lack of specification has given less meaning to death rates as indicators of health status of the aged. Neither do these death rates correspond to the extant morbidities or utilization of services for the remainder of the population, nor, most likely, do they for the aged as well (24, p. 174).

Dependence of Health Status Measures upon Health Definitional Frame of Reference

How health status is measured depends on how health is defined. Health definitions are products of theoretically or pragmatically derived formulations developed from the current context of the society's health problems and capacity of the society to solve them. The definitions range from a unified concept of health and disease as freedom from disease to broader multifaceted views that incorporate dimensions of social and psychological functioning as well as overall qualities of "happiness" and "quality of life" (27). An example of the latter is the World Health Organization definition: "Health is a state of complete physical, mental and social well-being and not merely the absence of disease or infirmity" (28). The far-ranging construct of this definition has made it a repeated target of the criticism that it is too broad for useful measurement purposes. The question of how far ranging the definition of health should be is a matter of empirical concern. Germane to this point is a conceptualization of mental health wherein it was noted that "the phenomenon of a superstate of good mental health, well beyond and above the mere absence of disabling illness, has yet to be scientifically demonstrated" (29, p. 112). Allied to the issue of a superstate of health is consideration of the analytic relationships between the overall global sense of life quality and "life domains," such as housing, leisure, family life, and health. There is now some empirical evidence that suggests a separateness and distinction between "health" and "quality of life." A continuing investigation that had posited a substantial interaction between a global perception of quality of life and specific life domains has so far found none. The investigators had thought that if a person were in poor health this might dominate his sense of overall life quality, regardless of how he felt about his housing, leisure pursuits, or family. Since the data do not support this hypothesis (30), it becomes evident that there is a need to empirically justify suprahealth dimensions in a conceptualization and measurement of health.

The pragmatist approach to health assessment has been primarily concerned with the efficacy of the provision of medical care services. While this disease orientation and provider focus has pervaded the conceptualizations of health definition and health status measurement, it is increasingly recognized that supplementation with social and economic orientations and a consumer focus will be required. At present, beyond the traditional mortality measures and prevalence and incidence rates, there are measures which attempt to account for severity and duration of illnesses. Some of these link biological states or symptoms to utilization of medical services and resources, and some account for sickness time or lives lost to premature death. More recent in conceptualization are behavioral measures that are addressed to social and physical functional limitations on role performance. The general picture, however, is of measurement procedures which often focus on relationships of interest, in ingenious ways, but nevertheless handicapped by lack of an operational definition of health that treats the assessment of health status as a problem of social analysis. Health, as any social phenomenon, changes its meaning over time. An operational definition of health that recognizes the changing character of social phenomena must be capable of incorporating a variety of health definitions (31). To this end the following classification is suggested.

A CLASSIFICATION SCHEMA FOR SOCIOMEDICAL HEALTH STATUS INDICATORS

During the present century in the United States an historic development of frames of reference for defining health and attendant measurement has been accompanied by three predominant disease patterns. The broader patterns have been infectious diseases and chronic degenerative diseases of aging, and most recently the trend is to modern life-style-associated diseases. While at any time one pattern may characterize an era by being the predominant pattern of health problems exhibited in the society, these patterns are not mutually exclusive. The following attempt to characterize them along various dimensions should not obscure the fact that these frames of reference are all part of the current work to develop health status indicators. The dimensions used to describe the different disease patterns are: (a) a generic health definition,[1] (b) a definitional frame of reference, e.g. therapeutic-medical (health as freedom from disease), (c) the content and impact of therapeutic technology, (d) the implicit or explicit

[1] At the *organic* level the reference is to organic and physiological disorder described as *disease* (if in process), or as *impairment* (if static and persistent); at the functional level the reference is to a subjective state of psychological awareness of dysfunction described as illness (if in process), or as disability (if static and persisting); at the social level the reference is to a state of social dysfunction, a social role assumed by the individual, described as sickness (if in process), or as handicap (if static and persisting). Organic and functional conditions are confined to the individual, whereas social roles are defined by the societal expectations and extend beyond the individual (32).

assumptions in selection/design of measures, (e) what the measures indicate, and (f) measurement criteria.

Infectious and Communicable Disease Patterns and the Organic Definition of Health

The infectious pattern is characterized by an organic definition of health. The provider focus is evidenced by a medical-therapeutic frame of reference where health by implication is negatively defined as freedom from disease or impairment. The medical and sanitarian therapeutic technology is specifically directed at the underlying mechanism of disease. Technologies that are directed at the cause of the disease that have the capacity to alter its course, and effect cures, have been called "high technologies" (33). In a society or group where the preponderance of health problems are solvable primarily by application of "high technology," health status is a direct outcome of either having or not having received the therapy. Thus health status is equatable to both receipt of services and diagnostic label. Use of a direct measure of the impact of care suffices to describe as well as explain health status. As noted in the first section, "Traditional Health Indicators," the ideal outcome measures that serve these uses are the death rates. Associated with the diagnostic taxonomy of the International Classification of Diseases, they are precisely measurable and amenable to social arithmetic. As application of therapeutic technology is expanded, it is only necessary to track changes in the downward direction of the rates to see general improvement in health. These trends have been significant, remarkable, and unambiguous. The collection and promulgation of age-specific death rates by cause of death is a technical and political process that identifies leading causes of death and serves as input to the formulation of health goals and program policy for the society (34).

Early gains in the conquest of infectious disease increase the number of survivors who live longer with increased risk of nonlethal acute disease. In the transitional period to the predominantly chronic era, morbidities as measured by incidence and prevalence rates suffice to supplement death rates as population health indicators. Overall, this is also a period where health problems are acute, easily diagnosable, and accompanied by specific therapies. The significant changes in mortality and morbidity, measurable in the short run, are directly linked to medical care and by implicit assumption mortality and morbidity patterns are equatable.

Criteria for a health status indicator at this stage are relatively straightforward as the measurement issue primarily relates to the processes of reporting, collecting, and compiling vital statistics and designing epidemiological studies. Rather than theoretical and methodological issues, relevant criteria are concerned with administrative use of health statistics: (a) they should be relevant to the country's needs; (b) they should be based on reliable data whose collection is practicable within the country's resources; and (c) they should be based on data which can be processed promptly, and directed readily to people who can use them (35).

Chronic Degenerative Diseases of Aging and Acute Nonlethal Disease Patterns and the Functional Definition of Health

The chronic degenerative diseases of aging and acute nonlethal disease patterns are characterized by (a) a functional definition of health embodied in a concept of illness as deviant behavior from normative standards (36), and (b) a view of health as a capacity for role performance (37). The provider focus is evidenced by measurement of dysfunction in terms of illnesses and disabilities. At this stage of development medical technology is a mix of high and halfway technologies. Halfway technologies are not specific cures. They are designed to deal with the consequences of disease or postpone death (38). These technologies are applied over longer time periods and/or with greater use of manpower and capital resources than the high technologies. Measurement, influenced by the infectious patterns' direct equating of outcome measures to therapy services and conditions, accounts for the impact of illness and disability by a general translation of the impact as the time away from role performance. Classified groupings of illnesses are linked to the utilization of medical services or resources, or to measures of time lost from activities of living due to illness, or to specific dysfunctions that compromise efficient participation in daily living. These are measures that, particularly during the earlier stages of the transition to an older-age population, would appear to allow combination of mortalities and morbidities to arrive at an estimate of the population's health. The measures represent binary valuations that enable equating the impact of morbidities to the presence or absence of individuals in the society as in the death rate alive or dead measurement possibility. They are also directly quantifiable into economic valuation, the dollars that value time lost, and/or any resource charge. However, when chronic disorders become the dominant pattern, new measures are necessary for health status assessment. This is necessary because morbidity measures of incidence or prevalence of acute or chronic conditions are essentially descriptive counts that do not account for the dimensions of severity, intensity, and duration of these disorders.

The initial measurement solution to the dimensions of morbidity within a function-performance focus was developed in the early stages of the household health surveys. While the disease category is still the reference unit of measurement, it is expanded to include either a resource use dimension, or a temporal dimension, or a physical dysfunction/disability dimension, or a scaled continuum dimension.

Resource Use Dimension. The early approach to the chronic pattern measurement problem was the development of a great variety of utilization of services and resource use statistics to serve as proxy measures for the impact of medical care techniques upon health status outcome. The intuitive assumption is that use is cure, and amount of use equates with severity of condition. It is now recognized that utilization of services varies with socioeconomic status (39). This variation and the fact that we lack a means of distinguishing the impact of medical care use from impacts of social and economic factors upon a population's health status, compromises these utilization counts as proxies for outcome measures of health status.

A further problem in the usefulness of utilization measures as outcome proxies is the content of medical care technology. Medical technology developments of the 1950s have been characterized as the doctor-saving (40) high technologies of antibiotic therapies and chemotherapies. As noted previously, the application of high technologies results in an older-age population whose chronic impairments need to be increasingly doctored by the expensive doctor-using "halfway" technological development of the 1960s. These halfway technologies have been termed "nontechnologies" which elude measurement of their capacity to alter the natural course of disease or its eventual outcome since they do not involve activities directed at the underlying mechanism of disease (33). Hence, while disease impacts are ameliorated they are not eradicated, and postponed death is eased by costly supportive therapies. All the services of supportive technology comprise a large and growing proportion of utilization of medical care services measurement. Consequently, by use of utilization measures we cannot demonstrate the impact of the provision of medical care services upon a population's health status.

Temporal Dimension. Another early measurement solution to the dimensions of morbidity is the undifferentiated disability days derived from survey findings that serve as currency for a variety of actual or suggested health indexes. Many of these global-type indexes have been described elsewhere (41). They attempt to directly account for the time involved in survivable illnesses, or the inverse—the amount of time one remains healthy. Illness time is then equated to productive time lost to the society from deaths, or to the inverse—life expectancies. This framework has direct comparability to an economic valuation of a lifetime based on earnings. An index developed by Chiang (42) is a representative example. Days lost to illness are equated to days lost to death in a summary index, thereby accounting for the temporal dimension of morbidities, but neither qualifying them nor qualitatively commensurating them to death. Another example is the Q index (43) which through the mechanism of productive years lost combines elements of mortality and morbidity for a normative reference population. Comparisons of target populations to the normative reference population are to be used in decision making for setting health programming priorities. The necessary implication that both populations be comparable in impact response to illness limits the application of the Q technique. It should be noted that there is, however, no general use of global indexes by administrators for setting programming priorities (44).

In addition to health status indicator criteria requirements for the infectious pattern, other criteria appropriate to this stage have been specified for an index of health by Moriyama (23, p. 593):

- It should be meaningful and understandable.
- It should be sensitive to variations in the phenomenon being measured.
- The assumptions underlying the index should be theoretically justifiable and intuitively reasonable.
- It should consist of clearly defined component parts.

- Each component part should make an independent contribution to variations in the phenomenon being measured.
- The index should be derivable from data that are available or quite feasible to obtain.

Physical Dysfunction/Disability Dimension. Since the above summary global measures do not directly link to disease categories and service program planning, additional information becomes necessary for administrative purposes. Information is also necessary because with incomplete knowledge about causes of diseases and pathogenesis, direct measurement in terms of organic change in illness state is difficult. The use of proxy measures in terms of degrees of physical dysfunction or disability linked to disease categories was initiated in the studies of the Commission on Chronic Illness (45). Physical dysfunction or disability can be measured objectively and is sensitive to illness changes. Function measures are therefore by implication indicators of severity and the changing course of illness (46). They have been used to describe target patient populations in terms of basic biological and physiological function (47), as well as to measure morbidity in the total population (48).

Scaled Continuum Dimension. The more recent development is one which arises from an implicitly defined continuum dimension of health from none (death) to optimal (absence of disease or disorder). With the incorporation of a health continuum into the function and role performance frame of reference, measurement methodology requires an equal appearing interval scale upon which to place different degrees of illness and dysfunction. With this methodology differentially rated function states are commensurate and therefore additive. There are two basic approaches to scaling, the psychologists' psychometric scaling (49) and the economists' utility maximization scaling (50). These are similar approaches of a general attempt to devise a valuation system for nonmarket activities analogous to the market system dollar valuation. This methodology is exemplified by the psychometric scaling of function status level used in the Fanshel-Bush (51) and Patrick (52) Function Status Index that has been developed and validated during the present decade. The system of weights that are coupled with the scaled and medically defined descriptive functional levels is a professional estimate of the future course of regressions (transitional probabilities) associated with the dysfunctions. This methodology is cast in a cost-benefit analysis frame whereby all the commensurate measures in a future currency stream are discounted by an appropriate interest rate to a present value. The researchers are currently engaged in validation of the transitional probability weighting system. The Function Status Index portion has recently been validated (53). However, because of its specific focus on dysfunction, the Function Status Index is still not linked to specific disease rates, nor to determinant variables. This is necessary information for health planning in light of a population's Function Status Index rating. The additional methodological criteria for health status indicators that are based on a view of health as capacity for role performance and measured as health related dysfunction have been specified as:

- scalability: ordering of an individual on a health-illness continuum must be possible, levels of health or functional status must be recognized;
- population instrument: instrument development for administration to a representative sample of a designated population so that reliable inferences about health (function) status can be made;
- applicability: the measure must yield information both on the individual level and the population level;
- relevance-behavioral measures: it is through measures in terms of behavioral functioning, rather than from self or professionally perceived health or diagnoses, that the concept of health is most relevant to social system functioning (53, p. 272).

Modern Life-Style-Associated Health Problems and the Social Definition of Health

While the Fanshel-Bush function states are behavioral measures, they are not dissociated from the provider-diagnostic terminology. While they relate to role performance, it is at a basic general level that is applicable to all activities of daily living and not to the content of the many varied social roles individuals assume in their many and different areas of living. A more expanded view of health capacity for role performance in the individuals' social settings has been proposed by René Dubos (54): "The nearest approach to health is a physical and mental state fairly free of discomfort and pain, which permits the person concerned to function as effectively and as long as possible in the environment where chance or choice has placed him." This additional emphasis on functioning necessitates a removal from a provider-medical health definition and from medically oriented measures for the operationalization and measurement of "effective functioning in a social environment."

The life-style-associated health problems of postindustrial societies are characterized by a social definition of health. This corresponds to a general consumer conceptualization of health as adequate functioning in age-sex roles. The consumer health concept is derived from criteria relevant to physical activity levels, performance of activities of daily living, physiological conformation, degree of absence of pain and other symptoms, health-producing behavior, and informational feedback from the health care system (55). The technology applied to life-style-associated morbidities is focused on medical care technology, even though it is widely recognized that health problems, which derive in large part from the society's environmental determinants, could be solved through individual behavior modification in conjunction with reorganization of societal priorities and provisions (56). In spite of the recognition that solutions other than medical care actions are needed, current solutions to life-style health problems are mainly focused on the economics of financing medical care services. The lack of provision of an array of medical, social, and psychological technologies directed at life-style-associated health problems is further exacerbated by a perverse impact on curative technology due to the political urgency generated by the drastic sequelae of these disorders (57). This lack results in development of expensive halfway technology products of targeted research programs that seek cures for devastating diseases at the expense of basic scientific research and low-cost specific intervention prescriptives.

Implications of a Social Definition of Health

At the point where it is recognized that other factors besides medical care services determine health status, and when a consumer-focused health definition incorporates an expansion into social domains, there is implicit in such a health definition not only what input function it may serve to individuals' endeavors, or what the state of health may be, but also how it is attained.

Ramsøy (58) has described a social frame of reference in health measurement that is particularly germane to this point:

> [The social] frame of reference is today closely identified with such labels as social indicators, welfare indicators, and subjective indicators, as well as with the "quality of life," although I don't think anyone can formulate clearly just what strategies for collecting information on health status are implied by these labels. Perhaps one kind of guideline that one can detect is that people, in this frame of reference, are not to be thought of only in the role of patient or only as nameless members of a "population," or only as task-fulfillers. In some way, persons are to be active agents who may define and act on their own health statuses in such a way as to make their "health behavior" an interesting variable. Furthermore, persons are to be observed in a more comprehensive way than in any of the other . . . frames of reference, so that a full range of biological, social, and psychological characteristics and resources are relevant in evaluating health status.

It should be noted that expansion into the content activity of other social domains is not the same as expanding the health definition from a negative health orientation to one that seeks to measure positive health attributes. Expansion into other social domains is indicative of some health input role into areas of daily living. However, any attempt to expand into positive health areas, as opposed to areas impacted by some degree of health-problem-related disorder, may be fraught with conceptual and measurement frustration. This is analogous to the previously noted psychiatric disclaimer of attempts to measure positive mental health as other than freedom from mental illness (29, p. 112). It may be that poor health is remarkable, noticeable, and measurable, whereas good health, past the point of minimal dysfunction, is an unremarkable given.

Four related demands, or criteria, are made upon measurement as consequences of expansion of the health definition into the social domains and the attribution of health status to a multiplicity of causes.

- The first criterion is the form of the health status indicator. To enable a complete assessment of health status at this definitional level both causes and effect have to be viewed simultaneously. This necessitates expansion of the indicator into a multivariate social indicator model derivative from a social system model. Therefore, in this model, health status is the outcome-dependent variable.
- The second criterion is that it be an unbiased indicator, independent of, or as

free as possible of, the context of the medical care, social, economic, and other determinants in the model.

- A third criterion is that in addition to the objective measure of health status, each other component of the model be a viable and independent indicator.
- The fourth and final criterion is a consequence of the three previous criteria. The indicator must be useful for the formal planning function of resource allocation at the margin. Although it would have been desirable at earlier stages, it is only at this definitional level that the criterion of usefulness is possible.

Current Usage of Health Status Measures

The measurement implications derived from the social frame of reference are the agenda for the next steps in formulation of health status indexes. Meanwhile the users of health status indexes are not particularly preoccupied with theoretical formulations, albeit they make a practical eclectic use of measures that relate to the definitional frames of reference. They are pragmatists in search of a replacement for death rates, and rightly so, as social scientists have still not offered a currently usable health status measure for health planning and resource allocation (59, 60). In the main, techniques involve matching service utilization and resource use statistics to demographic characteristics for specified geographical areas and making inferences based on comparisons to similar descriptive data for other areas (61). Similar in concept are multivariate factor analysis techniques that have been suggested for large areas such as states or for the entire nation. These current efforts do not require theoretical bases for suggested compilations of proxy measures of community health levels from routinely available demographic and socioeconomic variables that best correlate with generally available health statistics of resource use and traditional health indexes (62). The proxy measures may be useful in monitoring health status (63), but lacking the chain of outcomes linked to conditions, to resource use, and to other determinants of health status, the value of the proxy measures for efficient resource allocation at the margin is moot. They can, however, be particularly useful for the identification of determinants of community health status that can be incorporated into future modeling efforts (62, p. 22).

The traditional economic inquiries into demand for medical care have used selection of similar measures in studies that relate utilization rates to health conditions, and to demographic, socioeconomic, and other determinant variables. These studies have been useful in programmatic comparisons of the effect of health insurance differentials upon resource use rather than upon health status outcome. More recently economic demand studies have examined the demand for health rather than the demand for medical care. Grossman's is the most sophisticated formulation of the demand for health (64). Based on the theory of household production of nonmarket commodities (65), whereby the individual combines his own time with inputs of market goods to produce his own health, it is a theoretical and empirical formulation of how health status is attained. This corresponds well with Ramsøy's conceptualization of the social frame of reference. In Grossman's model health status is the outcome variable. Health is viewed as a stock which requires maintenance as well as repair until the time when the stock is depleted. The demand for health is differentiated from the demand for medical care, the latter being one of the market inputs into the individual's production function for health. This distinction between the demand for health and the demand for medical care is useful and relevant to health status measurement and the placement of variables into a health indicator model. It may also be a method of analysis that will serve to explain the discrepancy between survey respondents' reports of health problems and clinical assessment.

Measurement focus has heretofore been concerned with the "set of classes of outcome variables that have been defined [by Elinson (66),] conveniently referred to as the Five Ds. These are death, disease, disability, discomfort and dissatisfaction." We may find that with development of health indicator models that incorporate a consumer definitional input and view of the individual as an active agent in producing his own health, the measurement focus may include the basic "characteristics" consumers seek (67) in medical care services such as, for example, repair, relief, and rehabilitation.

THE USES OF SOCIOMEDICAL HEALTH INDICATORS

Concepts, constructs, and general uses of sociomedical indicators have been reviewed elsewhere (34). This concluding section will assess their use in a health indicator model. The current work in sociomedical health indicators, which incorporates functional and social as well as organic measures of outcome, relates well to the conceptualization of a social indicator model. It also relates to the conceptualization of viable individual indicators and indexes as components in such a model for health, namely, a health indicator model. The facets of the social frame of reference that have been considered in the classification schema point to the need for integration of the social domains and concerns. The integration is on two levels. The first level is among the measured variables in the organic, functional, and social frames of reference as they differentially impact the health status of population groups under assessment. The second integration is among the broad social domains as they impact outcomes in the health domain. While the components in such a model could be the same in all cultures, they would receive different weights for specific cultures. The modeling objective may be described as an incorporation of all of these types of indicators "into an integrated model of a social process" (4, p. 23). Land has said (4, p. 31),

> [An] approach is to seek the solution to the problem of interrelationships, not at the institutional level, but at the level of distributive consequences for individuals. In particular, we propose that the interdependencies of the institutional components of society as measured by social indicators are best treated in terms of their distributive consequences as spaced over the life-cycles of individuals. As a specific example, consider health status. It is clear that conditions of health and illness of a society are affected not only by its health care activities but also by its other institutionalized activities. However, rather than attempt to specify interrelationships among the health care, family, economic, political, and cultural institutions, our suggestion is that such relationships be measured in terms of relationships among the distributed products of society, that is, in terms of interrelationships among the health, employment, income, schooling, and consumption properties of individuals.

The sociomedical indicators that form the content of this monograph, *Sociomedical Health Indicators,* can serve as the beginning of the process of build-up of the components of an analytic model. Before one can begin to operationalize such a model, it is necessary to be within grasp of an appropriate health status measure. At present there is development of such an outcome measure of health, the Sickness Impact Profile (22). Whereas the Fanshel-Bush Functional Status measure is of differentially preferred functional states, the measurement items in the Sickness Impact Profile were developed to be as free as possible of cultural and medical context. They are empirically derived consumer-focused measures of the impacts of sickness upon the individual's observable behavior in fourteen major areas of living or activity in which dysfunctional behavior takes place (68). While the Sickness Impact Profile has still not been used as part of a social indicator model as described by Land, such a role may be envisaged for this measure.

The unmet needs concept for health care measures (69) forms the type of sociomedical indicator that serves as a component variable in a health indicator model. They are measures of society's capacity for the provision of services. While the measures have been developed for delivery program comparison, the next development of the unmet needs concept requires a form that enables a determination of whether current knowledge is, or is not, being applied to individuals, selected groups, and to total populations. It will also have to be developed into a form that compares disparate populations as to the degree to which populations receive needed care and/or to the degree of neglect. Unmet needs is appropriate for use in evaluating health problems as it directly relates or links health problems to health services, and thereby enables cost comparisons for use in resource allocation. The unmet needs measures, while not measures of health status, are the component measures that link medical care services and the other inputs necessary to maintain the population's health stock to health status.

Consideration of consumer preference for health care quality criteria implies the utility of the consumer's differentially preferred health care quality criteria to the consumer's health behavior as it impacts upon his or her health status. Any systematic relation between health care quality criteria and health status is the substance of a sociomedical health indicator that serves as a component variable in a health indicator model. The need for unbiased derivation and assessment of these consumer criteria based on population samples rather than patient samples has been presented in this monograph (70).

An indicator model has to take into account that at various stages of the life cycle there is a need to assess age-specific health problems which have their own unique measurement requirements. The relationship between self-perception of health and health status is a distinct feature of adolescent health status (71), whereas in the aged, health status is best assessed by measures of basic sociobiological functioning (72). Another life-stage-associated measure is "reproductive efficiency." Developed as an alternative to "infant mortality" for developed countries, it assesses the impact of health and social services upon natality. Infant mortality is included as a component. However, the need for an updated measure in this area is evidenced by the relative order of importance of causes of unsuccessful births in the numerator adjustment for the index. They ranged from a high of 48.2 percent for fetal deaths to a low of 6.4 percent for infant deaths (73).

These suggested uses of sociomedical health indicators are derived from a view of measurement of health status as a problem of social analysis. The interaction of the changing nature of society's health patterns and their engendered health status measurement requirements influences and is influenced by the society's constantly changing health definition. As a consequence, an operational definition of health, for health status assessment, requires a construct that incorporates a variety of health definitions and the variety of determinant factors that contribute to health status.

Acknowledgments–I would like to thank Margery Braren, Jack Elinson, Sally Guttmacher, and Donald Patrick for their helpful comments on earlier drafts of this paper. I, of course, am responsible for interpretation of their comments. I also wish to express thanks to Gail Garbowski for her patience and care in typing the manuscript, and to Hannah Frisch for suggesting that it be written.

REFERENCES

1. Bauer, R. A., editor. *Social Indicators.* M.I.T. Press, Cambridge, Mass., 1966.
2. United States President's Research Committee on Social Trends. *Recent Social Trends.* McGraw-Hill, New York, 1933.
3. United States President's Commission on National Goals. *Goals for Americans.* Prentice-Hall, Englewood Cliffs, N. J., 1960.
4. Land, K. C. Social Indicator Models: An Overview. Paper presented at the American Association for Advancement of Science Meeting, Washington, D. C., 1972. (Printed in *Social Indicator Models,* edited by K. C. Land and S. Spilerman, pp. 5-36. Russell Sage Foundation, New York, 1975.)
5. Suchman, E. A. *Evaluative Research: Principles and Practice in Public Service and Action Programs.* Russell Sage Foundation, New York, 1967.
6. Weiss, C. H. *Evaluating Action Programs.* Allyn and Bacon, Inc., Boston, 1972.
7. Struening, E. L., and Guttentag, M., editors. *Handbook of Evaluation Research,* vols. I and II. Sage Publications, Beverly Hills and London, 1975.
8. Duncan, O. D. *Toward Social Reporting: Next Steps.* Paper No. 2, Social Science Frontiers Series. Russell Sage Foundation, New York, 1969.
9. Sheldon, E. B., and Freeman, H. E. Notes on social indicators: Promises and potential. *Policy Sciences* 1: 97-111, 1970.
10. Sheldon, E. B., and Land, K. C. Social reporting for the 1970's. *Policy Sciences* 3: 137-151, 1972.
11. Sheldon, E. B., and Moore, W. E., editors. *Indicators of Social Change: Concepts and Measurement.* Russell Sage Foundation, New York, 1968.
12. Campbell, A., and Converse, P. E., editors. *The Human Meaning of Social Change.* Russell Sage Foundation, New York, 1972.
13. Gross, B. The state of the nation: Social systems accounting. In *Social Indicators,* edited by R. A. Bauer, pp. 154-271. M.I.T. Press, Cambridge, Mass., 1966.
14. Olson, M. An analytic framework for social reporting and policy analysis. *The Annals* 388: 112-126, 1970.
15. Duncan, O. D., Schuman, H., and Duncan, B. *Social Change in a Metropolitan Community.* Russell Sage Foundation, New York, 1973.
16. Land, K. C. On the definition of social indicators. *The American Sociologist* 6(4): 322-325, 1971.
17. De Neufville, J. *Social Indicators and Public Policy,* pp. 40-56. Elsevier Scientific Publishing Company, Amsterdam, Oxford, New York, 1975.
18. Executive Office of the President, Office of Management and Budget. *Social Indicators, 1973.* U. S. Government Printing Office, Washington, D. C., 1973.
19. Parke, R. Introduction in *Social Indicators, 1973: A Review Symposium,* edited by R. A. Van Dusen, pp. vii-viii. Social Science Research Council, Center for Coordination and Research on Social Indicators, Washington, D. C., 1974.

20. Johnston, D. F. Social Indicators, 1976–A Progress Report. Executive Office of the President, Office of Management and Budget, April 14, 1975 (mimeographed).
21. Flexner, A. *Medical Education in the United States and Canada.* A report to the Carnegie Foundation for the Advancement of Teaching. Bulletin No. 4, 1910 (reprinted in 1960).
22. Bergner, M. Presentation before Seminar on Sociomedical Health Indicators, Columbia University, April 13, 1973, on the Sickness Impact Profile developed at the University of Washington, Department of Health Services, in cooperation with the Group Health Cooperative of Puget Sound.
23. Moriyama, I. M. Problems in the measurement of health status. In *Indicators of Social Change,* edited by E. B. Sheldon and W. E. Moore, pp. 573-600. Russell Sage Foundation, New York, 1968.
24. Logan, R. F. L. Assessment of sickness and health in the community: Needs and methods. *Med. Care* 2(3): 173-190, 1964.
25. Sullivan, D. F. *Conceptual Problems in Developing an Index of Health.* Public Health Service Publication No. 1000, Series 2, No. 17. National Center for Health Statistics, Washington, D. C., 1966.
26. Stamler, J. Causes of the epidemic of coronary heart disease. *Bruxelles-Médical* 53(9): 473-501, 1973.
27. Lerner, M. Conceptualization of health and social well-being. In *Health Status Indexes,* edited by R. L. Berg, pp. 1-6. Hospital and Educational Trust, Chicago, 1973.
28. Constitution of the World Health Organization. In *The First Ten Years of the World Health Organization,* p. 459. World Health Organization, Palais des Nations, Geneva, 1958.
29. Barton, W. E. Viewpoint of a clinician. In *Current Concepts of Positive Mental Health,* by M. Jahoda, p. 112. Basic Books, Inc., New York, 1958.
30. Andrews, F. M., and Withey, S. B. Developing measures of perceived life quality: Results from several national surveys. *Social Indicators Research* 1(1): 1-26, 1974.
31. Fabrega, H., Jr. The need for an ethnomedical science. *Science* 189(12): 969-975, 1975.
32. Susser, M. Ethical components in the definition of health. *Int. J. Health Serv.* 4(3): 539-548, 1974.
33. Thomas, L. Notes of a biology-watcher, the technology of medicine. *New Engl. J. Med.* 285(24): 1366-1368, 1971.
34. Elinson, J. Toward sociomedical health indicators. *Social Indicators Research* 1(1): 59-71, 1974.
35. Knowledon, J. The collection and use of health statistics in national and local health services. *World Health Organization Technical Discussions* 1: March 9, 1966.
36. Parsons, T. *The Social System,* p. 431. Free Press, Glencoe, Ill., 1951.
37. Parsons, T. Definitions of health and illness in light of American values and social structure. In *Patients, Physicians, and Illness,* edited by E. Gartly Jaco, p. 168. Free Press, New York, 1958.
38. Ebert, R. H. Bio-medical research policy–A re-evaluation. *New Engl. J. Med.* 289(7): 348-351, 1973.
39. Suchman, E. A. Social patterns of illness and medical care. *J. Health Soc. Behav.* 6(1): 2-16, 1965.
40. Fuchs, V., and Kramer, M. *Determinants of Expenditures for Physicians' Services in the United States 1948-68.* United States National Center for Health Services Research, Rockville, Md., 1972.
41. Sullivan, D. F. *Disability Data Components for an Index of Health.* Public Health Service Publication No. 1000, Series 2, No. 42. National Center for Health Statistics, Washington, D. C., 1971.
42. Chiang, C. L. *An Index of Health Mathematical Models.* Public Health Service Publication No. 1000, Series 2, No. 5. National Center for Health Statistics, Washington, D. C., 1965.
43. Miller, J. E. An indicator to aid management in assigning program priorities. *Health Services Reports* 85(6): 725-731, 1970.
44. Goldsmith, S. The status of health status indicators. *Health Services Reports* 87(3): 212-220, 1972.
45. Commission on Chronic Illness. *Chronic Illness in the United States.* Vol. IV, *Chronic Illness in a Large City.* Harvard University Press, Cambridge, Mass., 1957.
46. Katz, S., Ford, A. M., Downs, T. D., and Adams, M. Chronic disease classification in evaluation of medical care programs. *Med. Care* 7(2): 139-143, 1969.

47. Akpom, C. A., Katz, S., and Densen, P. M. Methods of classifying disability and severity of illness in ambulatory care patients. *Med. Care* 11(2): 125-131 (supplement), 1973.
48. U. S. National Health Survey. *Chronic Conditions Causing Limitation of Activities, United States, July 1959-June 1961.* Public Health Service Publication No. 584-B36, Series B. No. 36, Washington, D. C., 1962.
49. Chen, M. Presentation before Seminar on Sociomedical Health Indicators, Columbia University, March 16, 1973.
50. Torrance, G. W., Thomas, W. H., and Sackett, D. L. A utility maximization model for evaluation of health care programs. *Health Serv. Res.* 7(2): 118-133, 1972.
51. Fanshel, S., and Bush, J. W. A health-status index and its application to health-services outcomes. *Operations Research* 18(6): 1021-1066, 1970.
52. Patrick, D. Measuring Social Preference for Function Levels of Health Status. Doctoral dissertation in sociomedical sciences, Columbia University, 1972.
53. Reynolds, W. J., Rushing, W. A., and Miles, D. L. The validation of a function status index. *J. Health Soc. Behav.* 15(4): 271-288, 1974.
54. Dubos, R. The mirage of health. In *Health and the Social Environment,* edited by P. M. Insel and R. H. Moos, pp. 439-450. D. C. Heath and Co., Lexington, Mass., 1974. (Also in *Man Adapting,* by R. Dubos, pp. 346-361. Yale University Press, New Haven, Conn., 1965.)
55. Hennes, J. D. The measurement of health. *Med. Care Rev.* 29(11): 1268-1287, 1972.
56. Somers, H. M. Robert D. Eihlers Memorial Lecture: Health and public policy. *Inquiry* 12(2): 87-96, 1975.
57. Strickland, S. P. Integration of medical research and health policies. *Science* 284(12): 1093-1103, 1971.
58. Ramsøy, N. R. Social indicators in the United States and Europe: Comments on five country reports. In *Social Indicators 1973–A Review Symposium,* edited by R. Van Dusen, pp. 51-52. Social Science Research Council, Center for Coordination of Research on Social Indicators, Washington, D. C., 1974.
59. Bush, J. W. Discussion. In *Health Status Indexes,* edited by R. L. Berg, p. 133. Hospital Research and Educational Trust, Chicago, 1973.
60. Goldsmith, S. A New Look at the Development of Outcome Indicators in Health Program Evaluation. Paper presented at American Public Health Association Meeting, Atlantic City, N. J., November 1972.
61. Wennberg, J., and Gittelsohn, A. Small area variations in health care delivery. *Science* 182(23): 1102-1108, 1973.
62. Levine, D. S., and Yett, D. E. A method of constructing proxy measures of health status. In *Health Status Indexes,* edited by R. L. Berg, pp. 12-22. Hospital Research and Educational Trust, Chicago, 1973.
63. Berg, R. L., editor. Discussion. In *Health Status Indexes,* p. 67. Hospital Research and Educational Trust, Chicago, 1973.
64. Grossman, M. *The Demand for Health: A Theoretical and Empirical Investigation.* Columbia University Press, New York, 1972.
65. Becker, G. A theory of the allocation of time. *The Economic Journal* 75(299): 493-517, 1965.
66. Elinson, J. Methods of sociomedical research. In *Handbook of Medical Sociology,* edited by H. E. Freeman, S. Levine, and L. G. Reeder, pp. 488-490. Prentice-Hall, Inc., Englewood Cliffs, N. J., 1972.
67. Lancaster, K. J. A new approach to consumer theory. *Journal of Political Economy* 75(2): 132-157, 1966.
68. Bergner, M., Bobbitt, R. A., Kressel, S., Pollard, W. E., Gilson, B. S., and Morris, J. R. The Sickness Impact Profile: Conceptual formulation and methodology for the development of a health status measure. *Int. J. Health Serv.* 6(3): 393-415, 1976.
69. Carr, W., and Wolfe, S. Unmet needs as sociomedical indicators. *Int. J. Health Serv.* 6(3); 417-430, 1976.
70. Kelman, H. R. Evaluation of health care quality by consumers. *Int. J. Health Serv.* 6(3): 431-442, 1976.
71. Brunswick, A. F. Indicators of health status in adolescence. *Int. J. Health Serv.* 6(3): 475-492, 1976.
72. Katz, S., and Akpom, C. A. A measure of primary sociobiological functions. *Int. J. Health Serv.* 6(3): 493-508, 1976.
73. Muller, C., Jaffe, F. S., and Kovar, M. G. Reproductive efficiency as a social indicator. *Int. J. Health Serv.* 6(3): 455-473, 1976.

CONTRIBUTORS

C. AMECHI AKPOM is an associate professor at Michigan State University. Previously he was an assistant professor at Case Western Reserve University School of Medicine and medical director of the Cuyahoga County Chronic Illness Center and Protective Services for Older Persons in Cleveland, Ohio. Dr. Akpom received his M.B.Ch.B. in 1963, his M.D. in 1974 from the University of Aberdeen, Scotland, and his M.P. H. from Harvard University in 1968. His research interests are in the area of long-term care, and his publications include *Measuring the Health of Populations and Methods of Classifying Disability and Severity of Illness in Ambulatory Care Patients.*

G. J. BORIS ALLAN is a senior lecturer in sociology in the Department of Social Science, Manchester Polytechnic, England, and a research consultant at the Department of Community Health, University of Nottingham. He has a B.A. in sociology from Kent University. He is especially interested in the relationship between macro indicators and perceptual indicators, and is the author of various publications in mathematical sociology and social statistics.

E. MAURICE BACKETT is chairman of the Department of Community Health at the University of Nottingham, Britain's first new medical school for nearly a century. His training is as a social scientist, epidemiologist, and clinician, and he was one of the first Nuffield Fellows in Social Medicine. He has worked for Britain's Medical Research Council, Guy's Hospital, London, and the London School of Hygiene and Tropical Medicine. He was formerly professor of social medicine and public health in Aberdeen, Scotland, and has directed two Health Services Research Units. He is currently a member of the World Health Organization Expert Panel on Health Manpower and Medical Education and chairman of the WHO Task Force on High Risk Strategies.

MARILYN BERGNER is associate professor of health services at the University of Washington. She received her Ph.D. in sociomedical science from Columbia University in 1970. She was Director of Planning for the New York City Health and Hospitals Corporation from 1970 to 1972. Her major areas of interest are in evaluation research, and health planning, and program development.

THOMAS W. BICE is professor of health services at the University of Washington. His research interests are in areas related to health services regulation, planning, and policy.

RUTH A. BOBBITT is a research professor at the University of Washington with primary research interests in the areas of design and in adapting and developing methodology for the study of developmental and social behavior and attitudes. Since receiving her Ph.D. at the University of Iowa in 1947, she has served on core and research staffs and as a consultant in psychology and psychiatry at a regional primate center, a child development and mental retardation center, and various agencies. Since 1972 she has served as senior methodologist on the Sickness Impact Profile Project, Department of Health Services, University of Washington. She has published in several books and the psychological journals.

ANN F. BRUNSWICK, Ph.D., is Senior Research Associate in Public Health at Columbia University, where she teaches a course on adolsecent health. Her research during twelve years at Columbia has been concerned mainly with the health of adolescents–physical, emotional, and social–particularly in a cross-section sample of Harlem youth. Currently she is director of the Adolescent and Young Adult Health Project, which is a follow-up interview study of more than 500 youths in the original Harlem adolescent survey. She is also a Senior Associate in the Columbia University Center for Socio-Cultural Research in Drug Use and chairs the National Task Panel on the Adolescent, sponsored by the Maternal and Child Health Section of the American Public Health Association.

WILLINE CARR is a senior research associate with the Center for Health Care Research, Meharry Medical College, and assistant professor in the Department of Family and Community Health at Meharry. She is co-principal investigator and study director for Meharry's Study of Unmet Needs. She teaches in the area of health care organization and health services evaluation. From 1967-1969 Ms. Carr was a research assistant with the Social Security Administration, where she worked in the area of health care financing and coauthored articles on private health insurance.

LOIS K. COHEN is a sociologist and the Special Assistant to the Director of the National Institute of Dental Research, U.S. Public Health Services. She was associated with the Division of Dentistry, USPHS, since 1964 as a research sociologist, Chief of Applied Behavioral Studies, Chief of the Office of Social and Behavioral Analysis and Special Assistant to The Director. Dr. Cohen completed her undergraduate work at the University of Pennsylvania in 1960. She received a Master's degree in Sociology from Purdue University in 1961, followed by a doctoral degree in 1963. Dr. Cohen has presented numerous scientific papers both in the U.S. and abroad, has authored and co-authored over sixty-five publications, and is co-editor of *Social Sciences and Dentistry* and *Toward a Sociology of Dentistry.* Her major interests are in the sociodental sciences and international health and she is currently co-project director of the USPHS/WHO International Collaborative Study of Dental Manpower Systems in Relation to Oral Health Status.

JAN DAVISON is a research fellow in the Department of Community Health, University of Nottingham. She received her Ph.D. in genetics from the University of Edinburgh, and subsequently spent three years at the University of Wisconsin, Madison, studying the genetic effects of irradiation in animal populations. This led to an increasing interest in problems in human populations and her research interests now include studies in primary medical care and the development and use of health indexes.

JACK ELINSON is professor, initiator, and first head of the graduate program in sociomedical sciences at Columbia University in which theory and methodology of the social sciences are applied to the probelms of health and health care. His work has dealt with the quantitative estimation of community health care needs, comparison of medical and sociological perspectives in conceptualizing illness, sociometric evaluation of the quality of medical and hospital care, and the development of sociomedical health indicators. He has served as chairman of the Section on Medical Sociology of the American Sociological Association; is a member of the Institute of Medicine, National Academy of Science; and is President-elect of the American Association for Public Opinion Research. He is co-editor of *Health Goals and Health Indicators: Policy, Planning, and Evaluation.*

BETTY S. GILSON is associate dean in the School of Public Health and Community Medicine and associate professor in the Department of Health Services at the University of Washington. She received her M.D. at the University of Minnesota in 1943 and served a residency in internal medicine at Case Western Reserve from 1943 to 1947. Her community practice in internal medicine and public health in Montana and Utah from 1948 to 1966 emphasized rheumatic and congenital heart disease. From 1966 to 1969 Dr. Gilson served on the faculty of the University of Utah. Her publications are in the fields of organization and standards for services in rheumatic and congenital heart disease, and behavioral measurement of health status.

JOSEPH GREENBLUM received graduate training in sociology at the University of Wisconsin (M.S.) and Columbia University and in social epidemiology at the Columbia University School of Public Health (M.P.H.). Specialized in research in the sociology of health and of ethnic group relations and contributed to journals and books in these areas. Now conducting a national followup study evaluating vocational rehabilitation programs for the disabled as well as studies of sociopsychological factors in disability based on national survey data.

FREDERICK S. JAFFE was president of the Alan Guttmacher Institute and vice president of the Planned Parenthood Federation of America, with which he was associated since 1954. A 1947 graduate in economics from Queens College, he is a coauthor of several books and has published extensively in numerous scientific journals. He was coinvestigator on studies of abortion need and services in the United States following the Supreme Court decisions, and of the demographic impact of publicly funded family planning programs in the United States.

JOHN D. JAGO, senior lecturer in dentistry at the University of Queensland, Brisbane, Australia, graduated in dentistry from the University of Melbourne in 1950. Following fifteen years of practice in Victoria, including ten in the Victorian Health Department treating handicapped children, Dr. Jago has been teaching pedodontics at the Dental School in Brisbane since 1966. He obtained the Master's degree in Dental Science from the University of Queensland in 1972, and is a doctoral student in public health at Columbia University. He has eleven publications in clinical and social dentistry, and his major research interests are in dental epidemiology and the sociology of dental care.

SIDNEY KATZ is professor and chairman of the Department of Community Health Science, Michigan State University, with a joint appointment in medicine. He received his M.D. from Case Western Reserve University in 1948 and trained in internal medicine. Formerly on the faculty of Case Western Reserve University, his primary research interests are clinical epidemiology and health services research. His publications cover outcome measures, the courses of chronic diseases, and controlled studies of service programs for chronically and aged ill people.

HOWARD R. KELMAN is professor of social sciences, Division of Social Sciences and Humanities, Department of Community Medicine, Health Sciences Center, and adjunct professor of sociology at the State University of New York at Stony Brook. Formerly on the faculties of the Columbia University School of Public Health and Administrative Medicine and New York Medical College, his major teaching and research interests include health services organizations, studies of long-term illness and disability, and evaluation of health services programs.

MARY GRACE KOVAR is Chief, Analytical Coordination Branch, in the Division of Analysis at the National Center for Health Statistics. Her work has been primarily in survey methodology and analysis of data on infant mortality, fertility, and the health and use of health services of elderly people and children.

SHIRLEY KRESSEL is associated with Government Studies and Systems, a consulting firm specializing in health planning and in evaluation of developmental disabilities services. Ms. Kressel has a B.A. in Russian literature from Brandeis University and an M.P.H. from UCLA. She was a research associate at Los Angeles County–USC Medical Center from 1969 to 1972, designing and conducting evaluation studies of various inpatient programs. During 1972-1973, she was a research associate on the Sickness Impact Profile Project in the Department of Health Services, at the University of Washington. This was followed by two years at San Francisco General Hospital, where she was involved in the evaluation of outpatient care.

CARLOS J. M. MARTINI, is a Professor of Preventive Medicine and Professor of Family Medicine at the University of Colorado Medical Center in Denver. He is also Director of the Division of Community Health at this medical school. Previously he was a senior lecturer in the

Department of Community Health, University of Nottingham, and deputy director to the Health Services Research Group within the same department. After completing his medical degree in 1961, he studied public health and social medicine at the University of Buenos Aires, Yale University, and the University of London. Dr. Martini has worked on the organization and management of medical care programs and in teaching and research at several universities in Argentina, England and the U.S.A.

JOANNE R. MORRIS is an interview supervisor with the Sickness Impact Profile Project in the Department of Health Services of the University of Washington. She received her B.A. in English from the University of Washington in December 1971, and has a Washington State Provisional Teaching Certificate for Secondary Education. During 1971-1972, she was a substitute teacher and director of a federally funded Human Relations Project with the Seattle Public Schools.

CHARLOTTE MULLER is associate director of the Center for Social Research and professor of economics at the Graduate School of the City University of New York. She is an economist who has specialized in health care research and who has been studying physician reimbursement under Medicare for the Health Care Financing Administration. Since 1969 she has been involved in the areas of fertility-related services and women in health care. Dr. Muller serves on the board of the Medical and Health Research Association of New York City and is a trustee of its pension fund. She is also on the National Council of the Alan Guttmacher Institute. She holds a B.A. from Vassar College and an M.A. and Ph.D. from Columbia University. Dr. Muller is a member of the Study Section on Health Care Technology of the National Center for Health Services Research.

DONALD L. PATRICK is Senior Lecturer and Head of the Social Science Section in the Department of Community Medicine, St. Thomas's Hospital Medical School, University of London. He received his B.A. in Social Psychology from Northwestern University and an M.S. in Public Health and Ph.D. in Sociomedical Sciences from Columbia University, where he completed his dissertation in "Measuring Levels of Well-Being for a Health Status Index." Formerly, he worked on the Health Index Project at the University of California, San Diego. He is currently leading an investigation of social networks and function status of the physically disabled for the Department of Health and Social Security in the U.K. His major interests are health measurement, evaluative research, resource allocation and primary care.

WILLIAM E. POLLARD is currently an assistant professor in the Department of Psychiatry at Emory University School of Medicine and is Director of Research, Evaluation and Planning for the Psychiatry Department at Grady Memorial Hospital and Central Fulton Community Mental Health Center in Atlanta, Georgia. He received his Ph.D. in Psychology from the University of Washington in 1973 and was a research associate on the Sickness Impact Profile Project in the Department of Health Services of the University of Washington from 1972 to 1975. He was a NIMH post-doctoral fellow in methodology and evaluation research at Northwestern University from 1975 to 1977 and an assistant professor in the Department of Psychiatry at Northwestern University Medical School from 1977 to 1978. His major areas of interest are evaluation research and decision analysis.

ATHILA E. SIEGMANN is a research associate in the Division of Sociomedical Sciences of the Columbia University School of Public Health. She holds graduate degrees in psychology, administrative medicine, and sociomedical sciences (health economics), all from Columbia University. She organized and administered a union health center for seven years, and was engaged in hospital administration for another five years. She has been consultant to various governmental agencies dealing with costs, management, and evaluation of health facilities, and most recently, health planning. For the past two years she has been on assignment from Columbia University as technical advisor to the Office of the Director, Division of Planning Methods and Technology, in the Bureau of Health Planning and Resources Development of DHEW, in the areas of health economics and the use of economic, medical and social indicators in health planning. She is the author of several articles and co-editor of two monographs on newer sociomedical health status indicators.

SAMUEL WOLFE is professor of public health and head of the Division of Health Administration at the Columbia University School of Public Health, and is also co-principal investigator for the Meharry Medical College Study of Unmet Needs. Earlier, he was at Long Island Jewish-Hillside Medical Center and the State University of New York at Stony Brook and, before that, was director of Comprehensive Health Care Programs at Meharry. Dr. Wolfe has worked in Canada as a practicing physician, as a commissioner of Saskatchewan's Medical Insurance Plan, and as director of the Saskatoon Community Clinic. He is the author of numerous articles and essays on the organization of health services and, with Robin Badgley, has coauthored two books, *The Family Doctor* and *Doctor's Strike*, and edited *Organization of Health Workers and Labor Conflict.*